Dr. D. James Kennedy
and
Coral Ridge Ministries Media, Inc.

present this special volume to you from

THE KENNEDY COLLECTION
1999

LED BY THE CARPENTER

Finding God's Purpose for *Your* Life!

D. JAMES KENNEDY

THOMAS NELSON PUBLISHERS
Nashville

Published in Nashville, Tennessee, by Thomas Nelson, Inc.

Library of Congress Cataloging-in-Publication Data

Kennedy, D. James (Dennis James), 1930–
  Led by the carpenter: finding God's purpose for your life! / D. James Kennedy.
     p.   cm.
  Includes bibliographical references.
  ISBN 0-7852-7039-6 (hardcover)
  1. Christian life. I. Title.
  BV4501.2.K4294 1999
  248.4—dc21   99–37814
                                                    CIP

Printed in the United States of America

1 2 3 4 5 6 QPM 04 03 02 01 00 99

To my wife, Anne, and our daughter, Jennifer,
who have made the trip more delightful as I have attempted to
follow the lead of the Carpenter.

ACKNOWLEDGMENTS

I am thankful to my faithful secretary, Mrs. Mary Anne Bunker, and to Dr. Herbert Lee Williams and Debbie Revitzer for their excellent assistance in editing and research.

I am also grateful to Mr. Dan Scalf, who helped bring this book into existence.

CONTENTS

1

GOD'S PURPOSE
FOR YOUR LIFE

You are the salt of the earth; . . . you are the light of the world.
(MATT. 5:13–14)

Why did God create you? What is your purpose for living? What did God put you on the earth to do?

I don't imagine these questions were uppermost in Carolyn McKenzie's mind when she picked up the phone to call her local radio station with a concern. Yet, at the moment she made that call, she set in motion events that answered those questions in a profound way for her own life.

The power of a concerned mother

Carolyn McKenzie is a Memphis, Tennessee, homemaker, wife to her husband, Mark, and mother to their four sons. "One night," she recalled, "my youngest child, who is handicapped, was playing with the radio, and I overheard an advertisement for a topless club. One thing that caught my attention was that the advertisement invited young women to come in on Wednesdays to strip for amateur night. Every woman who participated would receive fifty dollars and the winner would be paid a three-hundred-dollar prize. I thought, *It's such a shame that they would have that on a radio station with such a young listening audience.*

The next day Carolyn picked up the phone and called the radio station to complain about the ad—but the station refused to do anything about it. So Carolyn listened to the radio each night, wrote down the names of businesses that ran ads around the ad for the topless club—and then she called those businesses. "I'm a concerned mother in the community," she said, "and this ad for a topless club is running back-to-back with the ad for your business. Is this the kind of thing you want your business to be identified with?"

She went on to tell these business owners that the topless club had attracted the attention of the vice squad and the health department because it contained peep show booths where patrons engaged in anonymous sex acts. Trained as a healthcare professional, Carolyn was concerned not only about the moral threat posed by such businesses, but also about the health risks to the community. "If you're as concerned about your community as I am," she said, "please let the radio station know how you feel about this advertiser and the damage it does to your company's image."

Change didn't happen overnight, but Carolyn was persistent. She kept listening to the radio station, she kept calling local businesses—and before two months had passed, the ads for the topless club disappeared from the airwaves.

But Carolyn's work wasn't finished. She talked to the district attorney about prosecuting such businesses. He told Carolyn that many of the businesses were operating illegally, but that pursuing violations against them was a low priority in his office. "Every call I made, every question I asked," she said, "was met with, 'We don't have enough manpower; we don't have enough money.' To me, that was no excuse for inaction."

Carolyn contacted a group called the National Coalition for the Protection of Children and Families, and she discovered what other people had done to clean up their communities. "I learned about a bill that had been passed by the state of Delaware, requiring that doors be removed from so-called 'peep booths' so that the booths no longer offered any privacy. Though it was still legal for people to go into the booths and watch dirty movies, they could no longer engage in sex acts, either alone or with other people."

She got other people in the community involved, she got the D.A.'s office involved, and she went to the Tennessee state legislature, testifying before legislative committees. A doctor with her group documented the fact that he had found dried and fresh semen and human waste on the floors, walls, and chairs in the peep booths. As a result, a strong bill was enacted by the state legislature, over the loud protests of the rich and powerful pornography industry.

"My daughter is a topless dancer"

Sometime later, as Carolyn McKenzie was doing a radio interview on a call-in show describing her battle against pornography in her community, a woman called the show. "My daughter is a topless dancer," said the caller. "She wants to leave, but she has tremendous credit card debts and she makes good money as a dancer. She doesn't know how to get out of the business. Can you help her?" Carolyn agreed to meet with the caller's daughter.

When Carolyn met with the young woman, she told her, "If you promise to leave the strip club now and never go back, I'll help pay your bills." Carolyn and her husband were not wealthy and had no idea where the money was coming from—but she felt God telling her that He would provide. "My heavenly Father has always met my needs," she told the young woman, "and I know He is going to meet your needs too. I'm not going to ask you to go to church or a Bible study with me right now—but I'm going to pray for you. Then we'll see together if God provides for you."

"Carolyn was just so bubbly and positive," the young woman later recalled, "that she made me feel like everything was going to be okay. She put her arms around me, and I could feel the love."

Carolyn and her husband provided short-term help for this young woman, but ultimately the solution to her problems was found in answered prayer. The young woman found a job, and her husband—who was AWOL from the navy—turned himself in and was reinstated. Within a year this young woman and her husband had paid off all their credit card debt and were paying their bills on time—without having to sacrifice this young woman's morality and dignity. Most importantly, these two young people committed their lives to Jesus Christ.

And that was just the beginning! Since then Carolyn has helped a dozen or more young women escape the trap of the pornography industry, and many of them have accepted Jesus Christ as their Lord and Savior. Their stories are heartbreaking: Some started dancing topless as young as eighteen; some were single mothers; some were forced into prostitution. Lured by the promise of easy money—as much as a thousand dollars a week—they soon found themselves in degrading circumstances, unable to escape, surrounded by filth, violence, drugs, disease, and men who wanted only to use them. Many of these young women drank or used drugs to anesthetize themselves to the pain of their hopeless condition. The strip club managers constantly berated them by asking, "Who would ever hire you to do anything but strip?"

But Carolyn found a local businessman who trained and employed many of these young women so they could leave the dark world of pornography and come into the light. "Carolyn helped me become a human being again," reflected one of the young women Carolyn rescued. "Without her, I know I would be in a strip club tonight."

And it all began when Carolyn McKenzie picked up the phone to call a radio station.

Why did God create Carolyn McKenzie? What did God put her on the earth to do? Certainly He desired for her to be a follower of Christ, a life partner to her husband, Mark, and a mother to her four boys—but clearly He also created her to be salt and light in a corrupt and dark world. By the grace of God, Carolyn McKenzie has discovered God's purpose for her life, and she is allowing God to use her in a mighty way to redeem her little corner of the world and to bring others into a saving relationship with Jesus Christ.

Creatures of purpose

You and I are conscious and rational beings. We cannot live without a sense of purpose and meaning to our lives. Whether it is clearly understood or only implicit, everything we do is activated and motivated by a sense of purpose. This is not to say that every human purpose and motivation is a good and noble one. Some of us are motivated by greed, hate, revenge, or lust. For some of us the only purpose for living is to acquire money, fame, power, or sex. Whether our purpose is evil and debased or noble and exalted, whether it is a conscious purpose or a hidden and unconscious drive, every act of every human being is tinctured through and through with a sense of purpose. So it's important that we examine and ask ourselves, "What is the purpose for my life? What is my motivation for the things I do?"

If it is true that an unexamined life is not worth living, I think it is even more profoundly and biblically true that an unexamined life may lead us into great conflict with God. He is our Maker, and He created us with a specific purpose in mind. If we outline a purpose for our lives that does not square with His, then our own self-willed purpose is doomed to be self-destructive. A computer and a hammer are both tools, but their creators have designed them with very different purposes in mind. If you attempt to use a computer to fulfill the purpose of a hammer, the result will be the destruction of the computer! So it is with us. We must put ourselves to the purpose for which God designed us—or our lives will ultimately be wasted and ruined. It is critically important that we find God's purpose for our lives so that we can find true meaning and fulfill our reason for existing.

You and I are mortal human beings. We are rushing at a constant and inexorable rate of sixty seconds per minute, sixty minutes per hour, toward the Final Reckoning, toward the Great Assize, the Ultimate Judgment. When we stand before the One who has made us, He will ask, "How have you used the time I have given you? Have you fulfilled the purpose for which I placed you on the earth?"

What will our answer be?

If we do not want to be ashamed on that day, then we need to determine God's purpose for our lives *right now, today,* while we still have time to fulfill it and be used by God. We have to ask ourselves, "What am I living for? What is the purpose of my life?"

The secular humanist world in which we live has an answer for the question. It is a deceptive answer, but it is repeated loudly, and it assaults our senses day and night: "There is no purpose to life—no purpose at all! There is no God who gives you purpose. You are simply an accident in time and space. All you have is this moment, so enjoy it while it lasts!"

This philosophy is shouted at us in all sorts of ways in every information and entertainment medium we encounter. The beer commercials put it this way: "You only go around once, so grab all the gusto you can!" (The advertising sloganeer who came up with that one is in for a big shock when he wakes up in eternity and finds out that you go around forever!) The English mathematician-philosopher Alfred North Whitehead stated this philosophy with dreary, desolate conciseness: "Human life is a flash of occasional enjoyments lighting up a mass of pain and misery." And the famed American eccentric, Gertrude Stein, put it this way: "There ain't no answer. There ain't going to be any answer. There never has been an answer. That's the answer." Well, that's no answer at all—and it's certainly not God's answer.

GOD'S ANSWER: THE TWO MANDATES

If I asked you what the purpose for your life is, what would your answer be? I suspect that if I asked fifty people, I could get fifty different answers. And each of those answers would suffer from a single defect: They would all be partial.

But is there one complete, absolute, all-encompassing answer to the question of human purpose and meaning? Can I know *God's* purpose for my life? My friend, the answer is *yes!*

God's answer to the question of human purpose and meaning centers around the two great mandates He has given us in His Word. A mandate, of course, is a directive or command that points us in a specific direction. The first of God's two mandates—the Cultural Mandate—is found at the very beginning of the Old Testament, in Genesis 1:26–28:

> Then God said, "Let Us make man in Our image, according to Our likeness; let them have dominion over the fish of the sea, over the birds of the air, and over the cattle, over all the earth and over every creeping thing that creeps on the earth." So God created man in His

own image; in the image of God He created him; male and female He created them. Then God blessed them, and God said to them, "Be fruitful and multiply; fill the earth and subdue it; have dominion over the fish of the sea, over the birds of the air, and over every living thing that moves on the earth."

Here we see that God had a discussion within the confines of the Trinity—the Father, Son, and Holy Spirit—and He made a decision: "Let Us make man in Our image, according to Our likeness." This was God's original intention: to make human beings in His own image. And He blessed human beings and made them His "vice-regents"—that is, His corulers over His creation with authority given by Him to act in His name and in His stead. And He instructed human beings, "Be fruitful and multiply; fill the earth and subdue it; have dominion" over all the creatures of the earth. We are, in effect, God's junior partners. He has given us the command to multiply and fill the earth, and He has given us the responsibility to have dominion and sovereignty over all the earth in the name of the living God.

That mandate is still in force today. As the vice-regents of God, we are to bring His truth and His will to bear on every sphere of our world and our society. We are to exercise godly dominion and influence over our neighborhoods, our schools, our government, our literature and arts, our sports arenas, our entertainment media, our news media, our scientific endeavors—in short, over every aspect and institution of human society.

God commanded us to advance—and we have disobediently retreated. Instead of exercising dominion in the name of God, we have abdicated and relegated this world to the control of the dark and bloody god of this world, Satan. In so doing, we have robbed God of His rightful glory in the world He has made.

You don't have to look far to see the result of our retreat from the Cultural Mandate. Unbelief has replaced belief as the cultural norm. On our television screens, which once presented a godly image of the family on such popular shows as *Father Knows Best* and *Leave It to Beaver*, it is now difficult to find a single healthy, intact, churchgoing family. Is it because healthy families don't exist? Were the families of Jim and Margaret Anderson or Ward and June Cleaver hopelessly unrealistic? No, of course not. But today's culture—which is bent on tearing down Christian moral values—would like us to think so. Prime-time TV is a nightly moral meltdown of adultery, fornication, and homosexuality—and rarely can we find even a hint of healthy, married sexuality as God intended.

Step away from the TV in your own family room, visit the local cineplex or bookstore or magazine rack, and you will find that the corrupting influence of unbelief is just as pervasive there. Tragically, the response of all too many Christians has been to abandon these centers of cultural influence to the dominion of Satan. That is a major mistake—and an act of disobedience against God's Cultural Mandate. We need to have an effect for God in those areas of influence. The first mandate, the Cultural Mandate, was given at the dawn of creation. The second mandate, the Great Commission, was given at the dawn of the *new* creation, at the very beginning of the Christian era, soon after the death and resurrection of Jesus Christ. We find the Great Commission in Matthew 28:19–20:

> "Go therefore and make disciples of all the nations, baptizing them in the name of the Father and of the Son and of the Holy Spirit, teaching them to observe all things that I have commanded you; and lo, I am with you always, even to the end of the age." Amen.

Here again, we see one of the reasons for the mess the world is in today—and once again we have to confess that it is our failure as the Church of Jesus Christ to carry out God's second mandate, the Great Commission. Here again, God has commanded us to advance and we have retreated. We would like to blame the world's ills on the atheists, the ACLU, the NEA, NOW, on other godless institutions—but a great share of the blame belongs squarely at our own doorstep, because we have disobeyed the Great Commission to share the Gospel of Jesus Christ.

The solution to the world's problems

We cannot complain about the weeds of godlessness that have sprung up in God's garden—because *we* have allowed it to happen! The majority of young people in this country neither know where Jesus Christ was born, nor where He died, nor could they name half of the Ten Commandments. That is *our* failing, *our* disobedience, and no one else's. We who claim to be followers of Jesus Christ have allowed this to happen because we have not witnessed to the world about the wonderful message of hope that we have received.

A glance at polling data will show that, while the Church has not been totally inactive, it has not been nearly as effective in carrying out the Great Commission as it *could* and *should* have been. According to the Gallup polling organization, the number of Americans who claimed to be born-again Christians in 1994 was 35 percent. A year later it was 39 percent—an increase of about 8 million adults. By 1998, it was 42 percent. Now that's good news and bad news. The good news is that we see a positive trend—more and more Americans cross the threshold into God's kingdom every year. The bad news is that *most Christians did absolutely nothing* to carry out the Great Commission!

Think about it: If every Christian in America had simply led *one person* to Christ during 1998, the number of born-again Christians would have *doubled* from 42 percent to 84 percent in one year! By the year 2000, according to this simple mathematical calculation, the entire nation would have been converted, and Christians would have had to fan out past our borders to find unsaved people to evangelize!

You may say, "Well, that's not a realistic way to look at things! Certainly some people are so hardened against the Gospel they would never respond to it—there would always be at least a few agnostics, atheists, or adherents to other faiths." Well, let's accept that argument for a moment. Suppose that with every Christian leading just one other person to Christ per year, we reached a saturation point—and only 90 or 95 percent of Americans became born-again Christians. Our nation would still be overwhelmingly Christian, and nearly all of the problems of our society—crime, immorality, domestic violence, addiction, abandoned and abused children, and so forth—would vanish like frost before the rising sun.

The solution to the desperate problems of our world is for us to become involved in our culture and to proclaim the Gospel of Jesus

Christ. If Christians would do those two things, our nation—and ultimately our world—would be transformed almost overnight.

Our three duties

From these mandates—and particularly from the Cultural Mandate—we can draw three specific Christian duties that constitute our purpose in life according to God. We see these three duties spelled out, one by one, in the Cultural Mandate:

1. God expects us to participate and cooperate with Him as He seeks to refashion us into His image, after His likeness. This duty is embodied in the first section of the Cultural Mandate: "Then God said, 'Let Us make man in Our image, according to Our likeness.'"

2. God expects us to be fruitful and multiply—that is, we are to evangelize. This duty is embodied in the next section of the Cultural Mandate, when God blesses human beings and says to them, "Be fruitful and multiply."

3. God expects us to subdue the earth and exercise dominion over it in His name, as His vice-regents. This duty is embodied in the final section of the Cultural Mandate, where God says, "Fill the earth and subdue it; have dominion over the fish of the sea, over the birds of the air, and over every living thing that moves on the earth."

I have been a minister of the Gospel for more than forty years, and in all that time, in a thousand different ways, I have tried to make the point that Christians are *called* to make a profound difference in the world—and that Christians are *empowered* to make a difference if they will only be obedient to these duties under the Cultural Mandate and the Great Commission. To my astonishment, I have seen this simple message—which is so utterly biblical and basic to what the Christian faith is all about—met with an amazing level of resistance!

I don't know how many more years God will give me to proclaim this message, but I can tell you this: When it is my time to leave, amid all the many encouraging and fond memories I will take with me, the greatest and most puzzling disappointment I will feel is the fact that many hundreds of Christians who have listened to me speak or have read my books will remain as useless and ineffectual in the kingdom of God as when I encountered them.

Are you fulfilling God's express and explicit purpose for your life—or are you living in silent rebellion to His command, day after day, year after year? If you are choosing the latter course, you have no right to complain about the problems of your world, because those problems are directly traceable to your rebellion and the rebellion of Christians just like you. My friend, I say this with all compassion and love for you in the hope that your conscience will be afflicted and your heart moved to obedience.

Judgment must begin at the house of God.

Is it really such a burdensome thing God asks of us, that we heed these two commands, the Cultural Mandate and the Great Commission? Is it such an overwhelming challenge He places before us, that we be involved in our community and our world, and that we lead just one person to Christ per year—just one? Jesus' commands to us are so simple: In Matthew 4:19, He says, "Follow Me, and I will make you fishers of men." And in Mark 16:15, His last command is, "Go into all the world and preach the Gospel to every creature."

A passion for being salt and light should infuse all that we say and do every day of our lives. Our hearts should burn with a passion to win people to Jesus Christ; a passion to be fruitful and multiply and to fill the land with men and women who reverently, adoringly bow the knee to Christ; a passion for carrying out God's mandates in every sphere of life and activity, reclaiming and refashioning this foul world to its former beauty and glory, conquering and subduing and having dominion over it in the name of God who made everything. That is the purpose God calls every one of us to fulfill. That is God's purpose for your life.

In the pages to come, you will find that there is no need to flounder, hesitate, or wonder about God's purpose for your life—He has clearly spelled it out for you in His Word! When you understand that purpose, when you give yourself daily to fulfilling that purpose, you will discover what it truly means to live each day with a sense of joy, exhilaration, and satisfaction. Together in these pages, you and I will explore:

- What it means to be made in God's image, how that image was fractured and marred within us—and how it can be restored;

- How to live true to God's purpose for our lives;

- How to fulfill our Lord's command to be salt and light in a dark and corrupt world;

- How to live boldly and courageously, challenging the false beliefs and corrupt power structures of this world; and

- How to fulfill God's purpose for our lives in all the arenas of life—in our marriage relationship, in our parental role, in our workplace, in our church, in our society, and in our world.

Friend in Christ, I invite you to come with me on an adventure—the greatest adventure imaginable, the adventure of living your life in the center of God's will, fulfilling His purpose for your life, carrying out His grand eternal plan! As you discover what it means to be God's salt and light in this corrupt and dark world, you'll encounter the thrill of seeing Him transform your life into a walking benediction, a sweet fragrance of His grace moving through the world and drawing other people to Himself.

Are you ready to accept the challenge? Then come along! Turn the page—and prepare yourself for the dazzling vision of what God is about to accomplish through your life!

2

MADE AND REMADE
IN HIS IMAGE

For this is the will of God, your sanctification . . .
(1 THESS. 4:3)

Her name is Grace. It's a fitting name, considering the wonderful story of God's grace in her life.

If you are a fan of the classic TV series *Star Trek*, then you would certainly recognize her face and hair—especially the hair! The woman who wore the trademark blonde beehive hairdo of Yeoman Janice Rand was actress Grace Lee Whitney.

Before *Star Trek*, Grace enjoyed an exciting show business career, having worked with such stars as Marilyn Monroe, Jack Lemmon, Robert Stack, Groucho Marx, Phil Silvers, and many others. She appeared on Broadway and in scores of movies and television shows. But with the role of Yeoman Rand on *Star Trek,* she finally had a continuing role on a weekly dramatic series—a dream come true. But halfway through the first season, Grace was sexually assaulted by a studio executive. A few days later her role on the series was dropped—perhaps because the executive wanted no reminders of what he had done to her.

The pain of the assault, the pain of losing her dream role aboard the Starship *Enterprise*, plus the memories of childhood pain she had carried for years, tipped Grace into a self-destructive binge of alcoholism, drug addiction, and compulsive sexual behavior. She drank booze, took pills, and allowed herself to be sexually exploited because she wanted to blot out the hurt—and she wanted to die. Over the next ten years or so she nearly succeeded in destroying herself.

As she approached the end of her drinking, her gums bled, her hair came out in clumps, she was incontinent, and she experienced constant feelings of fear accompanied by frequent hallucinations and blackouts. The woman who had once toured the galaxy with Captain Kirk and Mr. Spock was reduced to sitting on a skid row curb in downtown Los Angeles, drinking gin and cheap wine straight out of the bottle. Finally, racked with delirium tremens and dehydration, she was admitted to a hospital in LA. There the doctor told her that the gin she was drinking had eaten a hole in her esophagus, and her liver had become dangerously enlarged and distended. "If you don't stop drinking right now," he told her, "you're going to be dead."

"How soon?" she asked. "Months?"

The doctor shook his head. "Days."

Scared to death, Grace thought, *I have to stop drinking—but I don't know how to stop drinking! The alcohol is stronger than I am!*

Amazing grace!

A few days later a friend invited Grace to a twelve-step recovery group meeting. There she met other people who were also powerless against their addictions but who had been able to make a clean break with alcohol by relying on God as their strength. After years of rebellion against God, Grace had discovered that God was there and He cared for her. Her drinking stopped the very first night she attended a meeting. That was in 1981.

Two years later Grace went to Israel to visit her son, who was studying at Hebrew University. He took her on a walking tour of the hills outside Jerusalem. They crossed the Kidron valley and went up toward the Mount of Olives, where the hills are studded with ancient churches and elaborate tombs. At last they came to a wall and a gate, beyond which was a grove of gnarled olive trees. A sign by the gate identified the place as the Garden of Gethsemane. Grace vaguely remembered that the garden had something to do with the story of Jesus.

While her son stepped away to take some pictures, Grace put her hands on the bars of the gate and looked through. Suddenly she felt a weakness come over her, as if she was about to faint.

And then she saw Jesus. He was kneeling in the garden praying. Though she had been raised in a Methodist home, she had converted to Judaism years earlier when she married a Jewish man, so she was shocked to see a vision of Jesus in the garden. Her first thought was, *But I'm Jewish!*

As if He could read her mind, Jesus looked at her and said, "So am I."

For two years, from the time she had gone into a twelve-step meeting and found recovery from alcoholism until the moment she experienced a vision of Jesus at the Garden of Gethsemane, Grace Lee Whitney had been like the Athenians whom Paul addressed in Acts 17 when he said, "Men of Athens, I perceive that in all things you are very religious; for as I was passing through and considering the objects of your worship, I even found an altar with this inscription: TO THE UNKNOWN GOD. Therefore, the One whom you worship without knowing, Him I proclaim to you" (vv. 22–23).

For two years, Grace had been relying upon "the unknown God" of her recovery to keep her sober on a day-to-day basis. Throughout that time, she had been sober without being saved. But in Israel, at the gate of the very garden where Jesus had prayed the night before He was crucified, Grace met the One who could bring her not only sobriety, but also eternal life, wholeness, and peace. A few days later, when she returned to California, God brought a Christian into her life who explained what the vision meant: Jesus was calling her to salvation. Soon thereafter, Grace Lee Whitney received Jesus as her Lord and Savior.

Today Grace is an ambassador for Christ. She appears at *Star Trek* conventions, does radio and TV interviews, goes into recovery group meetings and women's prisons, and sponsors and counsels other women with addictions. She is not only a woman named Grace, but she is also the very fragrance of God's grace, testifying wherever she goes to the power of God to transform and redeem a human life. Her autobiography, *The Longest Trek: My Tour of the Galaxy*, tells how God reached into the Hell of her life and moved her out of darkness and into the light of

His grace. In the foreword to the book, her friend and *Star Trek* costar Leonard Nimoy (Mr. Spock), paid her this glowing tribute: "I call her Amazing Grace. She rejects that name and denies that she is amazing, but I insist, because she *is* . . . It is a blessing to all of us that she has put this life of hers to such generous use."[1]

God has taken the bitterest experiences of Grace's life—her childhood pain, the experience of being sexually assaulted and unfairly removed from a television series, the degrading experience of being addicted to booze and pills and sex, of nearly ending her life in a skid row—and transformed them into the sweetest fragrance of His own grace. And that is what He wants to do in your life, regardless of your past and your sin. God's purpose for every human life is not merely that we would be saved for the great hereafter, but that we would be salvaged, restored, and put into service in the great here and now!

A race of wrecked Cadillacs

A small boy was drawn to the kitchen by the whirring of an egg-beater. He found his mother at work over a mixing bowl. He peered over the edge of the mixing bowl and asked, "What are you making?"

"A chocolate cake," his mother replied.

Well, he certainly liked chocolate cake! So he reached out with his finger and tasted some of the raw ingredients—and he grimaced! "Ugh!" he complained. "That doesn't taste like chocolate cake! That's bitter!" Then he looked around at the array of ingredients his mother had set out on the counter: sour milk and vegetable oil and baking soda. Baking soda? That's the horrible stuff she had once given him for an upset stomach! Why was she putting all these horrible, bitter things in a chocolate cake? She'd ruin it! "If you put all that stuff in the cake, I'm not eating any," he declared.

"We'll see," said his mother.

After dinner, she put a slice of cake on a plate and set it before him. He cautiously nibbled a tiny piece. Not bad! He ate a forkful. Then he ate a lot of forkfuls. Then he licked his plate clean! It was wonderful! He wanted another piece!

And that is how God's grace works in your life and mine. A lot of seemingly bitter, "yucky" ingredients seem to go into the making of a life—yet God, in the marvelous alchemy of His grace, is able to turn our bitterness into a sweet fragrance, our leaden worthlessness into a life of precious, 24-karat-gold value and worth.

That is His purpose for our lives. In fact, that has been His purpose for us since the beginning of time, since the moment of creation. He said, "Let Us make man in Our image, according to Our likeness." His original intent was to create a whole world of men and women, boys and girls, fashioned in His own image. That is a desire and a motivation that you and I can understand at least in part, because all parents know something of the desire to have children who are made in their own image, who reflect their best qualities.

But even though that was God's desire for our lives, something terrible happened soon after creation: Adam, the first man, sinned. Through him the entire human race fell. The image of God that was stamped upon our race at the moment of our creation was marred and distorted. It was not destroyed—we still bear the image of God today, even though it has been perverted and twisted and rendered largely unrecognizable by the effects of sin.

Imagine that you are invited to the General Motors plant in Detroit to pick out a shiny new Cadillac. You go and examine the production line and you select the most beautiful, flawless, impressive Cadillac on the line. They hand you the keys, you slide in behind the driver's seat, breathe in the luxurious "new car" smell, and smile. After fastening your seat belt, you turn the key and drive off the GM lot and onto the street. What a wonderful ride! The car purrs like a contented kitten!

A few miles out of town, you pass a warning sign without bothering to read it: DANGER! ROAD ENDS AHEAD! As a result, you drive your brand-new Cadillac right over the edge of a five-hundred-foot cliff.

The air bags deploy, the seat belt holds you in place, and you survive the crash—but as you climb out of the wreckage and survey the damage, you notice that the car doesn't look quite the same as it did when it came off the production line. The appearance of your brand-new Cadillac has been *altered*—to say the least! No, it hasn't become a Yugo or a Ford Pinto or a '57 Edsel. It's still a Cadillac—but it's a wreck. Yes, it's a *noble* wreck—it's the Cadillac of wrecks! But it's still a wreck.

You and I are just like that Cadillac at the bottom of the cliff. We are noble wrecks. We were stamped at the moment of our creation with the "Cadillac" of all images—the image of God. But we have suffered a fall, and we have been wrecked by sin. So God in His grace has made it possible for us to be repaired and refashioned in His image; in fact, He *calls* us and *commands* us to be remade in His image through the Cultural Mandate!

The wreckage of our lives must be towed into the garage so we can have the fenders pounded out, the frame straightened, the motor fixed, and all the other things that need to be done. In contrast to what many people seem to think, we aren't "fixed" at the moment of conversion. Conversion was simply the moment when the wreck was towed into the garage and the first hammer hit the fender! We still have a long way to go.

Your frame may still be bent. Your tires may be flat. Your fenders may be twisted all out of whack. If so, I know just how you feel—sometimes my motor hardly works at all! We need to be continually refashioned and reshaped into the image of God, so that God can walk with us and talk with us and have intimate communion with His children who have been made in His image as He originally intended. This was His grand design at the beginning of creation, as the New Testament tells us: "For this is the will of God, your sanctification . . ." (1 Thess. 4:3). And, "For whom He foreknew, He also predestined to be conformed to the image of His Son . . ." (Rom. 8:29).

Sanctification means to be put to the use or purpose for which we were designed and created. How, then, do we become sanctified for God's use? By cooperating with Him as He works to refashion us into His image—which is the image of His Son, Jesus. By applying ourselves to the study of God's Word. By applying ourselves to prayer. By worshiping God and following His commandments. That is what it means to daily seek to become more and more like Jesus Christ. And how vital this is in our lives!

Friend in Christ, you and I are a couple of wrecks! The entire human race is a race of wrecked Cadillacs! But thank God, He has not left us in the wrecking yard to rust and fall apart. He has made a wonderful decision about our lives, and He wants to restore us and make us as good as new. Some of us, unfortunately, are not very cooperative with God. We don't even allow the car to be in the shop very long so He can work on it! How much time are you giving God so that He can refashion you and restore you to the Cadillac image that was yours at creation?

God's extravagant grace

Perhaps you don't feel very much like a Cadillac right now. Perhaps life has been beating up on you, making you feel useless, incompetent, inferior—like a failure. Perhaps you have made so many mistakes in your life and committed so many sins that you feel hopeless, unlovable, and unforgivable. You've taken that plunge off life's cliff; you've hit bottom with a resounding crash; you've been wrecked and smashed and bent out of all recognition. You may think, *My life is beyond repair. No amount of hammering and straightening and buffing and repainting will ever make a shiny new car out of me!*

I once received a letter from a young man who said, "I quit—I give up on life." He felt that he had made too many mistakes and that life had kicked him in the teeth once too often. So he was ready to "go belly-up." Over the years I have counseled many people who have felt absolutely overwhelmed by the sins and failures of their past or by the pressures and unfairness of the world.

Have you ever felt that way? Have you ever felt as though it would be easier to quit and die rather than to go on living and struggling? I think everyone has felt that way at one time or another. I know I have at times in my life. Robert Service, the poet laureate of the old Yukon, once penned some lines for all those who might be feeling like giving up on life. In "The Quitter," he writes,

> When you're lost in the wild and you're scared as a child,
> And death looks you bang in the eye;
> And you're sore as a boil, it's according to Hoyle
> To cock your revolver and die.

But the code of a man says fight all you can,
And self-dissolution is barred;
In hunger and woe, oh it's okay to blow—
It's the hell served for breakfast that's hard.

It's easy to cry that you're beaten and die,
It's easy to crawfish and crawl,
But to fight and to fight when hope's out of sight,
Why, that's the best game of them all.

And though you come out of each grueling bout,
All broken and beaten and scarred—
Just have one more try. It's dead easy to die,
It's the keeping on living that's hard.

There is a lot to be said for the kind of true grit Robert Service commends to us. God has built into every human being an ability to go on and on, even in the face of great odds. But with all respect to these lines by Robert Service, I believe God has a better idea about dealing with our feelings of failure, defeat, and hopelessness. He has a better idea than mere grit. It's something called *grace*. We can never know true peace or fulfill God's purpose for our lives until we first experience God's grace.

Do you truly know God's grace, not merely as a religious-sounding word or a theological concept but as the cornerstone of your life? Grace is not something we can earn—it is God's unmerited, unearned, undeserved favor toward us. He loves us not because we are lovable, but because He is Love. He accepts us not because we can in any way make ourselves acceptable to Him, but because He is acceptance and forgiveness personified. Until we have humbly received His grace, His free forgiveness, His undeserved pardon, His extravagant mercy, we can never know what it means to have peace and a real sense of purpose. Grace comes to us from God our Father through the Lord Jesus Christ.

Sin, failure, and defeat can make us lose sight of God's grace. When we fail in business, in ministry, or in marriage, or when we commit some sin or moral failure, we easily lose sight of our God-given purpose. We lose sight of God's goodness and forgiveness. We think that God has abandoned us and that we are unworthy of His love and kindness. We think, *I can't do it. I can't make it. It is not going to work out. God can't use me. The future looks bleak.* When we see ourselves as unforgivable, useless failures, we cancel out the grace of God. The truth is that God's grace is tailor-made for failures like us! God gives us His grace for the express purpose of canceling out our sin, failure, and hopelessness.

Many people are set up for feelings of failure and hopelessness during their childhood years. From the time they are small, they are told they really don't amount to much. They receive such messages as, "Can't you do anything right?" Or, "How could you be so dumb?" You may have heard such words yourself when you were growing up—or you may have said them as a parent. I don't often talk about it, but there were times of great pain in my own childhood, the result of having a mother whose personality was often distorted by the influence of alcohol. I remember things that were done and words that were said to me when I was a child; they reverberate in my memory as if they were spoken only yesterday. Children often carry such hurtful messages with them long into adulthood.

Then we get up in life and find there are people around us who delight in telling us we will never succeed. It may be someone at the office or in the neighborhood, an old schoolmate, or even someone in the church. It may even be our spouse. There are, it seems, too few cheerleaders in life—and too many jeerleaders.

"You're a dunce!" said the teacher. "And I'm going to fail you!" Those were the words of the teacher who failed Albert Einstein in mathematics! I ask you: Who was truly the dunce?

"I'm sorry to have to tell you this," said the choir director, "but you lack talent. We don't have a place for you in our choir. Please leave and don't come back." That choir director was speaking to a young Jerome Hines, who later became the greatest basso profundo in the history of the Metropolitan Opera!

Refuse to believe lies. Don't listen to the lies of your past performance. Shut out the defeatist messages from the enemy. Listen to God and His promises. "I can do all things through Christ who strengthens me" (Phil. 4:13).

So what if you've failed? So what if you've failed two or five or fifteen times? That was then. This is now—and *now* you can do all things through Christ who strengthens you! Think of some of the greatest success stories of our time. Do you know that most of them have experienced failure?

Walt Disney went broke seven times before he succeeded. Thomas Edison made fourteen thousand experiments that failed before he developed the incandescent light. Babe Ruth amassed the largest record of strikeouts in the history of baseball, but he was always in there swinging! Nobody remembers the failures of those individuals. History is the story of their successes—but we should never forget that failure is often a prerequisite to success. No one ever succeeded without first making an attempt—and very few people ever attempted anything great without failing at least once. The most tragic lives are lived by people who exist in the gray twilight of timidity, never attempting great things because they are afraid to fail.

There is never a lack of people to tell you, "Look at the mess you've made of your life so far. You've never done anything worthwhile. But then, you can't make a silk purse out of a sow's ear." If anyone has said such a thing to you, I want you to know that we have a God who owns a pig farm and specializes in silk purses!

God is in the grace business, the forgiveness business, the business of lifting us out of the messes we make of our lives and putting us back into service for Him. Remember the story of actress Grace Lee Whitney? God was able to raise her from a skid row curb when she nearly drank herself to death, and reveal Himself to her at the Garden of Gethsemane. He filled her with joy and a new purpose, pointing her steps toward recovery meetings, *Star Trek* conventions, and women's prisons where she now shares the story of her new life in Christ.

God can do something just as wonderful in *your* life!

No matter what your sin, no matter what your failure, He is "able to do exceedingly abundantly above all that we ask or think" (Eph. 3:20). He is a God of abundant, extravagant grace. Do you believe that? If not, why not? Is it because you have never taken hold of the power that is appropriated by faith—the power of the Holy Spirit? We are told in the Scripture that faith is the victory that overcomes the world. What does this mean?

It means simply this: Whom do you believe? Do you believe the people who have told you all those negative things about yourself—or do you believe God? Do you believe that your past determines your future—or do you believe God when He tells you that He has a completely *new* plan and a *new* purpose for your life? God tells us that He has an entirely new story to tell us. If you belong to Him, if you have been redeemed, then you have been regenerated and reborn. "Therefore, if anyone is in Christ, he is a new creation; old things have passed away; behold, all things have become new" (2 Cor. 5:17).

God tells you that you are a child of the King—and therefore you are a prince or princess of possibilities! You are a son or daughter of the Most High. He promises that He will always lead you in triumph. "I can do all things through Christ who strengthens me," says Philippians 4:13. So whom are you going to believe? The defeatist messages of the past— or God's promise of the future? The condemnation of people—or the commendation of God?

Where is your confidence?

Sometimes we fail in life because of circumstances beyond our control, but the most devastating failures are the ones that are directly due to our own sins. When we sin and fall flat on our faces, we know there is no one else to blame but ourselves. We easily become overwhelmed by guilt, shame, and self-condemnation. We feel dirty and worthless and our sense of purpose and usefulness to God is shattered. That is an opportunity Satan never hesitates to exploit.

Our enemy comes to us with a devastating one-two punch. First, he tempts us to sin; then, when we succumb to his temptation, he lands his second punch—a message whispered in our ears: "You see how useless you are? You've blown it again! You'll never be worth anything to God! You're useless! You might as well go all the way, indulge in every sin imaginable! Come on! Join *my* side!"

I know there's a familiar ring to those words—you've heard that whispered message before in some moral and spiritual low point in your life. That message didn't just come out of nowhere—it was one of the enemy's fiery arrows, meant to derail you from God's purpose for your life. But God wants you to know that His grace is so great, it reaches down into even the lowest valleys of your experience. We have a God who is willing to forgive and cleanse us no matter what we have done, no matter how low we have fallen.

Once, when I was in school, I did something I knew was wrong, and afterward I was terribly overwhelmed with guilt. There is no point in laying out the nature of my sin in embarrassing detail. It is enough to say that, because of what I had done, I felt God would never use me in the ministry. I was certain I had completely invalidated God's purpose for my life. Then one day I went to chapel and heard a Scottish preacher give a message from Romans 8 where God says, "Who shall bring a charge against God's elect? It is God who justifies" (v. 33). And as the preacher proclaimed those words, a burden that would have crushed Atlas was lifted from my heart. I went out of that chapel rejoicing that we have a God of grace who forgives—not merely once but over and over again. We have a God who lifts us up and restores us to His purpose and plan for our lives.

Most of the motivational books on the shelves these days will tell you that the key to success is confidence. People who fail, they say, do so because they need to develop more self-confidence. Sounds reasonable, doesn't it? But I submit to you that such advice is dead wrong! You don't need more self-confidence—you need less! That statement may startle you, but it's the truth. In fact, the Bible tells us that self-confidence is a curse and a sin:

> Thus says the LORD:
> "Cursed is the man who trusts in man
> And makes flesh his strength, . . .
> Blessed is the man who trusts in the LORD,
> And whose hope is the LORD." (Jer. 17:5, 7)

I am not saying that we should not have confidence—of course we need confidence. But we must make sure that our confidence is not misplaced. The confidence we need is not *self*-confidence but *Christ*-confidence! We must make sure we invest our trust in someone who is worthy of that trust, not in a broken reed that will not support us. The word *confidence*, remember, comes from the Latin words *con fides*, which mean "with faith." Whatever failures may lie in our past, we can live boldly and confidently in the present, stepping eagerly and assuredly into the future because we have faith—not in ourselves, God forbid, but because we have faith in Christ! "I can do all things through Christ who strengthens me" (Phil. 4:13). That is a confident statement—but the confidence is focused on Christ, not on self.

I used to have a painful sense of inferiority when I was growing up. I suffered with it until I found Jesus Christ. Then I found out who I really was: a child of God; a child of the King. I learned that I was made for eternity, that I would outlive the stars, and that my life has a significance that transcends anything in this world. That is the perfect remedy for feelings of inferiority! It is a matter of believing God—trusting what He says in His Word—instead of believing the false messages of our own hearts, the whispered lies of Satan, or the condemnation and criticism of others. The truth of God's Word is the antidote for all those messages that would poison our souls.

There is nothing more disagreeable and offensive to the human senses than manure—but carefully applied by a skilled gardener, manure becomes a rich fertilizer out of which fragrant, beautiful flowers grow. God is the gardener of our lives, and He wants to take all the manure and misery of our past and use it to grow the beauty of His character and the fragrance of His grace in our lives. He did that for me. He did that for an actress named Grace Lee Whitney. He can do that for you.

From degeneration to regeneration

I once knew a man who had an unimpressive C-plus record in college. Then he gave his life to Christ and went to a theological school—and there things were altogether different! The change did not happen overnight, but his newfound faith in Christ and his newfound sense of God's purpose for his life enabled this young man to become more disciplined in his studies. By the time he graduated he was earning straight A's. He then went on to further graduate work.

Watching the amazing transformation in this young man, one of his professors said, "In the educational world, the most certain predictor of how a student will do in the future is how he has done in the past. But you have confounded that rule of thumb, transforming yourself from a C student to an A scholar! What happened?"

"Sir," the young man responded, "I was converted by Jesus Christ, by that One who makes all things new."

It's true—Jesus really does make all things new. Through Him, that which was born of the flesh can be *born again*—regenerated—made new in Christ. The message of the Gospel is the message that old things are passed away and all things are become new. We are not stuck in the old mess we have made of our lives; we are part of a new plan—God's plan— and that is what gives our lives purpose and meaning. We have received this Good News into our own lives—and now we have been commissioned to spread this Good News to everyone in our sphere of influence.

It has been said that the whole message of the Bible is one of *generation, degeneration,* and *regeneration.* You see these three themes woven throughout Scripture, from Genesis to Revelation, from the earliest human beginnings all the way to the culmination of human history. God *generated* the human race at creation, stamping us all with His perfect image. Humanity *degenerated* through the Fall, when sin marred the image of God. Now, God, through Christ and by His Spirit, is *regenerating* the human race and restoring the image of God within us. Jesus Christ said, "You must be born again" (John 3:7). We who have been reborn are in the process of being refashioned, regenerated, and remade into new creations through the transforming power of Jesus Christ.

Through biological reproduction—through the corruptible seed of man—we bring forth corruptible, degenerate, fallen human creatures. But through *spiritual* reproduction—through the process of evangelizing and spreading the incorruptible seed of God's Word—we bring forth incorruptible, regenerated creatures. We bring forth new creations in Christ. The Great Commission tells us to go and make disciples of all nations, to preach the Gospel to every creature, to be witnesses unto Jesus Christ. And in this way, by the incorruptible seed of God, we take part in God's great purpose of taking people who have fallen into sin and refashioning them into the image of God. We take part in the grand design of God's grace.

And here we begin to catch a glimpse of just what God's design of grace is all about: He is transforming the world—one heart at a time. That is so different from the way we human beings try to change the world, isn't it? People love big, institutional solutions to problems. Whenever we see a problem in society, what do we do? We create a government task force. We create a government program. We pass a federal law. We organize a massive public relations effort. As human beings, we are so small, yet we think so big!

The irony is that God, who is so big, thinks small! He changes the world one heart at a time, one life at a time. And the difference between God's approach and our approach is—God's approach works! All our massive, expensive governmental, legislative, and public relations efforts usually result in making the problem worse! But God understands something that we easily lose sight of: You can't change a society unless you change the *people* in that society. If you want a spiritual revolution in this country, you must first revolutionize individual human hearts. And when enough spiritual transformations take place in a society, you soon have a majority!

Forget about being a part of the Baby Boom Generation, or Generation X or Generation Y or Generation Z. Become a part of the *Regeneration Generation*—the people involved in the new creation, in a revolution to completely reshape our culture—one human heart at a time. I am excited about what is already happening in the world as Christians catch a glimpse of what God wants to do through their lives. And you know something? You won't see a word about this revolution in your newspaper or on CNN.

(Shhh! It's a secret! The world doesn't even know it's happening! It's our own little conspiracy!)

Friend in Christ, we are going to turn the world upside down! In the book of Acts a group of ungodly people said this of the early apostles: "These who have turned the world upside down have come here too" (Acts 17:6). May the same be said of us—or better still, may they say that we have come to turn the world right side up for God!

3

LIVING TRUE TO
OUR PURPOSE

But be doers of the word, and not hearers only,
deceiving yourselves.

(JAMES 1:22)

The youth pastor checked his watch as he stepped onto the front porch and knocked on the door of Allie's house. Yes—he was right on time.

Allie was a high school senior and one of the most faithful kids in the youth group. She was a leader and a role model for the rest of the young people in the church—and the youth pastor wasn't surprised. Her mother was a Sunday school teacher, and her father was a leading businessman in the community.

The front door opened; it was Allie. "Oh, thanks for letting me catch a ride to church with you!" she said. "My car wouldn't start!"

"No problem," he said. "It's right on the way, and I was—"

Whatever else the youth pastor was about to say was suddenly cut off by a stream of the vilest profanity he had ever heard, coming from the back of the house. Moments later Allie's father appeared in the living room, the stream of curses dying on his lips when he saw the youth pastor standing in the doorway.

Allie reddened, embarrassed almost to tears. The youth pastor stood stunned and openmouthed, not knowing what to say. Allie's father lapsed into an awkward silence for a few moments, then laughed nervously.

"Well, you know how it is, Pastor," the foulmouthed father said with a shrug. "I have my Sunday-morning mode and I have my real-life mode. You sort of caught me in my real-life mode."

What a tragic admission for any person to make who claims to be a Christian! Trapped by his own unchristian behavior, this father had to admit to being "two-faced." He had a hypocritical, fraudulent "Sunday morning" face and a "real-life" face.

If we would be true to the purpose to which God has called us, we must be people of integrity. A person of Christian integrity is a person who is the same inside and out; the same on Saturday night and Sunday morning and every day of the week; the same whether the whole world is watching or no one is watching. A person of integrity never has to worry about being caught in the act of being himself, because he is the same in private as he is in public.

I am convinced that we cannot truly fulfill our purpose in life if we are not people of complete integrity. To have a sense of purpose is to have a strong, singular sense of direction. When you know God's purpose for your life, you are seized by it and drawn in one direction only—toward the fulfillment of that purpose and toward complete obedience to the Cultural Mandate and the Great Commission. But a person without integrity is not drawn in one direction—he is torn in two! His "Sunday morning" self and his "hidden self" are at war with each other. While one part of him puts on a public display of "Christianity," the other part of him is constantly being tugged into the orbit of sin. All the while, both parts are aware that he is only playing a role, that he is not authentically carrying out God's purpose for his life. The book of James tells us,

> For he that wavereth is like a wave of the sea, driven with the wind and tossed. For let not that man think that he shall receive any thing of the Lord. A double minded man is unstable in all his ways (James 1:6–8, KJV)

Notice that phrase "he that wavereth" in the King James translation. Most translations render that phrase "he who doubts." The original Greek word in that passage is *diakrino*, which suggests much more than mere doubting. It suggests a deep striving and hostile opposition within oneself; to be at variance or incongruity or discord with one's own self. It means, I believe, to lack integrity and wholeness and unity within one's own self—which is why verse 8 amplifies the thought by saying, "A double minded man is unstable in all his ways."

If we wish to receive God's blessing for our lives, if we wish to discover and fulfill God's purpose for our lives, then we cannot be unstable in our ways. We cannot have two halves of ourselves warring against each other. That's not to say that we will ever reach sinless perfection in this life. Even people of integrity will slip and fail and sin from time to time. They will constantly encounter the tug of temptation. But people of integrity know with absolute certainty who charts the course of their lives and who their true Master is.

And they will follow Him with a single mind and a stable purpose.

"Is it safe?" versus "Is it sin?"

In order to have integrity, in order to live true to the purpose God has called us to, we need to have a very clear understanding of what sin is. In today's world, drenched as it is with secular humanism and New Age philosophy, we have lost sight of the real meaning of sin. A recent (and shocking) survey showed that 83 percent of Americans now believe that "man is basically good"—a belief that flies in the face of the biblical truth that human beings are born in sin.

To listen to the blather on our news and talk shows today, you might come to the conclusion that "sin" has ceased to exist in America. Oh, there's still plenty of sin to be seen on our TV screens—but the word *sin* is never mentioned. *Newsweek* columnist Meg Greenfield once wrote a piece called "Why Nothing Is 'Wrong' Anymore," in which she noted that we don't use such terms as *wrong* and *sin* these days. We don't think in terms of "right and wrong" anymore—we think in terms of being "smart or dumb."

For example, we don't talk to young people about morality, chastity, and virginity anymore. We give them condoms and tell them to be "safe—not stupid." We don't encourage virtue—we promote "safe sex." And if a major entertainer or sports figure such as Magic Johnson contracts the AIDS virus through illicit sex, we don't say, "He was immoral," or, "What he did was sinful"—we say it was dumb or that he should have practiced "safe sex."

When I look in my Bible, I don't find any advice to practice "safe sex"—but I find a lot of advice like, "Flee sexual immorality" (1 Cor. 6:18) and, "Flee also youthful lusts" (2 Tim. 2:22). While the world tells us the only consideration is, "Is it safe?" the Bible demands that we ask ourselves, "Is it sin?" The world doesn't care about righteousness—only about escaping consequences. So we are bombarded by messages promoting "safe sex" and "safe abortions." As a culture, we want our sin to be nice and neat, without guilt or unpleasant results. Tragically, many of us in the Church are succumbing to such thinking. We are losing our sense of right and wrong, of righteousness and sin, of Christian morality, virtue, and integrity.

In 1998, when the nation was rocked by a presidential sex scandal, we had much the same national dialogue—the problem wasn't "sin" but "stupidity." The "lesson" of the Oval Office sex scandal, according to an op-ed piece in the *Dallas Morning News:* "You're never too old to be stupid about sex." Asked the *St. Louis Post-Dispatch:* "How could a clever politician be so stupid?" *USA Today* led coverage of the scandal with these words: "The most common response heard . . . was, 'How could he be so stupid?'" Man-on-the-street interviews published by the *Los Angeles Times* included such comments as, "I wonder what [the president] is thinking right now—probably, 'How could I be so stupid?'" A caller to National Public Radio's *Talk of the Nation* had the same concern: "With his history, if he did do this, it's incredibly stupid."

I submit to you, however, that all of these comments have utterly missed the point of the Oval Office sex scandal. It was not an act of stupidity; it was an act of sin. The president was not *mentally* challenged, but *morally* challenged.

Know your own heart

To be a person of integrity, you must first know your own heart—and the evil of which your heart is capable. Are you basically good? If you think so, you are in great danger! For a sober assessment of our own sinfulness, we must turn to the Word of God. Looking there, we see that the greatest saints of history have acknowledged themselves to be the greatest of sinners.

So it was with Job, who said to God, "I have heard of You by the hearing of the ear, but now my eye sees You. Therefore I abhor myself, and repent in dust and ashes" (Job 42:5–6). So it was with Isaiah, who said to God, "Woe is me, for I am undone! Because I am a man of unclean lips" (Isa. 6:5). So it was with the apostle Paul, who wrote, "Christ Jesus came into the world to save sinners, of whom I am chief" (1 Tim. 1:15).

The unregenerate live in darkness, however, so they cannot see their own sin and uncleanness. Sin is the only thing I know of that the longer you practice it, the less you are able to recognize it. So those who are the most deeply enmeshed in sin are also those who most strenuously deny it—both to themselves and to others.

But what is the judgment of God's Word? "The heart is deceitful above all things, and desperately wicked; who can know it?" (Jer. 17:9). "For I know that in me (that is, in my flesh) nothing good dwells . . . I find then a law, that evil is present with me, the one who wills to do good" (Rom. 7:18, 21). "If we say that we have no sin, we deceive ourselves, and the truth is not in us" (1 John 1:8). Jesus Himself is in agreement with these pronouncements of the Old and New Testaments, saying, "For out of the heart proceed evil thoughts, murders, adulteries, fornications, thefts, false witness, blasphemies. These are the things which defile a man" (Matt. 15:19–20).

So the Scriptures teach that man is *not* basically good; Christ taught that man is *not* basically good; and history confirms that man is *not* basically good. Anthropologists tell us that one-third of all human beings who have lived on this planet have died at the hands of their brothers—that mankind has killed one-third of the human race. Consider some of the atrocities committed in this very century in which we live: We have seen the Spanish Civil War, the Nazi Holocaust, the Japanese prison camps, the Russian gulags, the atrocities of African tribal warfare, Pol Pot's massacre of a million of his Cambodian countrymen, 135 million people slaughtered by the communists, ethnic cleansing in Bosnia and Kosovo, and on and on and on. If man is basically good, then how do we explain humanity's bloody history? It is utterly astonishing to me that any thinking person could cling to such an irrational, demonstrably false position.

CBS News's *60 Minutes* once aired a story about Adolf Eichmann, one of the chief architects of the Holocaust. In that program, Mike Wallace interviewed a Holocaust survivor—a Jewish man named Yehiel Dinur. Wallace showed a film clip from the Nuremberg trials in which Dinur testified against Eichmann. As Dinur walked into the courtroom past the place where Eichmann was seated, the Jewish man turned and eyed the Nazi butcher—then he suddenly began to sob uncontrollably. Moments later he collapsed.

Was Dinur overcome by hatred? Fear? Horrible memories? No, it was none of these. As Dinur explained to Wallace, he was suddenly seized with the realization that Eichmann was not an inhuman monster—he was a totally ordinary man. "I was afraid for myself," said Dinur. "I saw that I, too, am capable of what this man did. I am no different from Eichmann."

Mike Wallace's chilling summation of Dinur's terrible discovery is true of you and me as well: Eichmann is in all of us.

To be people of integrity, it is critically important that we understand this: We are not basically good. Our hearts are capable of enormous sin and evil. The closer we draw to the Light, the more clearly we see our uncleanness and filth.

But thank God, He has not left us in our uncleanness and filth! Sin is a reality—but it is not the end of the story. We have redemption from sin in Jesus Christ, whom God has set forth to take away the sin of the world—your sin and mine. When John the Baptist announced the coming of Jesus, he said, "Behold! The Lamb of God who takes away the sin of the world!" (John 1:29). We are born in a fallen state, a state of sin and depravity—but God in His love chose to place all our sin upon His Son, Jesus. He punished that sin—not upon us by consigning us to Hell, but upon His own beloved Son, Jesus, on the cross.

Yet if we deny the sinfulness of our own hearts, we cut ourselves off from the redemption of Christ Jesus. We become like the man in the Lord's parable of the wedding feast in Matthew 22. In that story, the king comes into the wedding feast and looks upon all the guests arrayed in white robes—all but one man who has no wedding garment. The white robes, of course, represent the righteousness of Jesus Christ—and the man without the robe arrived dressed in the vileness of his own supposed righteousness. "But," as the prophet Isaiah observes, "we are all like an unclean thing, and all our righteousnesses are like filthy rags" (Isa. 64:6).

So the king says to the unrobed man, "Why are you not dressed in a wedding robe?" The man looks down, sees himself in all his wretchedness and filth, and he is speechless. So the king turns to his servants, orders the man bound hand and foot, and has him tossed into "outer darkness," a place of wailing, despair, and separation from God. May it never be so with us!

Sin is a disease—a far more fatal and disfiguring disease than AIDS or cancer. It is a disease that every human being on the planet has contracted—but God has provided us with the cure. As the words of the great hymn tell us,

> There is a fountain filled with blood
> Drawn from Immanuel's veins;
> And sinners, plunged beneath that flood,
> Lose all their guilty stains.[1]

Once we recognize the reality of our own sin, the deceitfulness of our own human hearts, and the wonderful cleansing and healing God has provided for us through His Son, Jesus, we have a foundation for living lives of integrity and moral, spiritual wholeness. We are ready to live true to the purpose God has for our lives.

"Eyeless in Gaza"—a lesson in temptation

The Old Testament hero Samson was a man with a deep sense of purpose. He knew exactly what God wanted him to do with his life. He was the strongest man who ever lived—yet Samson had a fatal weakness that ultimately destroyed him.

Samson is not a fictional character in a tragic myth. He was a real man, born the son of Manoalt and his wife of the tribe of Dan in Israel. Most people know little of his life beyond his unfortunate escapade with Delilah, but he is actually one of the most fascinating figures in biblical history. The birth of Samson was announced by an angel. He was gifted by God and called by God to be consecrated to a high and holy purpose: to deliver the people of God from the forty-year-long oppression of the Philistines. He was set apart to be a Nazirite—separated and consecrated wholly unto God, and because of his Nazirite vows, no razor was to touch his head, and no strong drink was to touch his lips.

Samson was one of the judges of Israel, and he judged that nation for twenty years. He led the people of Israel, he heard them, he judged them, he fought for them, and he was even betrayed by them. At one time they delivered him bound into the hands of the Philistines. His is an exciting, multifaceted story.

The name Samson comes from the Hebrew word *shemesh,* which means "sun"—or more precisely the diminutive form: "little sun." Samson was the light of day, the dawning hope of the Israelites who had long suffered under the tyranny of the Philistines. But when Samson met a woman named Delilah, the sun in Samson's life went out for good. Yet it is important to understand that the woman was not his downfall. The source of Samson's downfall was within himself. He had two major character flaws that ultimately destroyed him: (1) He had an eye for women; and (2) he was overconfident, and this overconfidence led him to flirt with temptation.

Is there anything wrong with confidence? No. The Bible calls us to be confident—but not overconfident, not self-confident. We are to be Christ-confident, God-confident, secure in the confidence that comes with faith and trust in God. Samson's confidence was misplaced. He leaned on the broken reed of his own human strength, he flirted with temptation—and he was ultimately destroyed by it.

The woman who tempted him was named Delilah. She was of the feminine gender—but she was no lady. Her name meant "desire" or "lustful." Though Samson was a man who had killed a thousand Philistine soldiers with the jawbone of a donkey, this one woman would prove to be his undoing.

God had given Samson a strong, clear sense of purpose—a mandate to deliver his people from the Philistines. His mission in many ways parallels our own: By fulfilling the Cultural Mandate and the Great Commission, we are to play a part in delivering the people around us from the tyranny of sin, death, and immorality. But Samson had a problem that you may be all too familiar with in your own life: He was lured and enticed by the attractions of the surrounding culture. He visited the cities of the Philistines, looked around, and liked what he saw.

It is important for you and me to understand that we live in a Philistine culture, surrounded by barbaric but alluring and enticing temptations. The entertainment media that bombards our senses is drenched in the lure of sensuousness and sex, wealth and materialism, power and status, selfishness and greed. Temptation is all around us. In our own self-confidence, we engage in much the same self-destructive arrogance that Samson did—and we set ourselves up for a fall.

Samson continually allowed himself to be lured and enticed by the godless culture around him. First, he fell in love with a Philistine woman who pleased him well, and he married her—but that relationship led to all sorts of problems, and she ended up not with Samson but with Samson's friend and best man (Judg. 14). Then he went to Gaza, where he spent time with a prostitute and forsook his consecration to the Lord. When he was dallying with a prostitute, he was not carrying out the purpose God had laid out for him—and he almost lost his life. When some of the men of Gaza learned that Samson was with the prostitute, they plotted to kill him. He foiled their plot when he picked up the gates and post with which the men of Gaza tried to trap him, and he carried all of that masonry on his back to the top of a hill to demonstrate his strength and his contempt for his enemies.

Next, he met and fell in love with Delilah, a woman in the valley of Sorek. Where was the valley of Sorek? It went down from Jerusalem right to Philistia! Moreover, it was wine country. Wine and women were a bad combination for Samson. He never should have ventured near that valley, because he could not handle those temptations. In his arrogance and misplaced self-confidence, he believed that nothing was too difficult for him. But Samson didn't reckon with Delilah—and with the weakness of character within his own soul.

Though it is never stated, Delilah was apparently a Philistine. Certainly her sympathies lay with the Philistines. When the lords of the Philistines realized that Samson loved her, they came to her and plotted with her against Samson—and she was ready and eager to betray him. She asked Samson the source of his strength, planning to give that information to Samson's enemies so they could entrap him. Now Samson wasn't a complete fool. He had already been deceived and betrayed by another Philistine woman—his wife—so he was careful not to reveal the secret of his strength to Delilah.

On one occasion he made up a story that if he was bound with seven undried bowstrings, he would be as weak as any other man. On another occasion he told her that if he was bound with new ropes, he would be helpless. On yet a third occasion he told her that if she wove his long hair with a cloth-making loom, he would be helpless.

Each time Samson told Delilah the "secret" of his strength, she betrayed him—but it didn't do the Philistines any good because each "secret" was a lie. Samson knew she was betraying him, yet he didn't turn away from her. He didn't "flee temptation"—he lay down with it! He continued to stay with her and be enticed by her. And that gave Delilah every opportunity she needed to destroy him. With all the wiles of a well-experienced woman, she pestered him day and night, pleading and coaxing and cajoling and seducing him.

Finally, just to be rid of her pestering, he told her his secret—the truth this time. Any schoolboy would have had enough sense to avoid this trap, but Samson tumbled into it with his eyes wide open. He told her, "No razor has ever come upon my head, for I have been a Nazirite to God from my mother's womb. If I am shaven, then my strength will leave me, and I shall become weak, and be like any other man" (Judg. 16:17).

Delilah lulled Samson to sleep, had his hair shorn, then called to him: "The Philistines are upon you, Samson!" He awoke and said to himself, "I will go out as before, at other times, and shake myself free!" (v. 20).

But Judges 16:20 goes on to record this tragic statement—which, it turns out, was Samson's epitaph: "But he did not know that the LORD had departed from him." He had violated his vows and betrayed the purpose God had planned for him—and the Lord had departed from him.

The next thing Samson knew, the Philistines were upon him and he did not have the strength to fight them off. They threw him to the ground, bound his arms and legs with bronze fetters, then put out his eyes. Blind, bound, and weakened, Samson was put to work pulling a grinding stone in a Philistine prison—an image of utter despair and hopelessness, prompting the poet Milton to write,

> O glorious strength
> Put to the labour of a beast, debased
> Lower than bond-slave! Promise was that I
> Should Israel from Philistian yoke deliver;
> Ask for this great deliverer now, and find him
> Eyeless in Gaza at the mill with slaves,
> Himself in bonds under Philistian yoke . . .[2]

Think of it! Here was the man of God's great purpose—the man God had chosen to free the Israelites from bondage to the Philistines. Yet he ended up in bondage himself, his own eyes put out, turning a heavy millstone in a prison under the watchful eyes of his enemies. But in the midst of utter despair came a ray of hope. His hair began to grow. His strength slowly returned.

One day he was called into the great amphitheater-temple to provide entertainment for a crowd of three thousand Philistine lords and ladies, dukes and duchesses. When they had drunk their fill, they praised their own demon god and brought out Samson so they could torment him and laugh at his pain. No doubt the most bitter agony of Samson's darkness was the knowledge that he had broken his vow, he had succumbed to temptation and breached his integrity, and he had betrayed God's purpose for his life. As a result, he had allowed the enemies of God to triumph and to make a mockery of himself and his Lord.

A boy led Samson by the hand, and Samson said to the boy, "Let me feel the pillars which support the temple, so that I can lean on them" (Judg. 16:26). The boy led him to the pillars, and Samson leaned against them and bowed his head, while the people mocked him. Then Samson prayed, "O Lord GOD, remember me, I pray! Strengthen me, I pray, just this once, O God, that I may with one blow take vengeance on the Philistines for my two eyes!" (v. 28).

Finding the pillars, he placed one hand upon one and the other hand upon the other—then he pushed with all his might. The pillars toppled and the temple collapsed. The crash of marble and the shrieks of the doomed Philistines were heard for miles around. Samson himself perished under the rubble. Scripture records that "the dead that he killed at his death were more than he had killed in his life" (Judg. 16:30).

This is a tragic, heartbreaking story, and I fear that Samson's life could easily become a metaphor for our own lives—*if* we fail to heed the lesson of his story. We, like Samson, have been chosen by God and given a purpose to perform. We have been called to a high and noble calling. We have been consecrated and set apart unto God who calls us to live a holy life. God, speaking through the writings of Paul, tells us,

> "Come out from among them
> And be separate, says the LORD.
> Do not touch what is unclean,
> And I will receive you."
> "I will be a Father to you,
> And you shall be My sons and daughters,
> Says the LORD Almighty." (2 Cor. 6:17–18)

Like Samson, we have been given a great and glorious calling—the calling to fulfill the Cultural Mandate and the Great Commission. God has called us to be refashioned into His image, after His likeness; to be fruitful and multiply through evangelism; and to subdue the earth and exercise dominion over it in His name. We do not have the muscle and might of Samson—but we have something much more powerful: the Gospel of Jesus Christ, which is the power of God. Tragically, we have all too often and too easily compromised our vows, we have flirted with sin, we have yielded to the surrounding godless culture—and we have set ourselves up for a terrible fall.

Dealing with temptation

We, like Samson, have a tendency to be overconfident where temptation is concerned. We approach it. We flirt with it. And we end up destroyed by it. The Bible is very clear about temptation:

- We are to flee it! We are to run like crazy! "Flee sexual immorality" (1 Cor. 6:18).

- "Flee from idolatry" (1 Cor. 10:14). "For the love of money is a root of all kinds of evil . . . But you, O man of God, flee these things" (1 Tim. 6:10–11).

- "Flee also youthful lusts" (2 Tim. 2:22).

Again and again, we are told to flee temptation—the temptation to sexual immorality, to greed, to idolatry.

Many people have supposed they could flirt with temptation. How many addicts to alcohol, tobacco, drugs, sexual perversion, pornography, gambling, and the like have thought: *Oh, it will never get the best of me. I am too strong*? Isn't that what Samson thought? Are we stronger than Samson?

Dwight L. Moody once said, "Give me ten men who love nothing but God and hate nothing but sin, and I will change the world." Those words are still true today. Would you be willing to be that kind of man or woman for God? Would you be willing to love God enough and hate sin enough that you would remain true to your purpose, that you would fulfill the Cultural Mandate and the Great Commission, that you would go out and change the world for Christ? Are you still consecrated to God—or are you compromised with evil?

How greatly our lives would change if only we understood that character determines destiny. There is no way around it, over it, or under it. Godly character is created by Christ. Any integrity, honesty, purity, or virtue in our lives comes from Him. When we compromise His character in our lives, we ask for the hand of judgment to descend upon us.

When I was a new Christian, in the first few weeks of my Christian life, I came across a text in Romans that had a great impact on my life. Up to that time, I had been living in a very godless, worldly way. The words I read were these: "Or do you despise the riches of His goodness, forbearance, and longsuffering, not knowing that the goodness of God leads you to repentance?" (Rom. 2:4). No doubt Samson thought that the long-suffering patience of God shows that God really doesn't care about sin, so Samson continued to place himself in situations of moral risk and temptation. He continued to partake of wine and women—two temptations that would lead to his ultimate downfall. Maybe you have had the same easy attitude toward God's grace, goodness, and patience.

But there is a limit to the patience of God. Samson got away with it once. He got away with it twice. He got away with it three times.

Then came a day of reckoning, when the presence of the Lord left him and his strength was taken away from him. His eyesight was blotted out, and he was left eyeless in Gaza. Yes, God was gracious to Samson in the end—but look at the terrible price Samson paid.

How long has the mercy of God been extended toward you? Think back over this past week and ask yourself: "What have I engaged in that is a violation of my consecration to God?" If you are honest with yourself and with God, I'm sure you can think of something—possibly many things—you have done to betray God's purpose for your life.

God's guardrails

The Scriptures place before us a number of fences for the various degrees of sin we face. Each fence protects us as we move closer and closer to the precipice that will cost us our reputation and our lives. There are fences in Scripture against evil thoughts. We are told that we are to bring every thought into captivity unto Jesus Christ. There are fences against evil looks. We are told that he who looks upon a woman to lust after her has already committed adultery with her in his heart. There are fences against evil words and lascivious speech. There are fences in Scripture against sinful acts—the acts of adultery, fornication, prostitution, and sodomy.

Notice how these fences are erected at various stages in the progression from thoughts to looks to words to acts. Many people will climb over the first fence, flirting with adultery, covetousness, or some other sin in the privacy of their thoughts. They say to themselves, *No one will know. What harm can it do to think about it, to mull this temptation over in my mind, to silently savor it for a while?* They are still a little way from the precipice of actually committing the act—so they climb the first fence, confident of their Samson-like invulnerability.

But once they cross the first fence, they quickly encounter the next fence. *What harm can it do to look?* they rationalize—and over they go. Then, *What's wrong with a little harmless flirting—a smutty innuendo, a lewd remark? What's wrong with a few harmless words?*

Before they realize it, they are climbing over the final fence—and crashing to their doom. They've been discovered. They've lost their reputation, their family, their career. And then in their denial they say, "I never intended for it to go this far! It just happened before I knew it!" But the truth is that they had to willfully, deliberately cross several protective guardrails before they got to that final fence. It didn't "just happen." They flirted with the temptress, with Delilah—in whatever form she came to them—and the end of that flirtation was destruction.

You cannot climb even the first of those fences and remain safe. God erected those fences for a reason, and the only safe place for you is on the righteous side of the very first fence. Once you cross that first guardrail, you have left the place of safety.

Those fences have never been more important than they are today. We live in a time of unparalleled temptation—not only sexual temptation but all forms of temptation. The lure of greed, covetousness, lust, fornication, adultery, and more is continually thrust in our faces in books, magazines, films, and television. To keep our thoughts on God's side of the fence may require that we close the books and magazines others around us read without a second thought, that we avoid the films that everyone says are a "must-see," that we turn off the television and find other forms of entertainment and information.

I am not saying we have to withdraw from the world—but we would be wise to keep some of the world's images and messages from penetrating and saturating our minds and thoughts. We need to maintain God's perspective on sin and morality, and that is not always easy in the world we live in. For example, fornication is no longer looked upon as sin in our culture; it is simply a "lifestyle choice." As a result, even many young people who were raised in the Church do not see anything wrong with "shacking up," living together, and having sexual relations outside of the holy sacrament of a marriage covenant.

Today, many people who call themselves Christians look upon it as strange and impractical to expect people to live a chaste and moral life.

Many Christians feel no twinge of conscience engaging in supposedly lesser forms of sexual immorality—the lustful thought, the prurient look, the smutty joke or innuendo. But if we are going to be Christ's people, living true to His purpose for our lives, if we are going to be the bond servants of Jesus Christ rather than slaves of lust, then we must bring every thought into captivity to Him.

If we are going to be the servants of Jesus Christ, we must deal with the matter at the very heart. We must deal with temptation and sin before it becomes a habit. Each time we yield to a certain temptation we become weaker and weaker. But every time we resist that temptation we become stronger and stronger. We have the promise of Scripture that greater is He is in us than he who is in the world (1 John 4:4); we have the promise of Scripture that if we will resist the devil, he will flee from us (James 4:7).

The longer I live as a Christian, the more I see that the most significant thing about any sin is how it affects my personal relationship with Jesus Christ. The key to victory over sin is to make Jesus Christ the absolute, sovereign Lord and King of our lives. When we have enthroned Him in our minds, in the things we choose to look at, in the words we speak, and in all of our actions, then—and only then!—will we truly conquer the sin and temptation that seek to destroy us and divert us from our purpose. Do not be deceived—nothing less than absolute surrender to Him will suffice. When our relationship with Jesus Christ is the most important thing in all the world to us, it becomes much easier to bring every thought, every look, every word, and every act into conformity to His good and perfect will for our lives.

Friend in Christ, a day of grace now shines upon you. The Son of righteousness is in the sky. If you have never known Him, you are cordially invited—no, *urgently* invited—to come to Christ, to know Him and to experience that grace. If you have known Him, but you have compromised your consecration and your God-given purpose in life, then you are invited to return to Him and repent. As Paul said in Romans 2:4, "The goodness of God leads you to repentance," not to license and greater sin. There is no higher calling in life than the calling God has issued to you. Live true to your purpose—don't miss out on God's great and wonderful plan for your life!

4

A PINCH
OF SALT

*You are the salt of the earth; but if the salt loses its flavor, how
shall it be seasoned? It is then good for nothing but to be thrown
out and trampled underfoot by men.*

(MATT. 5:13)

Today, Jeremiah Denton is a retired navy rear admiral, a former
United States senator, and the head of an international humanitarian aid
organization, the Joint Relief International Denton Operations. But
there was a time in his life when Jeremiah Denton's entire world was a
four-by-four concrete square.

On July 18, 1965, Denton, a forty-one-year-old navy pilot, took off
from the deck of the USS *Independence*, leading a group of twenty-eight
planes in an attack on enemy targets in North Vietnam. His plane was
shot down and he was captured. He would not see his family again for
nearly eight years. He spent almost half of his captivity in solitary con-
finement, chained in a four-by-four-foot cell hardly larger than a coffin,
with no windows, only a ten-watt bulb for light, and only spiders and
roaches for company. How did he survive? "Jesus was with me all the
time," Denton answers.

At one point he was tortured for ten days and nights. He reached a
point where he could no longer think or even pray. All he could do was
surrender—not to his captors but to God. "If there is anything more that

needs to be done, God," he said, "You will do it." At that moment, the pain left him and he felt a sense of God's peace and comfort flood into his soul.

Jeremiah Denton endured a great deal during his eight years of captivity in Vietnam—but nothing could prepare him for the shock that awaited him when he was released and allowed to go home to America. Arriving back in the naval city of Norfolk, Virginia, in 1973, he was appalled to discover what had sprung up in the downtown area during his absence: block after block of sleazy massage parlors and X-rated bookstores and movie houses. As he drove past dozens of these seamy establishments, he turned to his wife, Jane, and asked, "What's all this? What's a 'massage parlor'? What does 'X-rated' mean?" Denton was not naive—he knew what a "house of ill repute" was, but he had never before seen an area of an American city that had been completely overrun by sex-oriented businesses. Such a thing was simply unheard of in the America he had left in 1965.

"Over the next few months after I arrived home," Denton later recalled, "I was to absorb the whole picture of how far our country had strayed from its moorings during the time I was gone." Only someone like Jeremiah Denton, who returned to America after a long absence, could have noticed the dramatic, tragic downturn in America's moral standards.[1] In a short span of time, we have grown to accept the unacceptable and to tolerate the intolerable. The moral foundation of our Western culture has crumbled beneath our feet—and we have been totally unaware! Our nation is sinking into decay and corruption right beneath our noses—and what are we doing about it?

God has given us a mandate to act as salt in the world, working to preserve human society against the forces of corruption and decay. He calls us to move our culture from a declining course to an inclining course. If we ignore what is happening in our society, if we refuse to become involved in the battle for godliness and morality in our world, then we are denying God's lordship in our lives. We are choosing rank disobedience to His mandate and His purpose for our lives.

We have a duty to fulfill—and a choice to make. We will either be used by God as His salt in the world—or we will be fit only "to be thrown out and trampled underfoot by men." What will you choose?

What it means to be "the salt of the earth"

A man walked into a little mom-and-pop grocery store and asked, "Do you sell salt?"

"Ha!" said Pop the proprietor. "Do we sell salt! Just look!" And Pop showed the customer one entire wall of shelves stocked with nothing but salt—Morton salt, iodized salt, kosher salt, sea salt, rock salt, garlic salt, seasoning salt, Epsom salts, every kind of salt imaginable.

"Wow!" said the customer.

"You think that's something?" said Pop with a wave of his hand. "That's nothing! Come look." And Pop led the customer to a back room filled with shelves and bins and cartons and barrels and boxes of salt. "Do we sell salt!" he said.

"Unbelievable!" said the customer.

"You think that's something?" said Pop. "Come! I'll show you salt!" And Pop led the customer down some steps into a huge basement, five times as large as the previous room, filled wall to wall, floor to ceiling, with every imaginable form and size and shape of salt—even huge ten-pound salt licks for the cow pasture.

"Incredible!" said the customer. "You really do sell salt!"

"No!" said Pop. "That's just the problem! We never sell salt! In twenty years you're the first person who ever came into my store asking for salt. But that salt salesman—Hoo-boy! Does *he* sell salt!"

If there's one thing this world needs right now, it's salt—and plenty of it! Salt is a preservative for a corrupt and decaying world—and for corrupt and decaying people. When a dying, degenerate, deteriorating human soul comes into contact with Jesus Christ, who is life itself, that soul is cured, cleansed, purified, made alive—and *transformed* into the salt of the earth. In Matthew 5:13, Jesus said,

> You are the salt of the earth; but if the salt loses its flavor, how shall it be seasoned? It is then good for nothing but to be thrown out and trampled underfoot by men.

When we think deeply about that statement, we begin to see what a truly astonishing statement it is. In the ancient world, salt was the only preservative known. The fishermen of Jesus' day caught their fish in the Sea of Galilee and shipped them for sale to such places as Samaria and Jerusalem. Before shipment the fish was dried and salted to prevent spoilage. So when Jesus said, "You are the salt of the earth," His hearers knew exactly what He meant: "You are a preservative."

Consider for a moment the setting in which Jesus made that statement: A handful of people stood beside a lake in Judea, a despised and nondescript corner of the far-flung Roman Empire. There Jesus said to them, "You are the salt of the earth." You are a force for preserving all of human society against corruption and decay. Amazing! Does something of the weight of that statement rest upon you? Jesus is saying, in effect, "There is a lot of moral and spiritual corruption over in Outer Mongolia—you'd better get going! And the situation is really deteriorating in Africa—get over there right away! Oh, and something is really rotten in the state of Denmark—we need a dash of salt to stop the rot from spreading over there!"

Jesus never said, "You are the salt of Jerusalem," or "You are the salt of these Judean hillsides," or "You are the salt of Palestine." No, He said, in effect, "You are the salt of the earth. I'm going to tip over this great saltshaker full of believers, and I'm going to sprinkle you all over the planet." And, as amazing as it may seem, this astonishing prophecy has come true. Christians have in fact proved to be—more than any other group or cultural force in the world—the preservatives of morality, compassion, and ethical conduct in the world. It is nothing less than incredible that Jesus would make such a bold, prophetic statement to such a small and ragtag collection of followers, yet over these past two millennia we have seen His statement proven true.

Christians are the salt of the world. Christians are to stand at the threshold of the door of our culture and say to everything that would corrupt, defile, and pollute, "Thus far and no farther." That is what we *ought* to be doing if we are the salt of the earth. Tragically, as Jeremiah Denton discovered when he returned to America from eight years of torture and captivity, Christians have not barred that door. Corruption and pollution have gushed into our society like a flood from a broken sewer pipe. Defilement is everywhere around us.

Why have we not had more impact on our society? Why, if Christians are called to act as preservatives in our culture, do we see so much defilement, corruption, and decay? I submit to you that it is because we have pulled back from involvement and contact with our world.

For salt to preserve meat from corruption, it must have direct contact with the meat. It cannot sit in the saltshaker. It must be shaken out. Have you allowed God to shake you and sprinkle you out onto the world? Have you become involved with the hurt and wretched condition of our world?

Today it seems many Christians choose to ghettoize themselves into tidy little Christian enclaves, completely walled off from the world and its needs. We have our own Christian churches, our own Christian schools, our own Christian societies, our own Christian sports leagues and teams, our own Christian health insurance providers, our own Christian fellowship groups, our own Christian everything—and I am not faulting a single one of those endeavors.

But I am pointing out that if we completely seal ourselves up in Christian endeavors, we may soon find that we never get out of the saltshaker—we never have any contact with the world. We may become so comfy in our own little Christian ghetto that we never involve ourselves with the needs of a hurting and lost world. We may begin to think, *Why would any decent person want to have contact with all that corruption? It's nice and safe right here—so here's where I'm going to stay.*

How many unbelievers do you have any real social contact with in any given week? Certainly we ought not to be seeking our fulfillment from them because they can't provide fulfillment. But if we are truly following Christ, we know that *they* need to find their fulfillment in Christ, and *we* are the ones who have the truth they need. They have a God-shaped void in their lives. Jesus, our example, went out among sinners in order that He might give to them, not in order that He might get from them. So must we. We need to have contact with the world in order to preserve the world—we must be *in* the world without being *of* the world. We should be actively involved, saying yes to those who need to hear the Gospel of Jesus Christ while saying no to all of the influences and forces that seek to corrupt and destroy our society.

When was the last time you said a resounding *yes* to those around you who need to hear the Gospel of Jesus Christ? And when was the last time you said a firm, unyielding *no* to those who would tear down the moral standards of our society?

Some years ago a woman came to me claiming to be a Christian and telling me that she was romantically attached to an unbeliever. Not only that, but the man was *married*—and she intended to break up his marriage! I was stunned.

"You tell me you're a Christian," I said.

"Yes, I am."

"You believe that the Bible is the inspired Word of God."

"Yes, I do," she said.

"But you realize," I said, "that the Bible states very clearly that believers are not to marry unbelievers—and that believers are *certainly* not to covet the spouse of another person, nor commit the sin of adultery. You undoubtedly see the contradiction between being a Christian and doing what you intend to do! It would be wrong, it would be sin, it would be a fatal step for any Christian to take!"

"Well," she said, "if it wasn't God's will for me to fall in love with this man and for the two of us to be together, then why did God allow me to cross paths with this man? Why did God *bring* us together if He didn't *want* us to be together?" She didn't ask this question in a wondering, inquiring way—she asked it contentiously, defiantly, as if throwing down the gauntlet of challenge and daring me to come up with an answer!

"Well," I said, "did it ever occur to you that God might be using this experience of temptation in your life to see if you are willing to be obedient to His Word? Because His Word is clear, and it would never be His will that you should violate what is clearly stated in the Scriptures. You need to recognize that you are following your own will, not God's. By this same twisted logic you have suggested, a person could say to himself, 'I know the Bible says, "Thou shalt not steal," but if I cross paths with someone who is holding a big, fat purse full of money, then it's okay to take it! Otherwise, why did God bring me and that purse together if He didn't want me to steal it?' Does that make any sense?"

She seemed momentarily shaken and speechless, as if she had no defense against that argument. But an instant later, she set her jaw and a fire of rebellion lit her eyes, and she said, "Well, I know that this man and I are meant for each other. I'm going to continue to pursue this relationship one step at a time—and I'm going to tell my Christian friends what I'm doing every step of the way. I'll just see what my Christian friends have to say, and if none of them object to what I'm doing, I'll know it's God's will."

She proceeded to follow her own desires—and tragically her Christian friends failed to object. They saw what she was doing, but they didn't want to "get involved," "butt in," or "be busybodies." So this woman broke up the other marriage, married the unbelieving man, and is today very far from a walk with Jesus Christ.

Isn't that the way the world goes? Down one step, and then down another and another, because the salt is not there to confront the decay and stop it in its tracks. The world is watching and waiting for us in the Church to react to each fresh outrage, each step further down into the cesspool of corruption—yet we say nothing! We do nothing. We confront nothing. We are not salt. We are silent.

What if this woman's friends had spoken up and challenged her sinful choices? I wasn't able to get through to her, but she obviously cared what her Christian friends thought of her. What if they had chosen to be obedient to the words of Paul in Galatians 6:1?

> Brethren, if a man is overtaken in any trespass, you who are spiritual restore such a one in a spirit of gentleness, considering yourself lest you also be tempted.

Had this woman's Christian friends spoken up and lovingly but firmly confronted her about her sin, perhaps she and this other family would have been spared a great deal of emotional, relational, and spiritual destruction.

We could do so much if only we would choose obedience and involvement. We could change our churches, our neighborhoods, and our society, and we could rescue many souls if we would just sprinkle some salt upon the decaying meat of our culture. As Vance Havner has observed, "Humanity is a decaying carcass awaiting the vultures of judgment."

So, friend in Christ, it really comes down to this: We are either the carcass or the salt. Which are you today?

More than a preservative

We have been looking at salt as a preservative. But salt is more than just a preservative, and I think Jesus may well have had other aspects of the salt metaphor in mind when He first told His followers, "You are the salt of the earth." Some examples:

1. Salt is precious. Yes, I know that salt is one of the cheapest commodities in any grocery store today—you can buy a whole pound for about fifty cents. But in Jesus' day, salt was an exceedingly valuable substance. In some places and times, salt has even been used for money—hence the expression of a man being "worth his salt." Salt has also been used in some cultures as a rare and precious gift. And the salt we have to share with the world is also a rare and precious gift—the gift of the Gospel, the gift of liberation from bondage to moral corruption and the death that sin brings.

2. Salt stings. Rub salt into a wound and—*ouch!* That hurts! In a society filled with wounds and sores and ulcers, we should not expect that our touch of salt will always be welcomed—it won't! I have discovered many times that the Christian Gospel, no matter how graciously and lovingly spoken, frequently produces enormous offense, hostility, and rage in our hearers. That should never stop us or silence us. We must simply recognize that salt stings—and that opposition and rejection just go with the territory of being a follower of Jesus Christ.

How does salt sting in the day-to-day experiences we all have? Here's an example. Suppose you are around the office watercooler and someone says, "I heard a funny story the other day—you've got to hear it!" You can simply say, "Great—I love a good clean joke." If your friend's joke was going to be clean, no problem. But if not—look out! He will have been stung. You will have innocently, righteously rubbed salt in the wound of his immorality. If your friend has no clean joke to tell, be prepared to tell one of your own.

Billy Sunday, who was the Billy Graham of the early twentieth century, preached boldly against sin and immorality in his day. One day a man came to him and said, "Mr. Sunday, you rub the fur the wrong way."

"No, I don't," Billy Sunday replied. "Just let the cat turn around, and his fur will be unruffled when I stroke it."

Yes! That is the message! Turn around!

I have always been impressed by the Lord's first public words to the people when He began his ministry: "Repent, for the kingdom of heaven is at hand" (Matt. 4:17). I think of the fact that God has waited and planned over billions of trillions of eons of time, and during all that time He foreknew that Christ would come into this world and speak God's own words to His creatures. No doubt He gave much thought to what He would say. When He appeared, the first thing Jesus said after pondering the matter for endless eons was, "Repent! Turn around!" The original Greek word for "repent" is *metanoeo,* which means to do an about-face and head in the other direction.

Just as Billy Sunday said, we only rub the fur the wrong way if the cat is turned in the wrong direction. If the cat will repent, turn around, and go in the other direction, our message won't irritate—it will soothe! Salt does irritate; it does sting—but only those who need to be stung for their own good so that they will repent and turn their lives around. That is why we are called to be salt.

Peter Marshall, the late chaplain of the United States Senate, said that when the apostles preached, there were either riots or regeneration. Today we pastors get a handshake and the words, "Nice sermon, Pastor." Nice sermon! If we are preaching a nonirritating, stingless brand of Christianity, there is something desperately wrong with our preaching! It is without offense and without effect!

Notice, my friend, that Jesus didn't call us to be the "sugar of the world." He called us to be the "salt of the earth." I have to confess, I would much rather be sugar than salt. Everybody likes sugar. Everybody speaks well of sugar. But *salt*—! That stuff stings!

Let me tell you, one of the most despised and persecuted classes of people in America today is the vocal, politically active Christian. Pornographers, perjurers, and sex offenders are not as reviled in America today as are Christians who try to live out their faith as salt and light in a corrupt society. Some examples:

- Liberal columnist Molly Ivins has labeled evangelicals "Shiite Baptists," and in a 1998 column referred to the religious right as the "theocratic right"—a movement she claimed was planning "to impose its religious views on others through government action. It is both unconstitutional and profoundly un-American."

- A 1993 *New York Times* editorial piece asserted that the religious conservative movement "confronts us with a far greater threat than the old threat of communism"—a statement that is all the more outrageous in that this nation was founded by religiously conservative evangelical Christians!

- Another *New York Times* columnist referred to the influence of evangelical Christians in one of our political parties with these words: "The crazies are in charge. The fringe has taken over."

- Yet another syndicated columnist, noted for his pro-tolerance, antibigotry stances (unless, of course, that bigotry is directed against Christians!) wrote that the government should "tax the **** out of the churches if they open their holy yaps one more time about abortion, prayer in the schools, or anything else." Opening our "holy yaps," by the way, is what the First Amendment calls "the free exercise" of religious freedom and "freedom of speech," and what Jesus calls being the salt of the earth and the light of the world (by the way, I thought it best to edit out the swearword that came from his unholy yap!).

- After the chairman of the Democratic Party suggested that the "religious right" should henceforth be called the "radical religious right," that new, more pejorative label began to appear with numbing regularity in print editorials, news stories, and broadcast reports. Is it any wonder that American Christians are feeling marginalized, demonized, and assaulted in their own country for simply practicing their beliefs and exercising their constitutional rights?

- Democrats and members of the liberal media are not the only offenders. A number of so-called "moderate" Republicans (such as Arlen Spector of Pennsylvania) have attempted to distance themselves from what they call "the extreme religious right" by issuing statements containing Christian bashing.

I have experienced Christian bashing firsthand—and I have to tell you, I don't much like it when people carry signs or publish statements describing me as a "Nazi" or a "hatemonger" or a "fascist" or a "Khomeini" or some other label or libel. But it happens to me on a regular basis. Who would enjoy that kind of treatment? On the level of my own personal feelings, I would much rather be a "sugar daddy" than the salt of the earth. But if I were to do so, I would betray God's purpose for my life. Jesus said, "Woe to you when all men speak well of you, for so did their fathers to the false prophets" (Luke 6:26). Instead, Jesus says, "Blessed are you when they revile and persecute you, and say all kinds of evil against you falsely for My sake. Rejoice and be exceedingly glad, for great is your reward in heaven, for so they persecuted the prophets who were before you" (Matt. 5:11–12).

The Bible tells us, "Yes, and all who desire to live godly in Christ Jesus will suffer persecution" (2 Tim. 3:12). How much persecution have you endured for Christ's sake? I don't mean being persecuted for being needlessly offensive or obnoxious or abrasive. I mean being persecuted for being salt, for following in the footsteps of our crucified Master. If you have to answer, "None," then perhaps you are not being salty enough!

3. Salt heals. Just as we are not called to be the sugar of the world, neither are we called to be vinegar. We are called to be salt because salt not only stings, but it also purifies and cures and heals. There is nothing like hot salt water for a sore throat, as every speaker and singer knows. So we should not only irritate and sting as salt often does, but we should also be a force for healing whenever healing is needed.

Have you ever noticed that many people who revile and persecute Christians suddenly change their tune when they get into trouble? When their world comes crashing down, when the grim diagnosis comes back, or when they suddenly face the consequences for some poor choices they have made in life—where do they go? Often, they go straight to Christians, to the only people they can count on to pray. "Please help me," they say. "Please pray for me!" They come to people who know the Source of all healing—and that is our opportunity to witness and reach out to them with the healing love and power of Jesus Christ. That, too, is what it means to be the salt of the earth.

4. *Salt seasons.* Salt gives zest and flavor to life—and so should we! All too many Christians see their purpose in life as one of being the wet blankets of the earth—but that is not the calling God has given us. "You are the salt of the earth," said the Lord.

A young boy once defined salt as "that stuff that tastes bad when it's not there." Amen! That is how the world should see Christians. When Christians are not around, non-Christians should feel that something is missing, something is lacking in their lives. Authentic Christianity always brings a lift to the heart, a smile to the face, a sense of genuine joy even in times of trial. Christ makes us happy. He makes us feel blessed—as we see in the Beatitudes in Matthew 5: "Blessed are those . . . , blessed are you . . . , blessed are the pure in heart." *Blessed* means happy, so Christians should wear a happy face. They should spice up the lives of the people around them with Christlike joy and love.

5. *Salt causes thirst.* You have heard the cliché "You can lead a horse to water, but you can't make him drink." I disagree! Any horse you can lead to water, I can make drink. It doesn't take a rocket scientist. I don't even know a whole lot about horses, but I am quite certain that if you place salt tablets in the horse's cheeks, you had better not stand between the horse and the nearest water trough, because that horse is going to get thirsty!

That is the effect Christians should have on the world. We should awaken a thirst within the people around us for the Water of Life, a thirst for righteousness and godly living, a thirst for Christ. How many people have you made thirsty for the Water of Life? How many people have come to you and said words such as: "I don't know what you have, but I want it!"? And how many times do we hear just the opposite: "If that is Christianity, I don't want any part of it!"?

I remember one couple I met some years ago. The wife had recently accepted Christ as her Lord and Savior, while the husband was clearly not a Christian. As we talked, the husband said to me, "Well, you know, my wife got religion not long ago. And she has been more forgiving and more joyful and more peaceful than at any other time in our marriage. I don't know what it is, but whatever she's got, I'd like to have it."

I said, "Praise the Lord! I just happen to have brought some with me."

Now that lady was the salt of the earth—and the salt of her home. That is what Christ calls all of us to be. As salt, we are to make people thirsty for the truth, thirsty to know this same Jesus we know. Then we will have the opportunity to share with them the sparkling, bubbling Living Water that leads to life everlasting.

"Keep your salt in the spice cabinet!"

Unfortunately, the world, which is dominated by Satan, seeks to keep Christian salt bottled up and shut away in the spice cabinet. One of the ways anti-Christian forces have blunted Christian influence in the world is by stealing the First Amendment from us. America's founding fathers had a view of the First Amendment much different from that which is now proclaimed in our courtrooms, classrooms, and newsrooms. By sheer sloganeering, the forces of cultural decay have been hugely successful in keeping Christians from being the salt of the earth. What is the slogan of these anti-Christian forces? "Separation of church and state."

Does the First Amendment decree that there shall be a wall of separation between church and state? If you put that question to the American people, 90 percent would respond yes—because the American people have been brainwashed into such a belief, and because few Americans have ever bothered to read the First Amendment for themselves.

The truth is that the First Amendment says no such thing. It is absolutely vital that we understand what the First Amendment to the Constitution truly says, because the relationship between these two "kingdoms"—the kingdom of God's Church and the kingdom of the state—has been a long and contentious one. Here is the entire text of the First Amendment:

Congress shall make no law respecting an establishment of religion, or prohibiting the free exercise thereof; or abridging the freedom of speech, or of the press; or the right of the people peaceably to assemble, and to petition the government for a redress of grievances.

Question: What does this clear, simple statement say about what the Church can or cannot do? What does it say about what the Church should or should not do? What does it say about what a Christian minister should or should not say? What does that say about what a Christian citizen should or should not do?

Answer: Absolutely nothing!

Having seen centuries of oppression of religion in Europe, the founding fathers deliberately created a society in which the government would be prohibited from interfering in any way with the free exercise of religious expression. They crafted the First Amendment with the clear and unambiguous intent of keeping the state completely out of the business of the Church—but they never, ever envisioned that the Church would be kept out of the business of the state!

Where, then, did we get this idea of a wall of separation between church and state? It is not found in any part of the Constitution or the Federalist Papers or the Declaration of Independence or any of the other founding documents of our republic. No, the concept of "separation of church and state," which so many have mistakenly adopted as if it were sacred writ, is actually a phrase from a *private letter* written in 1802 by Thomas Jefferson to the Danbury Baptists of Connecticut.

The phrase was largely unknown to the American public until it was quoted in a 1947 Supreme Court decision. Since then the term "separation of church and state" has been mindlessly parroted by those who would muzzle and neutralize Christians. Jefferson himself would be horrified to know how his words have been wrenched from their original context and turned against his own beliefs, as stated in the Danbury letter,

> Religion is a matter which lies solely between man & his God . . . I contemplate with sovereign reverence that act of the whole American people which declared that their legislature should make no law respecting an establishment of religion, or prohibiting the free exercise thereof; thus building a wall of separation between church and state.

Jefferson's purpose in writing these words was to assure the Danbury Baptists (who were a religious minority in largely Congregationalist Connecticut) that they would always be free to practice their religious faith without government intrusion. Jefferson never envisioned an America (like today's America) in which government would be hostile toward religion, nor an American government that would be shielded from being influenced by religious people. His "wall of separation" metaphor was a one-way barrier, intended only to keep government out of the churches, not to keep Christians out of their government.

As Justice Oliver Wendell Holmes once said, "It is one of the misfortunes of the law that ideas become encysted in phrases, and thereafter for a long time cease to provoke further analysis." To which Supreme Court Justice William Rehnquist adds, "The 'wall of separation between church and State' is a metaphor based on bad history, a metaphor which has proved useless as a guide to judging. It should be frankly and explicitly abandoned."[2]

What Justice Rehnquist suggests is nothing more than a return to the clear, original intent of the Constitution. All ten amendments of the Bill of Rights were written with a single purpose in mind: to restrain the federal government from interfering with the liberties of the people. None of them were written to restrain the people from influencing their government. The Bill of Rights was added to the Constitution because the framers of the Constitution feared (and rightly so) that the people of this country would not accept the new Constitution unless the rights of the people were defined and protected—and the power of the government was limited.

Today, however, the American people will swallow just about anything. If you ask the average person in the street where the phrase "separation of church and state" comes from, they will probably tell you it comes from the Constitution. The phrase is found in a constitution, all right—but *not* the U.S. Constitution! In Article 124 of the constitution of the now defunct Soviet Union you find this statement: "In order to ensure the citizens' freedom of conscience, the church of the USSR is separated from the state." Is that the kind of government we want—the government of the old USSR?

Today we are drifting irresistibly toward the Soviet concept of separation of church and state. Under the Soviet view, the Church is free to do anything the government is not engaged in—and the government is engaged in everything! So what is the Church free to do? It is free to remain within four walls, where believers may pray and sing hymns. But should the Church decide to become salt and light, exercising dominion over the world in God's name, then the Church must be crushed. That is the Soviet view—and it is rapidly becoming the prevailing view in America as well.

Today when you hear the phrase "separation of church and state," remember what it means: "Christians, stay out of matters of government and social policy—leave that to us, the atheists, agnostics, and humanists. Keep your salt in the spice cabinet. Let us run society as we see fit."

This view stands the First Amendment on its head. It's time we put the First Amendment right side up so that we as Christians can remain free to influence society, to be salt and light in a decaying and darkening world. This is what it means to subdue the earth and exercise dominion in His name.

The reign of unbelief is ending

I once appeared on a secular radio talk show. During the show, the phone lines were opened and one of the callers used blasphemous language in the course of stating his anti-Christian opinions. That caller was followed by a very dear Christian lady who politely said she wished the previous caller would not use such offensive language on a radio show. Shortly thereafter, we received a call from an abrasive humanist. "Who does that woman think she is?" he growled. "I'll use any kind of language I want, and nobody has the right to tell me not to swear or curse or blaspheme! I say what I want, when I want, in any way I like!"

On another occasion, I appeared on a talk show, paired up with an avowed atheist. We had a lively exchange of points of view, then the phone lines were opened for callers. Near the end of the show, someone called and asked, "Dr. Kennedy, can you tell me how I could become a Christian?" So I explained the plan of salvation and suggested to this caller that he get down on his knees, bow his head and heart before

Christ, and ask Him to come into his life to forgive him and make him a new creature.

The other guest, an avowed atheist and humanist, was clearly irritated by the counsel I offered and was chomping at the bit to give his advice to the caller. Finally, when I had finished speaking, he launched in, "Caller," he said, "my advice to you is that you get up off your knees, stand up straight, and lift up your head. Never bow to God or anyone else. Don't look to God to save you or forgive you. Stand proud and run your own life!"

That is the essence of human rebellion. That is autonomous humanity, a law unto oneself, defiant and proud like Milton's depiction of Satan, who said he would rather reign in Hell than serve in Heaven. The human heart has not changed a bit since the human race fell through Adam. Men and women are still infected by the same satanic lie that the serpent hissed into the ears of Eve: "Ye shall not surely die . . . ye shall be as gods, knowing good and evil" (Gen. 3:4–5 KJV). Today human beings still seek to be gods unto themselves—rebellious, arrogant, amoral, autonomous, accountable to no one, reigning supreme in their own universe. They resent the authority of God. They resent the restrictions of Judeo-Christian morality. They will have no one telling them what they can and cannot do.

Today unbelief occupies our land. The forces of unbelief do not fully control our culture, but neither does Christianity. Instead we see a great civil war, a moral and ethical war, a spiritual war, a culture war that rages throughout our society. It is the battle between salt and corruption. It is a good war, a just war. If Christians were not engaged in this war, committed to being salt in a dying culture, struggling to spread their healthful influence in a sick and diseased society, life would be unlivable. Without the salt that Christians bring, our world would become so abominable and the evils would be so great, the stench of evil would make it impossible to live in the land. As the "salt of the earth" we are to keep this earth from utterly decaying before the time comes when Christ shall return.

Consider what would happen if there were no Christians, no "salt of the earth," to hold back the flood of human evil in society! Imagine if there were no Bible-believing, Spirit-led Christians to oppose the politically powerful, well-financed movements of social decay and moral corruption that are abroad in our society. What would we see? The destruction of the sanctity of marriage and the family; the elevation of sexual degeneracy to the status of a "protected minority" with special "affirmative action" quotas and privileges; the legalization of adult-child "consensual sex" and child pornography; the replacement of the First Amendment with only officially approved, "politically correct" speech; a torrent of hideous "brave new world" practices such as infanticide, euthanasia, and physician-assisted suicide; and on and on. A world without Christians would be a continual feast of demons, a place filled with unimaginable horrors, terrors, and obscenities—a global Sodom to the nth degree!

We live in a world that appears to be out of control—a world of wars, famines, murders, rapes, thefts, lies, corruption in high places, immorality, and perversion of every sort. We look at our morning paper or the evening news, and we wonder how the world could get any worse than it already is. But we have not seen the worst of which human evil and satanic evil are capable. Only when Christians have either been removed from the world or have fully abandoned their mandate to be salt and light will the full force of evil be unleashed upon the planet.

While Christians remain on the earth as the salt of the earth, the great struggle rages—the struggle between light and dark, between salt and corruption, between the forces of God and the false religions and antichrists of the corrupt world system. The leading anti-Christian force in our society is a religion called humanism.

You may be surprised that I would describe humanism as a religion. Isn't humanism a secular movement—and an aggressively antireligious movement at that? Yes—but it is still a religion. You do not have to believe in God to have a religion. Buddhism, Taoism, wicca, and scientology are all examples of nontheistic religions; humanism—secular and atheistic as it may be—is a religion as well, and the goal of humanism is to supplant and replace Christianity as the dominant belief system in the world. Among the stated goals and tenets of humanism as enshrined in the 1933 and 1973 *Humanist Manifestos* are: a belief that the universe is self-existing and not created; a belief that science has rendered faith in the supernatural "unacceptable"; the assertion that "salvationism," "false hopes of heaven hereafter," and "fear of eternal damnation" are harmful and illusory; and the declaration that ethics and morality are a matter of personal autonomy and choice, not governed by God or church.

Humanism has, in fact, declared itself to be a religion without God. We see this stated nine times in the *Humanist Manifesto* of 1933 and also in the second *Humanist Manifesto* of 1973. In 1961, the Supreme Court handed down a decision in *Torcaso v. Watkins* that placed nontheistic religions on an equal footing with theistic religions; a footnote in that decision clarified what the court had in mind in regard to nontheistic religions: "Among religions in this country which do not teach what would generally be considered a belief in the existence of God are Buddhism, Taoism, ethical culture, secular humanism, and others." The same Supreme Court that has declared that our schools cannot teach any religion has declared that secular humanism is a religion!

Despite this fact, humanism—with its tenets of atheism, evolution, amorality, socialism, and one-world government—is taught in our public schools and legislated into power in our public square. While Christianity is being systematically attacked, marginalized, and forcibly removed from the marketplace of ideas, humanism has become the official state-sponsored religion of our nation. Tens of billions of our tax dollars are spent by the government every year to inculcate this state religion into the minds of our children in the public schools. Is this a deliberate strategy to brainwash an entire generation of young people into the godless religion of secular humanism? Read these statements by prominent humanists—and *you* decide:

> Education is thus a most powerful ally of humanism, and every American school is a school of humanism. What can a theistic Sunday school's meeting for an hour once a week and teaching only a fraction of the children do to stem the tide of the five-day program of humanistic teaching?
>
> —CHARLES F. POTTER
> *Humanism: A New Religion*, 1930

I think that the most important factor moving us toward a secular society has been the educational factor. Our schools may not teach Johnny to read properly, but the fact that Johnny is in school until he is sixteen tends to lead toward the elimination of religious superstition.

—PAUL BLANSHARD
"Three Cheers for Our Secular State"
The Humanist, March/April 1976

We must ask how we can kill the god of Christianity. We need only insure that our schools teach only secular knowledge. If we could achieve this, god would indeed be shortly due for a funeral service.

—G. RICHARD BOZARTH
"On Keeping God Alive"
American Athiest, November 1977

I am convinced that the battle for humankind's future must be waged and won in the public school classroom by teachers who correctly perceive their role as proselytizers of a new faith: a religion of humanity . . . These teachers must embody the same selfless dedication as the most rabid fundamentalist preachers, for they will be ministers of another sort, utilizing a classroom instead of a pulpit to convey humanist values in whatever subject they teach, regardless of the educational level—preschool day care or a large state university. The classroom must and will become an arena of conflict between the old and new—the rotting corpse of Christianity, together with all its adjacent evils and misery, and the new faith of humanism, resplendent in its promise of a world in which the never-realized Christian ideal of "love thy neighbor" will finally be achieved.

—JOHN J. DUNPHY
"A New Religion for a New Age"
The Humanist, January/February 1983[3]

Clearly, the atheists and humanists have been hard at work over the past few decades, putting their anti-God strategy into effect in our public schools. But I believe the humanists are wrong when they declare

Christianity a "rotting corpse." Christianity may have been slumbering, but it is not dead. Even now I see God breathing new life into these dry bones. Christianity is shaking itself awake and rising to its feet. Though the religion of unbelief now occupies the land, though the humanists have fortified themselves in a walled city like Jericho of old, and though we have in past times retreated from our responsibilities to fulfill the Cultural Mandate and the Great Commission, I have traveled this country, and I see what God is now doing. I can hear the ground shaking beneath the marching feet of the men of God, and I can hear the rumbling and trembling of the walls and towers of unbelief. Soon I believe we will hear the trumpets sound and the shout of victory—and we will see the walls come tumbling down. The forces of unbelief, I am convinced, are in for a big surprise!

Winning the war

You and I are involved in one of the greatest struggles in the history of the world: the struggle for the soul of America—the nation that has been called the "last best hope of mankind on earth." America, you remember, is the source of most of the missionaries and missionary money for furthering the Gospel of Jesus Christ around the world—and we are involved in a struggle for her soul! The tragedy is that many of us are still on the sidelines of that struggle. Many of us are merely spectators while the most exciting adventure the world has ever seen is raging before our eyes. It is time—it is past time!—that each of us as Christians take the plunge and get involved.

You may ask, "How do I get involved?" Here again, it comes down to the purpose God has set forth for our lives in the Cultural Mandate and the Great Commission. To get involved in this all-important struggle, you must determine that you are going to become an influence for God in your community and your world. How do you do that on a daily, specific basis? That is something you should set down as a matter of daily prayer:

Lord, please open my eyes to the opportunities that are all around me to have an influence for You and to be a witness to You. Lord, please bring situations

*and people into my life that I can touch for Your sake, so that I can be salt
and light in the world, so that I can fulfill the purpose You have given me.*

Of course, Christians must never seek political power for power's
sake. We should only seek to influence the country for good. The French
political philosopher Alexis de Tocqueville said, "America is great
because America is good, and if America ever ceases to be good, America
will cease to be great." Today, sin is fashionable in America; those who
would do good are condemned and ostracized. If America's goodness
departs, it is only a matter of time—and not much time at that—before
America's greatness departs as well.

I believe many Christians who were once asleep in complacency and
apathy have been awakened by the stench of a rotting culture. We are seeing more Christians writing articles and letters to the editor, more
Christians taking strong moral positions, more Christians running for
elective office, and more Christians voting in national and local elections.

The question naturally arises: How should Christians vote? First, I
believe that Christians should not be bound to any political party.
Instead, Christians should be bound by the Word of God. We should
search the Scriptures, ascertain what the Bible says about any issue facing our nation, and then vote our biblically informed conscience. As
Martin Luther said, "My conscience is bound by the Word of God. I can
do no other." That is how Christians ought to vote.

At the same time, we must recognize that being salt in our society
means much more than simply voting or becoming politically involved.
We must also become *personally* involved in defending morality and
godliness in our neighborhoods, our schools, and our communities.
Here are a few examples of things you could do to be salt in your own
little corner of the world:

Monitor the media. Be aware of the immorality and obscenity on
your TV screen, your radio, and your home computer—and fight back.
Target sponsors of immoral programming with letters and e-mail.
Contact broadcast and cable TV networks, as well as companies that
host offensive websites. Talk to the theater owners in your neighborhood
who show offensive or anti-Christian films. Talk to the radio station

managers who program obscene "shock jock" shows on your local air-waves—and let them know you will be filing letters of protest when the station's license comes up for renewal. Be aware of the influences that are impacting your community and the souls of your children.

Stand up for the First Amendment. When atheist pressure groups try to halt such events as student-initiated prayer at graduation exercises or other constitutionally protected religious expression, take a stand for God and for freedom. Don't be silent. Get involved. Talk to school administrators and school board members. Write letters to the editor. Contact and support the Rutherford Institute and other organizations that defend religious liberty.

Get involved with your local schools. Attend school board meetings and PTA meetings, and be aware of policies and programs that affect the moral and spiritual welfare of students. Above all, make sure the school's sex education program is focused on abstinence. Eve Jackson taught "family life" classes at Hamilton Southeastern High School in Indianapolis—but as a Christian, she had a crisis of conscience. As much as she wanted to talk about God and morality in her classes, the prevalent doctrine of "separation of church and state" forbade her from teaching God's truth about chastity in the public schools. So Eve Jackson, a Baptist, left the public school, developed an abstinence-based program rooted in Scripture, and introduced it into thirty-four parochial schools in Indianapolis.

Soon afterward, Indianapolis Mayor Steve Goldsmith decided the city needed Eve Jackson back! Facing a 40 percent rise in teen pregnancy over the preceding decade, the school system invited her to bring her abstinence program, "A Promise to Keep," into the public schools. The program builds credibility with students by using trained, committed high school students as teachers who are able to communicate that "chastity is cool." The program sends a clear message that young people should maintain abstinence until marriage. "That faith component is essential," says Eve Jackson, "because it gives them a moral standard to live by. Otherwise, it's anything goes."[4]

Get involved with your local library. Make sure your neighborhood library is "family-friendly." Most parents are unaware that their children can go to most libraries, access the Internet on public library computers, and download hardcore pornography or bomb-making information in full view of everyone—and most librarians will not stop them. In fact, this policy of wide-open Internet access for minors is *mandated* by the American Library Association's "Library Bill of Rights," which guarantees that no person's access to books, magazines, or material on the Internet shall be "abridged because of . . . age."

The ALA also has an express policy forbidding the use of filtering software to block out pornography on library computers—so a child in the public library is just one click away from the most incredibly vile images imaginable! The ALA's website (www.ala.org) even features links designed to take your young people to such websites as "Go Ask Alice," which offers raw, detailed, "nonjudgmental" instruction to young people in how to engage in the most nauseating and obscene sex practices imaginable (including homosexuality, sadomasochism, and bestiality). Another link on ALA's website takes young people to "Peacefire: Youth Alliance Against Internet Censorship," which shows kids how to disable Internet filtering software, such as SurfWatch and Cyber Patrol, so they can access pornography without their parents' finding out! Not all local libraries subscribe to the antifamily, antiparent policies of the ALA—but most do. By getting involved and showing you care, you can help make your own local library "family-friendly."

Fight abortion—one pregnancy at a time. You may feel powerless to overturn the *Roe v. Wade* Supreme Court decision that legalized abortion—but you still have the power to save a life. Every major community in America has a Crisis Pregnancy Center—a Christian ministry that offers counseling, care, and a Christian witness to women with unwanted pregnancies. These centers always need people to volunteer time and resources—so instead of moaning about the abortion plague, you can actually pitch in and help save lives.

Work for racial reconciliation. Work within your church to initiate special ministry relationships and worship events with ethnic churches. If you attend a predominantly white church, build bridges of friendship and cooperation with predominantly black, Hispanic, or Asian churches. Find ways to break down cultural barriers while embracing and supporting your brothers and sisters across racial and ethnic lines.

Become a community volunteer. Charles Colson tells about a group of Christians from several churches, plus other community leaders and citizens of goodwill, who joined forces to clear drug dealers out of a city park in Houston's tough Precinct Six. The citizens group, which called itself "the Little League Squad," was first trained by the Houston police department. Then the group bought baseball equipment and uniforms and started Little League teams at the park. Some two hundred volunteers worked as coaches and "volunteer cops," patrolling the park and keeping out drugs and alcohol. An antigraffiti squad helped stop vandalism.

By coaching Little League teams, these volunteers built relationships, provided positive role models, and offered healthy activities to kids who might otherwise end up as casualties of the inner city. And by moving crime and drugs out of the neighborhood park, they removed one of the corrosive elements that bring corruption and decay to our society. The results, according to Colson, were dramatic: "Homicides are down by nearly 50 percent. Robberies have dropped by 34 percent. Auto thefts are down 48 percent . . . Houston's Little League Squad [is teaching] citizens how to rebuild civil society, one block at a time."[5]

These are just a few examples of actions we can all take to become salt in our society and in our own neighborhoods. These examples are intended only as suggestions and ideas to spark your own thinking. I encourage you to take a good look at the needs and hurts and injustices in your own neighborhood—then ask God to open your eyes and show you what He wants you to do to act as His preservative, sprinkled out upon your corner of the world.

Political involvement is just one way of being salt in our society—but there are so many other ways! And perhaps the most important way we become salt is through the power of our witness, our Christian testimony. C. S. Lewis, the great scholar and lay theologian, once made a striking statement: "The most significant political action that any Christian can take," he said, "is to convert his neighbor." And he is exactly right! Our political beliefs are an expression of our worldview, and our worldview is a natural outgrowth of our religious beliefs.

When a person comes to Christ, his worldview changes—and frequently his political views undergo a transformation. I have seen such transformations myself. I once spoke with a high official in one of the political parties of our country. He told me he was converted to Jesus Christ in 1974, and in 1976 he changed his party affiliation. Our faith in Christ should touch every aspect of our lives and our thinking, including our views on how we should vote, how government should run, and how society should function.

Years ago a Christian said to me, "Do you really believe that Christians should get involved in political activities? That's dirty business!"

My tongue-in-cheek reply: "Oh, Heaven forbid we get our hands dirty by getting involved in our government! You're right—we should let the atheists take over and run the country! That way, we'll always have plenty to complain about—and we Christians would much rather curse the darkness than light a candle, wouldn't we?"

This well-meaning but misguided Christian got my point. If we do not get involved in our own government, who will? If we abandon the government to godless people, what right have we to complain when the world begins collapsing around our ears?

In recent years I have been encouraged to see Christians increasingly getting involved, putting themselves on the front line, seeking public office in city, county, state, and federal government, from school board member to U.S. senator. There are so many ways we can make our presence felt and fulfill our Lord's command to be the salt of the earth.

"But," you may say, "I'm just one person! How can one person be 'the salt of the earth,' and reverse the entire trend of corruption and decay that is going on in our society?"

Friend in Christ, you are just one person, I am just one person, the Christian next to you is just one person—but we are all in God's great saltshaker together! God is taking the saltshaker in hand, and even now He is pouring us out upon the world—a grain of salt here, a pinch of salt there, strategically placed in our own individual corners of this dying, decaying world.

In 1968, a young army surgeon named Kenneth Swan arrived in Vietnam and was instantly plunged into the bloody horrors of that war. One of the first cases placed upon his operating table was a nineteen-year-old soldier who had been horribly mutilated by a Vietcong grenade.

The young man's face was lacerated and his eyes were destroyed. Both of his legs were gone. Dr. Swan spent more than seven hours operating on the young man.

After the surgery, several of the other doctors—"old-timers" who had been in the "'Nam" far longer than the newly arrived Dr. Swan—said, "You shouldn't have wasted seven hours on a case like that. A kid like that is better off dead. Next time you get a case in that condition, just let him die." That advice jolted Dr. Swan—and haunted him for years to come. He often wondered if he had done the right thing in saving that soldier's life.

Finally, after two decades had passed and the war was long over, he decided to track down the soldier and find out whatever became of him. It took two years for Dr. Swan to locate the soldier—and what he discovered was astounding. As expected, the man was blind and spent most of his day in a wheelchair—but everything else about the man was totally unexpected! He was married with two daughters; he had earned a college degree and learned to scuba dive; and he had become an instructor to the disabled, helping others learn to cope with crippling injuries. Most important of all, this man had found peace with God and gave God credit for everything that had happened in his life.[6]

Sometimes, like Dr. Swan, you may wonder if your efforts to make a difference in the world are really worthwhile. There are probably times when you think, *Am I doing any good at all?* Well, maybe you can't change the entire world with the wave of a wand—but you can change your own little corner of the world if you are willing and obedient to allow God to pour you out of His saltshaker.

So don't worry that you are "only" a pinch of salt. When you are God's salt, poured out according to His plan, a pinch is just the right amount!

5

A RAY
OF LIGHT

You are the light of the world. A city that is set on a hill cannot
be hidden. Nor do they light a lamp and put it under a basket,
but on a lampstand, and it gives light to all who are in the house.
Let your light so shine before men, that they may see your good
works and glorify your Father in heaven.

(MATT. 5:14–16)

I was once interviewed on a television station in a large American city by a young woman who was the coanchor for the local evening news. In the course of the interview, she asked me a number of questions that got to the very heart of the Christian life—the kind of insightful questions not usually asked on secular TV. Near the end of the interview, she said, "You know, there are a lot of people watching right now who don't really know what a Christian is or what you mean when you talk about being 'born anew.' Why don't you explain that to them?"

So I explained what it means to accept Christ as one's Lord and Savior. Then we broke for a commercial. As the newswoman and I were chatting during the break, I asked, "Are you sure the station is going to run this interview?" I could hardly believe I had been allowed to give the entire plan of salvation on a major news broadcast.

"We just ran it," she replied. "This is a live telecast."

"In that case," I said, only half joking, "you'd better look for a new job because you're about to be fired."

She smiled and said, "I won't be fired. I'll tell you why later—we're back on in ten seconds."

We came back from the commercial and finished the interview. At the conclusion of the program, she explained her earlier comment. "The reason I'm not worried about being fired over this interview is simple. Do you see that man over there behind the camera? Five years ago, I led him to Christ. And my coanchor? I led him to Christ three years ago. I led my station manager to Christ two years ago. Four years ago, I led the owner of this station to Christ—and he owns five other TV stations as well. So, you see, I don't have to worry about losing my job for doing an honest live interview about the Christian faith."

This is a powerful example of what it means to be the light of the world, fulfilling the Great Commission. This woman was an influence on a one-to-one basis in her own workplace—and an influence on a mass basis through her work in the broadcast media. That is what God has called us to do as Christians—to use every atom of influence we have in whatever sphere we are in to reach others with the Good News of Jesus Christ.

I'm not suggesting that this should only be done through the media—far from it! I challenge you, however, to consider a career for yourself (or encourage your children to consider a career) in a strategic place of influence—a TV or radio station, a newspaper or magazine, a position in the government. And I challenge your church to adopt as its mission field, its target for prayer and witnessing, a local media outlet or government office. Begin to pray for the people in positions of power and influence, begin to meet with them and talk to them about Christ—and begin making a difference in this nation for Jesus Christ.

And whether you have a position of influence like the broadcast news anchor who interviewed me, you can share your faith with others, one-on-one, as this woman did with her coworkers and her bosses. When you do that, you will see that your witness and the new life of Christ within you will be multiplied many times over in the lives of those around you.

"You are the light of the world," Jesus said in effect, "so let your light shine!" That is our purpose for living! Are you shining the light of God's love and righteousness in your little corner of the world right now? Living as light in a dark world is the core duty we find in both the Cultural Mandate and the Great Commission. In Genesis 1:28, He told us, "Be fruitful and multiply; fill the earth and subdue it." That mandate is still in force today, as is our mandate, given to us by Christ in Matthew 28:19–20: "Go therefore and make disciples of all the nations, baptizing them in the name of the Father and of the Son and of the Holy Spirit, teaching them to observe all things that I have commanded you . . ."

As Americans, we want to see our nation renewed, revitalized, and restored to goodness and greatness. As Christians, we want to carry out our God-given purpose and fulfill His mandates for our lives. We want to restore moral sanity and spiritual responsibility to this nation that has fallen so far from what it once was and what it could be again. So our purpose as Christians is very clear, isn't it?

If every Christian would be obedient to the Cultural Mandate and the Great Commission, if every believer were faithfully living as salt and light in the world, we would soon see the most radical spiritual transformation and moral revolution in human history. So what is stopping us? I suggest to you that this revolution is hindered by two forms of resistance—the internal resistance that operates within many Christians and the external resistance of this fallen world. Let's examine these two forms of resistance in closer detail.

Resistance within

God has commanded us to multiply and replenish the earth with men and women who have been reshaped in God's image, in the image of His Son, Jesus Christ. Yet most Christians have been content to leave the task of evangelism to "the professionals," to the pastors and evangelists who evangelize from the pulpit or over the airwaves. Friend in Christ, that was *never* God's plan for evangelism! It was *never* God's purpose for your life that you be a spectator on the sidelines. *All* believers are expected by God to be in the middle of the arena—not sitting in the bleachers.

The Great Commission was not given to pastors and evangelists alone. It was given to every individual who follows Jesus Christ. Every person who is seeking to be refashioned into the image of Jesus Christ bears the responsibility for spreading the Good News of Jesus Christ to other people.

Tragically, surveys indicate that *more than 90 percent* of all church members in America have *never* led a single person to Christ—not one! This is a catastrophe and a failure almost beyond comprehension. If you are among the 90 percenters who have never led another person to Christ, odds are you are reading these words and feeling a rising sense of resistance within you at this very moment. You may be thinking, *But I don't have the spiritual gift of evangelism,* or *I'm too shy to go up to strangers and start witnessing to them,* or *I get tongue-tied—I wouldn't know where to begin evangelizing.*

While it's true that God has given a special, outstanding gift of evangelism to some Christians, He has not exempted the rest of His Church from the Great Commission—far from it! He expects *every* believer to be a witness, and He has enabled and empowered *all* believers to tell their story of how they came to know Christ. This is a duty you cannot escape—it is an essential part of being a Christian. If you resist this duty to be the light of the world, to be fruitful and multiply, and to share your faith with others, then you are resisting one of the most fundamental aspects of what it means to be a Christian.

It is clear that the Church has failed miserably in carrying out the ordinance God gave us at creation to reproduce other creatures in the image of God—otherwise, the world would be overwhelmingly Christian. We need to seize the day and accept our personal, individual responsibility for fulfilling this purpose of God.

Moreover, we need to understand that while evangelism is a duty, it is the most thrilling and joyful Christian duty of all. You will never know the depths of the rich and rewarding Christian experience God intended for you until you partake of the incredible privilege of being used by God to bring others to eternal life. No thrill ride at Disneyland, no experience of soaring aboard a space shuttle or walking on the moon, no sensual experience known to human experience can match the catch of the heart, the leap of the soul, and the lasting sense of joy, peace, and satisfaction that comes in watching another human being—a life God has used *you* to touch!—come into the kingdom of God and the experience of eternal life.

God has commanded His Church to light a torch and advance into the world. The Church has responded by placing its light under a basket and withdrawing in retreat! One of the main causes for this retreat is a defective view of Christianity called pietism. The pietistic view emphasizes a very personal and private spirituality to the exclusion of the rest of the world. Instead of witnessing boldly to the world around them, people of the pietistic persuasion confine their spirituality to their own lives. While claiming to love and serve and worship God, they ignore His two mandates.

The Christian withdrawal from the world has been going on for the better part of the twentieth century and sadly continues on into the twenty-first. By abandoning entire spheres of influence in our world to unbelievers, we have allowed a number of ominous trends to arise, threatening our religious freedom and the moral fabric of our society. When we look about us at the way our government has begun to suppress religious expression, or the way the Christian faith is being ridiculed and attacked in education, the arts, the media, the scientific community, and the social sciences, it is clear that the pietistic approach has contributed to today's amoral, nonreligious, anti-Christian society.

Everywhere in our world we see the glorification of evil and the exaltation of humanity where once God was glorified and His kingdom was advanced. Why? Because Christians have largely ceased to be salt and light in the world. We have retreated from our God-ordained duty to "go into all the world and preach the gospel to every creature" (Mark 16:15).

There is no limit to what God can do through us—if we will only let Him have His way in our lives. When we, as obedient individual members of the body of Christ, move out to accomplish God's will, the Church as a whole moves forward and accomplishes unimaginably great things in His name. Despite the failures, neglect, resistance, and retreat of the past, I genuinely believe that God is ready to revive His Church and move us forward into the greatest time of worldwide change and evangelization in human history—if we will only hear His call and obey it.

Resistance without

We have just examined the *internal* resistance that many Christians must overcome in order to fulfill God's mandates for their lives. Now let's look at the second form of resistance that hinders the approaching spiritual revolution in our world: the *external* resistance of this fallen world. Those who would be salt and light in our world today face an uphill battle on many fronts. Even our own government is working against us.

All around this nation, Christians are discovering that their right to freely exercise and witness to their faith is under increasing assault. Often these are stealth attacks. Many Christians in various parts of the country have been told, for example, that they cannot hold a small group Bible study in their home because it would constitute a "church," and their neighborhoods are not zoned for "churches." Tupperware parties, raucous Super Bowl parties, window-shattering beer parties with live rock bands—no problem! But eight to twelve people gathering quietly to study the Scriptures together? That violates the zoning ordinances!

That's what Pastor Orie Wenger of Simpsonville, South Carolina, discovered in 1998 when county officials slapped him with a $1,000-a-day fine for holding Bible studies in his home. Fortunately, this anti-First Amendment act of insanity was halted when the state's governor, David Beasley, interceded with the county. "As governor, I cannot stand silent while someone's basic fundamental rights are trampled upon," said Beasley. "It outrages me that anyone needs to be reminded that zoning regulations can never wipe out constitutional rights . . . We have a Bible study gathering in the governor's mansion. We also have them in my office. Apparently, I might need permission from a zoning board to study God's Word with some of my friends."[1]

Another modern-day battleground of religious liberty is our public schools. While the First Amendment guarantees every schoolchild the right of free religious expression, many school administrators and teachers have swallowed the "separation of church and state" notion and have tried to scour every trace of God and morality out of our public schools. A few examples:

Annie, a high school sophomore in Satsuma, Alabama, put up a poster on the school bulletin board that was available for students' use. The message of her poster: "Jesus died for you. Why not live for Him?" Annie was simply being salt and light on her campus—but the school principal told her that posters with Christian messages were prohibited. Annie countered by showing the principal that such messages were allowed according to the student handbook (not to mention the United States Constitution). The principal's reply: "I don't care what the book says. This is my school. This is a dictatorship. The poster comes down—case closed." The case was resolved in Annie's favor after Mathew Staver of the religious liberty advocacy group Liberty Counsel stepped in on Annie's behalf.

Though the Constitution requires government to guard the religious freedom of all Americans, students all over the country are experiencing a level of religious oppression and intolerance that once typified only Iron Curtain countries:

- In Melbourne Beach, Florida, a second grader was told that the Valentine's Day card he made in class violated separation of church and state. The message in the card: "Roses are red, violets are blue. Did you know that Jesus loves you?"

- In Pell Lake, Wisconsin, first graders were invited to bring in their favorite Christmas videos to show the class—but a girl who brought a video about Jesus was told it was "inappropriate."

- In Winter Park, Florida, a first grader was forbidden to pass out religious Christmas cards or pencils imprinted with "Happy Birthday, Jesus" to his school friends at Christmastime.

- In Mobile, Alabama, a fifth grader was told by his teacher and the principal that he could not bring his Bible to school, he could not bow his head in prayer at school, and he could not discuss his faith with any of his friends.

- In Belgium, Wisconsin, a second grader was told she could not bring her Bible to school, nor could she bring religious stories for show-and-tell.

- In Orlando, Florida, an elementary student was told he could not read his Bible during free time while he waited in the classroom for his school bus.

- In Clarkston, Georgia, students of the high school ACTS club (Active Christian Teens in Service) were forbidden to decorate school bulletin boards for Christmas with pictures of a nativity scene and the message "Without Him there wouldn't be a Christmas."

- In north Florida, a high school issued a policy stating that no campus clubs could use the words *Bible* or *Christian* in their name; the school demanded that the Fellowship of Christian Athletes chapter on campus change its name.

- At Milwaukee's High School of the Arts, the Christian Fellowship Club was barred from promoting a Valentine's Day "True Love Waits" campaign for sexual abstinence because it was a religion-based program.

Fortunately, all of these cases were resolved in favor of religious freedom—but only after Mathew Staver and the Liberty Counsel stepped in. Tragically, there is a widespread misimpression that people of faith are not protected by the First Amendment. This is incredible in view of the fact that the First Amendment clearly guarantees complete, unrestricted religious freedom—including the religious freedom of students in the public schools:

> Congress shall make no law respecting an establishment of religion, *or prohibiting the free exercise thereof* . . .

In view of the clear, unambiguous language of our Constitution, it is absolutely unthinkable that Christians are being told they do not have the right to exercise their faith; that they must be silent about their faith;

that they must leave their Bibles at home; that the Christian Gospel is taboo, banned, and void where prohibited. Yet that is what Christians are being told on a daily basis, from sea to shining sea. If we do not speak up today and assert our First Amendment right to freely exercise our faith, tomorrow may be too late.

An urgent sense of purpose

Many churches in America espouse a liberal theology, do not hold to the authority and inerrancy of Scripture, have no Gospel, and, in general, never see people converted. You see no regeneration taking place in such churches. People live for decades in those churches and die in their spiritual blindness. If they use the word *evangelism* at all in such churches, it is to spend twenty years in committees trying to figure out what the word means! For a church to still be dithering over the meaning of *evangelism* some two thousand years after the Great Commission is tragic indeed!

And what about the Cultural Mandate? Many liberal churches have turned the concept completely upside down! They may be involved with the culture—but their involvement makes matters worse, not better. Instead of applying God's standards to the world, they have adopted the world's standards and have prostituted and demeaned the Church. They have turned the Church into an arm of the liberal political establishment. They believe that the cure for all of society's ills is simply the expansion of socialism and the welfare state.

But I must hasten to add that conservative, evangelical, Bible-believing churches and Christians are not without blame either! Remember the three duties that are spelled out within the Cultural Mandate? They are:

1. Be refashioned into His image.

2. Be fruitful and multiply; evangelize.

3. Subdue the earth and exercise dominion in His name.

Many evangelical churches are good at carrying out the first duty. They preach the Gospel and people are converted to faith in Christ; as a result, a number of people in these churches are being at least partially refashioned into the image of Christ. Yet a lot of these churches fail to teach their people how to carry out the second duty, which is to reproduce and multiply spiritually—to evangelize. As a result, there is a tragic lack of balance in those churches.

There are many other churches that not only preach the Gospel, but also teach their people how to be fruitful and multiply, and how to share their faith with others. These churches have captured what it means to carry out the first and second duties under the Cultural Mandate. Yet, there is a lack of balance even in these churches. They have ignored the third aspect of the Cultural Mandate: that they are to promote what God has declared about education, culture, media, art, literature, government, business, and every sphere of life. As Christians, we are all too eager to limit the scope of the Bible to "religious" spheres and issues. But God does not stop there. He says that His Word applies to the whole world. Every sphere of human life and culture must be brought under the Word of God, cleansed for His use, and offered for the purpose of glorifying and magnifying Him.

How, then, do we become the light of the world as God commanded? The answer is simpler than most people think: Be a witness!

Get involved—and be bold!

Now this requires that you determine ahead of time that you will become an effective witness for Jesus Christ. You must make a decision to learn how to present the Gospel to others. You must make a decision to create and recognize opportunities and openings for talking to people about spiritual things. And you must make a decision to become bold and assertive in sharing your faith.

I can hear the objections forming in your mind as you read these words! *Oh, but that's not my personality! That's not my style! I'm not a bold person!* Then ask God for boldness. That's what the apostle Paul did. In Ephesians 6:19–20, he wrote, "[Pray] for me, that utterance may be given to me, that I may open my mouth boldly to make known the mystery of the gospel, for which I am an ambassador in chains; that in it I may speak boldly, as I ought to speak."

After all, why shouldn't you be bold? You have the best news anyone has ever heard! If you had a cure for cancer, wouldn't you share it with the world? Well, you have something even greater—a cure for the cancer of sin. You have the secret of eternal life. So why are you keeping it a secret? Why aren't you boldly telling the world? Why aren't you telling every person you meet where they can find the way, the truth, and the life?

These days it seems that everyone is coming out of the closet! The fornicators have left the closet and now parade their sinful lifestyle on our streets and television screens. They're not sinners anymore—they're swingers! They are proud of their sinful lifestyle, they demand their rights, they expect society to treat their "shack-up" relationship as the equivalent of marriage. The prostitutes, too, have left the closet and are now on the streets and in our courts, demanding their rights. The homosexual and lesbian activists are out of the closet and are marching down Main Street carrying signs demanding gay rights. Even the pedophiles are out of the closet, demanding that adult-child sexual acts be decriminalized and considered normal and healthy—and many in the psychological community, the media, and the government are ready to meet their sick demands!

Yet one group still hides in the closet, crouched in a dark corner behind the clothes rack. Who are they? Christians! Yes, the world is filled with silent, timid, closet Christians. They are afraid to come forth and speak about what God has done in their lives. Why? Are they afraid of being martyred, burned at the stake, crucified, thrown to the lions, or boiled in oil, as so many were in the early Christian era? No. They are just afraid of what people will think of them. They don't want other people to think them too forward, too pushy, or too fundamentalist—so they lock themselves up in their closet and hide in the shadows.

Are you a closet Christian? Are you afraid to come out and speak for the rights of your crowned King, for His proper sway over the souls of men and women? Are you afraid to speak boldly in His name? If so, why?

Let's examine for a moment what it means to be bold for Christ. Why should Christians boldly proclaim the mystery of the Gospel? When Paul used the word *boldly* in Ephesians 6:19 and 20, he used the Greek word *parrhesia*, which comes from the word *pas*, which means "all," and the word *rheo,* which means "to pour forth" or "to utter." The word literally means "all utterance," so that a person who has the boldness of Christ has absolutely no fear of speaking but freely utters the message God has given him to speak. He does not retreat into a craven silence (and remember, not all silence is golden; sometimes silence is simply a cowardly shade of yellow!). Rather, he seizes opportunities that are brought his way by the Holy Spirit.

Of course, it is hard for us to feel bold and courageous in our witness if we do not feel prepared. So we should prepare ourselves with prayer, daily asking God to live in us, embolden us, and bring us opportunities to share His Gospel with others. And we should prepare ourselves by memorizing the Scripture passages that relate to our need of salvation and God's provision of salvation by grace through faith, including John 1:12 and 3:16; Romans 3:23 and 6:23; Ephesians 2:8 and 9; and 1 Peter 3:18. As the apostle Peter tells us in 1 Peter 3:15, "Always be ready to give a defense to everyone who asks you a reason for the hope that is in you."

The time for boldness is now—not tomorrow, not next week. We do not know when the Lord will return for us, and then it will be too late for that unsaved neighbor. We do not know when death will come for that coworker we've been meaning to speak to—and then it will be too late. We do not know how long we will be free to speak without fear of reprisal or imprisonment—because our religious freedom is under constant assault from those in our society who would silence the voice of God and His people.

Right now, we can boldly proclaim the Gospel and the government cannot legally, constitutionally silence us. We don't know if that will be true tomorrow or the day after that—so let's boldly proclaim God's Word today while there is still time.

The friendliest man in Castle Rock

I'd like you to meet the friendliest man in Castle Rock, Colorado. If you were to pass him on the street, chances are he'd thrust out his hand, look you in the eye, and say, "Hi! I'm Art Fowler, how are you doing?" Art Fowler has a knack for meeting and befriending people. I don't know if it's a natural personality trait, or if it's something he has consciously cultivated. But I do know that *you* can do what Art Fowler does—*if* you make a priority of fulfilling the Great Commission, *if* you make a decision to share the Gospel, *if* you really put your mind to it. You see, anybody can be friendly. Any Christian can be a friend to someone who needs a friend.

Fowler's professional training is in counseling, but his purpose in life is to introduce people to Jesus Christ. He meets people anywhere and in just about any way imaginable—and even some ways you'd never imagine! For example, he likes to—well, maybe I'd better let Art explain it to you himself.

"One thing I like to do," he says, "is to pull police officers over. I get behind them, turn my headlights on, put my brights on, and sometimes I honk my horn. Policemen are very surprised when someone pulls *them* over—pulling people over is usually *their* job! The Lord uses this technique for me to get to the police officers and to get their attention, to get them to realize, *Hey, this guy has something to say to me.* I've seen many cops come to know Christ in a personal way—at least 150 to 200 cops.

"I've pulled them over in heavy traffic on the interstates, on city streets, on county highways, and on country roads in the dark of night. When I stop them they wait in their car for me to get out and approach them. They don't know who I am or what I want, so they are cautious and they usually just roll down the window a couple of inches. I usually don't know what I'm going to say to them until I'm up to their window, and I suspect when I come up to them that they probably have one hand on their gun—which is one reason I don't recommend this particular method of witnessing to everyone.

"There's always a bit of apprehension for the first few seconds, but then after I start talking, they figure out that I'm harmless, and we usually have a good conversation. Sometimes I give them my business card, and I try to encourage them. 'I know you guys have a tough job,' I sometimes say, 'and I just want to thank you for being there, protecting the people. I just want to support you guys. I know there are hurts and struggles in this line of work, and you almost have to wear a facade because you can't let your feelings be known. But I just want you to know I care.

"In all the times I've been doing this, not once has an officer ever gotten upset with me. They always seem to appreciate the words of encouragement. Sometimes we talk beside the car, sometimes they invite me in and we talk in the car, and sometimes I've even ridden along with them on patrol and we talked as they went about their jobs. On one occasion, I gave my business card to an officer who seemed troubled but was not ready to receive the Gospel. Some weeks later I got a call from his wife—she said that she and her husband were separating and that she had found my card on his dresser. She had no one else to turn to, so she called me. I met her in a restaurant and she received Christ on the spot.

"One officer gave me a CB radio to use in my car. He said, 'Art, you have a certain way of talking to people, a very direct way of leveling with them. I want you to use this CB for the Lord's work.' So I use that CB a lot, and I talk to people who drive on the job, like truckers, and I talk to people who are retired and driving around in their RVs. Sometimes I'll be talking to people and I can tell they would be open to sitting down and talking face-to-face, so I'll arrange to meet them in a restaurant or coffee shop. It's a good place to meet and talk freely.

"There was one fellow I met with at a coffee shop. His name was Ron, and he had been contemplating suicide. I told him I had something to share with him and that it was the answer to life's question. 'If you really want that answer,' I told him, 'I'm not going to tell you until you call me and say, "Hey, Art, I really want that answer!"' I wrote a note to Ron and said, 'I really do care.' And I jotted down my phone number."

Now Ron picks up the story. "I was driving around town sometime around midnight or one o'clock in the morning," Ron recalls, "and I gave Art a call. I said, 'Art, I need to talk.' He had been asleep, of course, but he said, 'Where would you like to meet?' He didn't care how tired he was—he was ready to meet me at a moment's notice. So we met at an all-night restaurant and Art said, 'I want to know, Ron—are you really willing to accept the answer I have for you?' And I said, 'Yeah, I am.' And we prayed together right there, and I accepted the Lord. Instantly,

I felt a total turnaround. I felt warmth, I felt real comfort. I felt I'd been washed clean inside."

"That's what Ron told me, just five seconds after we prayed," Art recalls. "He said, 'I feel so clean.' And then he got up and went to the pay phone and said, 'I've got to start calling people and telling them what happened, what's different in my life!' And there he was, after one in the morning, calling all of his friends, saying, 'Hey, I'm saved! I've got Jesus Christ in my life!'"

Art Fowler has literally touched and changed thousands of lives— one life at a time. His obsession for reaching the lost has taken him far beyond his hometown of Castle Rock, Colorado. In 1982, he picked up his newspaper and read about the imprisonment of former Miami Dolphins star running back Mercury Morris on drug trafficking charges. Though he only knew Morris by reputation, Art Fowler didn't hesitate to buy a plane ticket to Miami in hopes of getting to tell Mercury Morris about the love of Jesus Christ.

Art Fowler talked his way into the Florida prison where Morris was held, and he got to share the Gospel with the former football star—and Morris responded by committing himself to Jesus Christ. "Old Art Fowler!" Morris recalls. "He just came out of nowhere, and he seemed like kind of a hayseed to me. He came to me out of the love that he has through Jesus Christ—and that was really the important thing for me at that time in my life."

"When I talked to Mercury Morris," Art recalls, "he prayed there in the visiting cell to receive Christ, and then he said to me, 'Art, I want you to go see my wife, Bobbie, and tell her about Jesus.' So he drew me a little map to his house, and I went over and introduced myself. She and her kids were there, and she accepted the Lord too."

Morris, who played for the Dolphins in 1972, the year they went 17-0 and won Super Bowl VII, looks back and says, "I have a lot of trophies—they're all over the house. But the only trophies I have out on display are the ones that are the most significant to me. One of the things of significance I keep out is a plaque with a little football player on it that I got from Art Fowler back in 1987. It reads, 'I can do all things through Christ who strengthens me.' Now, this is important to me because it says to me, 'I'm your partner on the winning team.' Art Fowler is a teammate of mine now. He's a teammate in the spiritual sense that I didn't have before. Coach Don Shula and the Miami Dolphins, that's one thing. But Art Fowler and Jesus Christ, that's another."

At the urging of Mercury Morris, Art has recently been directing more and more of his evangelistic efforts at the "up-and-outers," the high-profile people in our world who need Jesus Christ. As a result, in recent years he has personally led many people to the Lord whose names you would certainly know—wealthy financiers and business leaders; a former U.S. senator, a governor, and numerous other political figures; people in the entertainment industry and the sports world; and more. Frequently, he simply makes an appointment to see people without stating his business—and he gets right in! Clearly the Lord is leading the way for Art Fowler.

Does Art Fowler do anything that you couldn't do? Does he say anything you couldn't say? No, he simply makes himself available as a servant to God and a friend to people. Nothing complicated—but look at the lives he touches!

"I'm not saying that the way I witness is the way everyone should witness," Art says. "I don't think God is calling everyone to stop police cars or hop on a plane and witness to high-profile people. Those are just some ideas that occurred to me. I believe God has given the Holy Spirit and a creative mind to all of us so that we can discover our own particular way of sharing Christ with others. I hope that when people look at what I do, they'll think, *Well, hey, if Art Fowler can stop police cars, maybe I can do this or that or some other innovative thing.* There are really no limits to the ways we can share Christ with people, if we will just open our minds to the possibilities."

Art Fowler is the salt of the earth, the light of the world. And so are you and I—if we will simply be obedient to the mandates God has given us.

Five steps to boldness in witnessing

What if every Christian in every church was as enthusiastic and open and obedient to God as Art Fowler? Imagine a church with 200 or

500 or 1,000 or 5,000 Art Fowlers in it! What he does is so simple—yet what God could accomplish through an army of Art Fowlers would be astounding! How can we develop that boldness and openness for Christ? Let me suggest some specific actions you can take:

1. Spend time with Christ in prayer and in His Word. In the New Testament, we read that when the learned men of Jerusalem "saw the boldness of Peter and John . . . they realized that they had been with Jesus" (Acts 4:13). There is something about spending time in the presence of the Nazarene that will put iron in our blood, steel in our backbone, and boldness in our witness for Christ. So we need to spend time learning of Him from His Word, drawing strength from His example, and praying for boldness on behalf of ourselves, our church, and all the Christians around the world. Pray that God would grant His people boldness to speak His message to the world.

2. Consider the example of Jesus. If you want to be more bold in your witness for Christ, consider what He endured for your sake. Do you ever feel embarrassed to mention Christ around other people? Are you concerned that others might think you a bit odd? I ask you: Was Jesus embarrassed to go to the cross for you? How do you think He felt being stripped and lashed, beaten and disfigured, a crown of thorns pressed into His brow, then being nailed to a rough wooden cross, thrust up against the sky to endure mockery and shame as His life's blood spilled out upon the ground? Do you still say you cannot risk being thought a little out-of-the-ordinary on His behalf? Do you still say you are embarrassed or ashamed to mention His name?

Many years ago, Frances Havergal, who would later write a number of classic hymns of the faith, was a young Christian student attending college in Düsseldorf, Germany. Arriving at the dormitory, she was surprised to find that she was the only Christian there. Her initial response was one of timidity. *I could never witness for Christ among all those non-Christian people!* she thought. *They're all so sophisticated and worldly, and they would only be hostile and make fun of me if I opened my mouth and talked about Jesus.* But then the realization came to her: *I am the only one He has in this place. Jesus has no one to depend on but me.* That thought gave her strength and boldness, and many of the young women in the dormitory came to know Christ because Frances Havergal was willing to be bold for her Lord.

3. Consider the lost condition of the people around you. If we will actually consider the stakes involved, we will be able to overcome the timidity that silences most of us. Jesus told us to love our neighbor as ourselves. But can we truly say we love someone if we are willing to let them go into eternity without Christ—just to save ourselves a little discomfort or embarrassment? How little we truly care if we give so little consideration to our neighbor's eternal soul!

More than a century ago, an incident occurred at an English train station that illustrates the plight of the people around you. A number of people stood on the train platform in an English village, waiting for the train that would take them to London. Among them were a judge, a number of businessmen, some well-dressed Victorian ladies, a lowly bootblack, and some other assorted people. As they waited, they were astonished to see an indigent man coming around the bend, walking on the tracks. He was dirty and ragged, and he looked down at the railroad ties at his feet, not meeting anyone's eyes.

As the man was passing the platform, his head down, his hands thrust into the pockets of his seedy secondhand coat, the people on the platform heard the sound of the approaching train. But the man on the tracks just kept on walking with his back to the train, seemingly unaware that death was chugging toward him and soon would be on top of him. People on the platform called to the man. "Sir! Sir! Get off the track!" The judge said to him, "My good man, don't you hear the train?" The businessmen waved their newspapers and shouted. The ladies in their finery called to him, "Oh, look behind you!" The bootblack pounded his shoeshine box against the platform, hoping to attract the man's attention but to no avail—because the man on the tracks was deaf.

Finally, one of the men on the platform, realizing that the man could not hear their warnings, leaped down onto the tracks himself, ran after him, grabbed him by the arm, and spun him into the dirt and cinders along the tracks. A split instant later, the train lumbered past, screeching to a halt at the station. If the one brave man had not acted as he did, the ragged man would have been crushed under the wheels of the locomotive.

The lesson of the incident is this: Everyone who saw what happened rejoiced that a life was saved. Not one went up to the rescuer and said, "You know, you were a little rough on that fellow. I hated to see you throw him on the ground that way. Rather impolite, you know. In fact, a number of us were commenting on how presumptuous you were; after all, you never even bothered to inquire whether the man wanted to be saved. He seemed perfectly happy right there on the tracks. I would encourage you not to be so brash and forward in the future."

Can you imagine a more ridiculous response under the circumstances? Yet many people today criticize those who are snatching souls from the fires of Hell (even though they themselves have never led a single person to Christ), saying, "Oh yes, I am in favor of witnessing, but I don't like the way you do it. We must not upset people. We must not be too presumptuous. We must not be too assertive." I ask you: If being too presumptuous or assertive is not an issue when saving a mortal human life, why would it be an issue when saving an eternal human soul?

4. Learn the skills that will enable you to witness confidently, comfortably, and effectively. The one factor that seems to stop most Christians cold, preventing them from witnessing, is a lack of confidence—a feeling that they do not know what to do or say, a fear that they will "mess up." The cure is simple: acquire the skills! Witnessing skills are really quite easy to learn and put into practice. If you have never undergone evangelistic training before (such as the Evangelism Explosion program we developed at Coral Ridge Presbyterian Church and which is now in use in thousands of churches in two hundred countries around the world) you will be amazed at how uncomplicated, easy to remember, and easy to use this approach can be.

The Evangelism Explosion (EE) approach gives you an easy, non-threatening way to open a spiritual discussion with another person, using two "diagnostic questions" to establish a connection. The answers to these two questions will give you a clear indication about whether an individual has a personal relationship with Jesus Christ:

- *Have you come to the place in your spiritual life where you know for certain that you have eternal life?*

The answer to that question is invariably either yes or no (a doubtful or hedging answer is a no).

- *Suppose you were to die today and stand before God, and He were to ask you, "Why should I let you into My heaven?"—what would you say?*

The answer to that question will always be based on either faith in Jesus Christ or a person's own "good works." That gives you the opportunity to explain that our own efforts are useless to save us, and leads directly into a discussion of such Scripture passages as, "All our righteousnesses are like filthy rags" (Isa. 64:6); "For all have sinned and fall short of the glory of God" (Rom. 3:23); and "For the wages of sin is death, but the gift of God is eternal life in Christ Jesus our Lord" (Rom. 6:23).

The EE approach also helps you learn how to give your own personal testimony in a succinct, compelling way. That, after all, is what it means to be a witness—you simply tell what God has done in your own life, just as a witness in a courtroom simply tells what he has seen and experienced. The beauty of sharing your personal testimony is that it cannot be refuted! No one can argue with your own experience of Christ. It is your own story, told in your own words. Sharing your testimony is a wonderful act of humility in that you place yourself on the same level as the other person: "I can empathize with you. I've been where you are. I don't have superior knowledge or power or spirituality—I'm just a sinner saved by grace." Someone has beautifully described sharing your testimony as "one beggar telling another beggar where to find bread." There is something very compelling and attractive in the simple act of sharing your own story.

We cannot all be preachers or teachers, but we *can* all be witnesses, because every Christian has a story to tell. And the beautiful thing about witnessing is that most people would rather listen to a simple, honest, open, straightforward personal witness than a preacher or teacher any day!

If you would like to know more about the EE approach, I invite you to read my book *Evangelism Explosion*.[2] To begin an EE training program in your church, order EE training materials, or to obtain information about Youth EE or a schedule of EE Clinics in your area, contact Evangelism Explosion International at P.O. Box 23820, Fort Lauderdale, FL 33307; telephone (954) 491-6100; fax (954) 771-2256. You will also find a very informative EE website at http://www.eeinternational.org/.

5. Finally, consider the account you must give of your faithfulness before the judgment seat of Christ. To overcome timidity and acquire boldness in witnessing, remember that to whom much has been given, much will be required. Each of us will one day account for the life we have lived, the opportunities we have been given—and the souls we neglected who were right within our reach and ripe for conversion, waiting only for a word of witness from us. Let us not waste any more opportunities. As Jesus said in John 9:4, we must do the work the Lord has given us to do *now*—"while it is day; [for] the night is coming when no one can work."

A personal issue

God may be prompting your heart right now, bringing to mind some person He wants you to speak to about the Gospel. You may be thinking, *Oh no! Not him! Not her! That person is too hardened, too hostile to the Gospel of Christ. It's pointless to even mention the name of Christ in that person's presence!* I remind you that the sovereign power of God can change even the most hardened sinner. He can use your bold witness as a lever to pry open that hardened heart—but only if you make yourself available to Him.

I mention this matter because it is a very personal issue in my life. Let me tell you a story to illustrate:

There was once a young man who was a professional musician. He was a rowdy sort of fellow who ran with a wild crowd of friends. But his brother went to West Point and there became a Christian. When the brother came home and shared Christ with this rowdy young musician, he, too, became a Christian.

Now this newly converted young musician had a very good friend with whom he had caroused many a time and he said to himself, *I think I need to talk to my friend about Jesus.* But then doubts crept into his mind: *Oh no, I couldn't do that. What would be the point? My friend is too hardened in his disbelief, too hostile to Christianity. He'd just get mad and throw me out!* So the musician never shared the Gospel with his friend.

The name of that hardened, hostile reprobate was Jim Kennedy.

That's right. Before I was a Christian, my newly converted musician friend gave up on me, decided I was a lost cause, and chose not to witness to me. He had concluded I was beyond the reach of the grace of God. Fortunately, God did not share that opinion, and He brought someone else into my life to share the Gospel with me and alter my downward course.

Who is the pre-Christian "Jim Kennedy" in your life—the person you have written off as beyond the reach of God's grace, the person who is headed for an eternity without Christ unless you speak boldly and candidly about the love and grace of Christ? Who is the person God wants *you* to reach right now?

We live in exciting times for the advance of the Gospel. The Christian Church is growing more rapidly today than at any other time in the history of the world. Consider this: At the Last Supper there were eleven disciples. On the morning of the day of Pentecost there were 120; by evening, there were three thousand. Shortly thereafter five thousand more were added, and then they multiplied exceedingly. By A.D. 313, when the Edict of Toleration was signed, historians tell us there were about 12 million professing Christians in the Roman Empire. By A.D. 500 it is estimated there were 25 million. By A.D. 1000 there were 50 million. By A.D. 1517, when Martin Luther nailed the ninety-five theses on the church door at Wittenberg, it is estimated there were 100 million professing Christians in the world. While it is undoubtedly true that not all possessed what they professed, there were at least that many "professing" Christians.

By 1795, when the modern Protestant missionary movement began, when William Carey went out from England to India, it is estimated that there were 200 million professing Christians in the world. By 1900 there were 500 million Christians. As of the year 2000, there are at least

2 billion professing Christians in the world! Let the meaning of that number sink in for a moment: It means that *more people have been added to the worldwide Church of Jesus Christ in the twentieth century than were added in the entire 1900 years before that time!* Indeed, it is an exciting time to be a Christian!

What's even more exciting is the fact that the *rate* at which people are coming to know Christ is *rapidly accelerating in our own era!* According to research conducted by the Center for World Missions in Pasadena, California, we are seeing the most astonishing advance of the gospel *right now,* at the turn of the new millennium.

In A.D. 100, there were only about one hundred new professions of faith per day worldwide. Over the centuries that followed, the rate of new professions climbed slowly, gradually, almost imperceptibly until by A.D. 1900, there were an estimated 943 professions per day worldwide. By 1950, the rate of new professions began to pick up steam, reaching a rate of 4,500 per day. By 1980, the rate was 20,000 new converts per day. By 1995, 100,000 new converts. By the year 2000, the rate is an astonishing *200,000 new believers every day*!

Now, think that over for a moment! Such a rate of increase—from fewer than a thousand new believers a day in 1900 to some 200,000 by the end of that century—is nothing short of miraculous! And in only the last five years of the twentieth century, the rate has doubled! Despite the fact that we as the Church of Jesus Christ have not done everything we could do, nor everything we should do, the Spirit of God has been moving through our world, actively drawing thousands of men, women, and children to a saving knowledge of Jesus Christ. You and I have been living in the middle of the greatest period of spiritual revival in the history of mankind—and we have not even been aware of it! That is why I say with confidence that *we are winning.* This is enormously encouraging news, and I share it with you in the hope that it will lift your heart, energize your spirit, and motivate you to do even more in the coming days to be God's salt and light in this fast-changing world.

This is a time when every Christian should overcome the fear of witnessing, a time when every Christian should be willing to boldly, courageously, enthusiastically share the Gospel. It is a time when God is doing great things. I believe that America is going to be changed. Yes, the culture war—the spiritual warfare between good and evil—will continue to rage, but we are seeing a great upsurge in the hunger for truth, morality, spirituality, and meaning. We are seeing lives changed and transformed and redirected by the Spirit of God and the power of the Gospel of Jesus Christ.

It is time for Christians to come out of the closet. It is time for Christians not to be ashamed of Jesus Christ. Someone has well said that every person is either a missionary or a mission field. Which are you? Christian, I implore you—come out of the closet!

Isn't it interesting that many Christians are so enthusiastic about sports that they can scream and yell and lose all dignity and self-control at a basketball arena or football stadium—yet they are afraid of being branded a "fanatic" by just mentioning the name of Jesus in a calm, quiet conversation! We can get so emotional and enthusiastic over a dunk shot or a touchdown—yet when it comes to Jesus Christ, the Savior of our souls and the Lord of creation, the only Person truly worthy of our devotion and enthusiasm—we suddenly become very quiet and restrained.

May God change our hearts! May He fill us with enthusiasm, excitement, exuberance, joy, and an eagerness to share Jesus with everyone around us!

Three centuries before the birth of Christ, there was a man who was very courageous and bold. Though he was a pagan man, not a believer in God, his life is a challenge to the way we live our lives. His name was Alexander, and history has appended a title to his name: "the Great." Alexander the Great conquered the entire known world by the time he was thirty—then wept because there were no more worlds to conquer.

One day Alexander was conducting court for his army in a great palace. Soldiers were lined up at attention along each wall, spears at their sides. Alexander, the king of the world, sat upon his throne while various soldiers were brought before him for judgment because of crimes they had committed in the king's service. He would pronounce summary judgment, and there was no appeal to the sentence he imposed, because there was no one greater than Alexander, the sovereign of the earth.

Finally, a young man was brought before Alexander—a Macedonian about seventeen years old. Alexander looked at the scared young soldier and his countenance softened somewhat. "What is this one's crime?" he asked.

The sergeant-at-arms read the charge. "He's a deserter, my liege," said the sergeant. "He fled the battlefield and was found cringing in a cave."

Alexander's face darkened. If there was one thing he could not stand, it was cowardice. He eyed the young man stonily. "Soldier," he said, "what is your name?"

The young man hesitated. "Alexander," he answered.

Alexander the Great rose from his throne. "What?" he asked in an offended voice. "*What* did you say your name is, soldier?"

"Alexander, sir."

Alexander the Great stepped down from the dais and advanced threateningly toward the young soldier.

"*What* is your name?!"

The young man was now visibly trembling as he stammered, "A-Alexander, sir."

The king reached out, grasped the young soldier by the tunic, lifted him from his feet, and snarled into his face, "Soldier! Change your *conduct*—or change your *name!*"

Now I turn to you and ask: *What is your name?*

You know the answer: Christian!

You bear the name of Jesus Christ. By the way you live your life, you bring honor or dishonor to that name.

Christian! Change your *conduct*—or change your *name*!

The time for timidity and excuses is long past. It is time to be bold—to live as the light of God in a dark and festering world. Do not say, "But I'm only one little ray of light." In a world as dark as ours, one ray of light can be seen for miles. And when all of us together live in obedience to the mandate and the purpose God has laid down for us, our individual rays of light combine to create a shining radiance—a wonderful blaze of illumination that reflects the brilliance and glory of God.

So may *your* light shine!

6

THE POWER
OF ONE

So he [Paul], trembling and astonished, said, "Lord, what do You
want me to do?" Then the Lord said to him, "Arise and go into
the city, and you will be told what you must do."

(ACTS 9:6)

Can one person really make a difference? Dr. Richard Lumsden, former professor of biology at Tulane University and Medical School and
former dean of the graduate school, understands the power of one—
because his life has been changed by it! The course of his life was totally reversed and his worldview was completely turned upside-down (or,
more accurately, rightside-up) by a single student in his biology class.
For most of his life, Dr. Lumsden—who studied at Tulane, Harvard,
and Rice Universities—believed that evolutionary theory is science,
whereas creationism is merely religious myth. That is what he believed
and what he taught his students.

When the Louisiana state legislature passed a law requiring that creation science be given equal time with evolutionary theory in the classroom, Dr. Lumsden was indignant. "Who did these legislators think
they were, telling us Ph.D.-level scientists how to teach and what to
teach regarding science? I thought the whole thing was absolutely
absurd. I was prompted at that point to give a lecture on the origin of
life, giving creation its due with as much mockery as I could summon.

For example, I would tell my students, 'In the beginning was the word, and the word was—*hydrogen!*'"

After one such class, a student of his, a Christian young woman, came to him and complimented him very sweetly and politely. "Great lecture, Doc," she said.

"Well, that got my attention," Dr. Lumsden recalls. "Flattery always did! 'But,' she went on, 'I have some questions.' And indeed, she did. She had a legal pad, and I could see that she had written line after line after line of questions. So we made an appointment to meet."

That appointment changed Dr. Lumsden's life.

"Now I'm not trying to challenge you or anything," the young woman began. "I just want to get my science straight."

"Fair enough," said the professor.

"A while back, you said that mutations are genetic disasters. So I want to understand how, by natural selection, mutations can produce new and better structures?"

"Good question," replied the professor. "I'll probably have to think more about that and get back to you."

"Okay," said the student, "but aren't the odds of the random assembly of genes mathematically impossible?"

"Well," said Dr. Lumsden, "let's see if we can figure that out." And he put down the various factors involved in assembling a single simple gene—and he realized that the odds against such a random event were roughly 10 to the 200th power, or a 1 followed by 200 zeros! "As this student and I were talking," he recalled, "it dawned on me that not only were we talking about a mathematical impossibility, we were talking about a physical and chemical impossibility. But I couldn't let the student know that she had stumped the professor! So I lamely replied, 'Well, the fact remains that we are here—and in reality the only way we could have gotten here is through the evolutionary process. So the fact that we are here really proves evolution, doesn't it?'"

But, of course, the fact that we are here proves no such thing! The young student knew it—and so did Dr. Lumsden. "For the first time in my life," he said, "I began to listen to what I was saying. And what I was saying wasn't making very good scientific sense."

They continued to talk about other problems with the evidence for evolution, such as the gaps in the fossil record. What was originally scheduled as a brief after-class meeting went on for around three hours. "She didn't argue with me," recalled Dr. Lumsden. "She just asked me questions, and the whole time we talked, I was trying not to betray to the student how full of holes my answers were!"

After the student left, Dr. Lumsden continued to think about the questions she had raised. "It dawned on me right then and there that evolution was bankrupt as a scientific theory. Well, if that were so, if life did not originate by naturalistic, materialistic, spontaneous processes, what was the alternative explanation? And then I said aloud, 'Oh my God!' And I said it not in blasphemy, but in awe."

In that moment, Dr. Lumsden's eyes were opened and a light shone in upon his soul. "What happened to me that afternoon was, first of all, a mortal embarrassment to me as a professor. Professing to be wise, the professor was made a fool. But second of all was the realization that God exists! And God created! Now that's enough to turn a corner in anybody's life!" The transformation in Dr. Lumsden's thinking was not instantaneous—he would undergo a great deal more study and soul-searching before he would finally be dragged, almost against his will, into the kingdom of God. He became a creationist first—and then a Christian.

"The one led to the other," he recalled. "The culmination was finding myself before the saving altar, on my knees, my stiff neck broken, in obedience asking Jesus to come into my life to be my Lord and personal Savior." Today, Dr. Lumsden's life moves in a totally new direction. He is a committed Christian and a committed creationist who takes every opportunity to debate evolution and teach the truth that "in the beginning, God created the heavens and the earth."

None of this would have happened if one student hadn't taken the time and the opportunity to speak up, to politely ask questions, to gently raise the issues that needed to be raised. That's the power of one!

Moments of self-doubt

I think everyone has experienced moments—or even years or decades—of self-doubt, of feeling insignificant or directionless or powerless. Everyone, when facing a big challenge, has thoughts of inadequacy, a sense of, "I'm just not up to this challenge." I believe every person who ever lived has been tormented at times by such doubts as these.

Picture George Washington standing at the Delaware River on Christmas night, 1776. We all know that Washington crossed the Delaware, defeated the British, and won independence for America. But we easily forget the context of that victory. What had Washington accomplished up to that point in the Revolutionary War?

After an initial victory over British General William Howe at Boston, which forced Howe's retreat, Washington pursued Howe to New York—and there he himself was forced into retreat. Washington's forces were driven out of Brooklyn and Manhattan. They were pushed across the Hudson River and sent fleeing into New Jersey. Washington's army suffered enormous casualties, demoralization, and desertions as he was forced all the way across New Jersey and into Pennsylvania, with the British forces at his heels all the way. Retreat after retreat after retreat, loss upon loss upon loss.

Now he stood at the edge of the Delaware River. Imagine the doubts that must have whirled through his mind that night as he looked across that ice-choked river, sizing up his own ragtag army versus the well-armed, well-supplied British and Hessian troops who camped on the other side. What would happen when he led his troops across that river? Would they be met by an alerted enemy force waiting on the shore to sink the American hopes in the river? I wonder if his officers said, "It'll never work. It's suicidal," when he told them of his daring plan.

The winter had brought a lull in the fighting because warfare in the bitter northern cold is such difficult and ugly business. Washington's only hope was the element of surprise. After a string of dispiriting defeats, this was Washington's last-ditch attempt to win America's freedom. If this battle was lost, America was lost. The burden of that decision weighed heavily on one man's shoulders. That night, Christmas night, he led his troops in small boats across the icy Delaware River—and he caught the British and Hessians by surprise at Trenton.

From victory at Trenton, he went on to defeat the British at Princeton, placing New Jersey under American control. After wintering at Morristown to rebuild his forces, Washington went on to lead his forces to victory at Brandywine Creek and Germantown, saving Philadelphia, then again to victory at Yorktown.

But none of those later victories would have occurred had Washington not dared to cross the Delaware and reverse the tide of war. He accomplished that by faith, believing that God would bring him through. Washington was a man of faith who believed God had called him for a specific purpose. He understood the simple spiritual-mathematical equation that one person plus God is an unstoppable force.

Do you have such a faith in God's power and God's Word? Do you believe that by His grace you can do all things by the faith He gives to you? What Washington did as a great military man and statesman, you and I can do within the sphere of influence where God has placed us. We can conquer the world in the moral and spiritual realm.

One man against the world

The problems confronting our world today stagger the imagination in their immensity and complexity. The world economy is a fragile row of dominoes waiting to be toppled; we have brushfire wars threatening to ignite global conflict; we have crazed dictators and terrorists who possess or will soon possess the means to wage massive chemical, biological, and nuclear war; we have intense racial and ethnic hatred around the globe and here in America; we have creeping atheism, bold humanism, and rampant socialism in our schools and our federal government; and that's only the beginning. What can one person do, given the crises that face our world on so many fronts?

I recall a tour that Billy Graham took a few years ago. He visited with the head of state of almost every nation in the free world, and he asked each of them about their hopes for the future. Without exception, every leader he spoke to told Dr. Graham that there was no foreseeable hope, no foreseeable solution to the world's problems. If those who direct the destinies of nations have no hope for the future, what hope do you have— just one ordinary person in a big wide world? Is there an answer to the questions that plague the human race? If there is, where would it be found?

I suggest to you that the answer exists—and that it is to be found by looking *backward* to the beginning of the Christian era. As hopeless as world conditions seem today, the Roman world in the days of the apostle Paul seemed no less hopeless and bleak. Roman society was already in a state of decline. The *Pax Romana*—the peace imposed upon the world by the oppressive military might of Rome—was weakening. Barbarians were clawing at the edges of the Roman Empire. While the old religions of pagan Rome had lost their force and the winds of agnosticism and atheism were blowing through the Roman world, Herod, Pilate, and Caesar conspired to destroy Christ and His new religion. Even the religion of the Jews had fallen to a low state. The world of that era was half slave and half free—much as the world is today. Infanticide was prevalent in that society, just as today. Popular forms of entertainment were drenched with blood, brutality, and sadistic violence, just as today. Sexual perversion was on the rise, approved by the philosophers as well as the masses, just as today.

What hope was there for a world in such a state? Who could have foreseen that the seed of hope for that world would be planted in the darkened heart of a hardened, murderous Pharisee named Saul of Tarsus? Who could have foreseen that this man—who was bent on destroying the Christian Church and eradicating all memory of the man named Jesus—would one day be the greatest missionary of the early Church? This man who had once had Christians bound, tortured, and killed suddenly encountered the power of the Lord Jesus on the road to Damascus—a power so great that the sun itself was dim by comparison, a power so great that it caused him to be thrown from his horse to the ground! And he heard a voice call his name: "Saul, Saul, why are you persecuting Me?"

"Who are You, Lord?" asked Saul, trembling with astonishment.

"I am Jesus, whom you are persecuting," came the reply.

In that moment, Saul was captured by a vision that would transform his life—and our world. Everything was changed in the brilliance of that light. Saul discovered that everything he thought was right was wrong—his faithfulness was treason, his truth was a lie, his zeal was rebellion, his enemy was his Lord. In that moment, the persecutor became the apostle. He fell to the ground a sinner; he arose a saint. He fell to the ground a sighted man who was blind; he arose a blind man who could see. He saw the greatest sight in all the world: he saw God as He truly is.

Perhaps the greatest miracle of that moment was the miracle of

Paul's submission to Jesus Christ. There is nothing harder for a human being to do than to wholly submit his will to another. For Saul to submit his will totally to the One he had set out to persecute is one of the greatest miracles of history. Only the infinitely strong hand of God could have bent the iron will of Saul. This was a conversion experience of the most radical kind. Skeptics through the centuries have tried to explain that conversion, but there is simply no explanation other than the supernatural, sovereign work of God.

The early Christians were well acquainted with this man named Saul—and they were astounded when they heard of his conversion. In fact, they refused to believe it. "Isn't this the man," they asked, "who destroyed all who called on the name of Jesus in Jerusalem and everywhere?"

Once Paul was brought into submission, he voiced a second question—a question that is always asked by anyone who truly encounters the power and love of Christ: "Lord, what do You want me to do?" Notice that Paul did not merely ask, "What do You want me to believe?" Paul's conversion was not merely a change of creed, but a dynamic change in the entire direction of his life, a change in the way he would live his life and conduct his life's work. As the apostle James has observed, faith without works is dead (James 2:20). Not only did Paul's faith change, but so did the works of his life.

The Scriptures teach that a faith that does not lead to a life of submission and service is no faith in Christ at all. The question "Who are You, Lord?" must lead to the question: "Lord, what do You want me to do?" Is that the honest response of your heart: "Lord, what do You want me to do?" Not a desire for a new idea or a new tradition or a new church to belong to, but an all-encompassing, consuming desire for the risen Lord Jesus Christ. Until we bend our will to His, until we surrender completely to Him as Master of our lives, we have not really exercised faith in Christ. Our daily prayer must be, "Take my life and lead me where You want me to go." Each new morning, our question to God should be, "Lord, what do You want me to do today?"

How different Paul's question was from that of Peter. In John 21, we see Peter asking Jesus a very different question. Instead of asking, "Lord, what do You want me to do?" he asked, "Lord, what about this man?"

meaning the apostle John (John 21:21). Whereas Paul was instantly concerned with his own responsibility to serve the Lord, Peter still had a lot of growing up to do, and his concern was to make sure others were carrying their share of the load! Peter's response is a lot like the response of many Christians today. Instead of instantly, obediently shouldering our own responsibility and carrying out the Lord's mandate and purpose for our lives, we look around and compare ourselves to others. We want to make sure the load is fairly distributed. We're eager to say, "Let George do it!" That is hardly the attitude of a servant of Christ.

That is why, when Peter asked Jesus about His will for John's life, Jesus replied, "What is that to you? You follow Me" (John 21:22).

Our attitude must be that of Saul/Paul who, when he saw the glory that is Christ, had no thought for anyone else. His only response was, "Lord, what do You want me to do?" He did not have time to complain about hypocrites in the Church or make excuses for himself. He stood soul-naked before the living God, and he wanted nothing but to do what the Lord wanted him to do. That is what happens in a human life when a person truly confronts Jesus Christ. The rest of the world just seems to disappear, and there is no one but Christ and your own soul.

When I think about Paul's first encounter with Christ, I am reminded of my own first encounter with Him—a day when I, too, saw a light. Isaiah 9:2 says, "The people who walked in darkness have seen a great light." Though I didn't see a blinding, visible light like Paul did, a light dawned in my soul that illuminated the inner recesses of my heart. I saw the glory that was Jesus Christ. I saw that it was *me* whom He loved and *me* whom He died for. I, too, was cast to the ground, right out of my chair with my face on the floor. In my heart I said in effect, "Lord, take my life. You bought it; You paid for it; You own it. What do You want me to do?"

When we ask God that question, there's no telling where He will take us—or what He will do through us!

The Lawndale miracle

"What do You want me to do?" Wayne Gordon, a white Christian high school coach, asked that same question—and the Lord's answer changed not only his own life but the lives of thousands of other people in inner-city Chicago. "I simply said to Christ, 'I'll do anything You want me to,'" Coach Gordon recalls, explaining his decision to move to one of the most dangerous mission fields in the world. "It wasn't that I had a dream or a vision or anything of that nature. But in my mind I knew that God was telling me that He wanted me to do something for Him. He wanted me to work with African-American people. So I started looking for a public school in the heart of the inner city and in a black community where I could teach and coach."

That was in the 1970s. Many of Wayne Gordon's friends tried to talk him out of his goal of moving into the violent heart of inner-city Chicago. They told him, "You can't live in that kind of neighborhood. It's too dangerous. You'll get in trouble, you won't make it, you won't survive." But despite the warnings of his well-meaning friends, Wayne Gordon chose to follow God's guidance for his life. He knew that God was leading him to a drug-infested, murder-ridden section of Chicago known as North Lawndale, where a violent crime is committed every three hours and a murder takes place roughly every three days.

Wayne first came to North Lawndale in the 1970s as a teacher and coach at Farragut High School. "I was the only teacher, black or white, who lived in the neighborhood," he recalls. "Nobody else at the school lived in the neighborhood, but I really felt I should. I talked to a lot of people—a lot of white people, black people, Christian people, non-Christian people—the story was the same across the board: You can't live in this neighborhood. It's too dangerous. People said, 'Coach, you can't live in this neighborhood because there are no whites in our community.' I ended up getting an apartment about a block from a little tavern known as the Bucket of Blood. The Bucket of Blood is a place where a murder happened about every other month. Some of my football players, I found out, were afraid to come to my apartment because I lived on such a dangerous street."

But Wayne Gordon was not deterred. He started a series of Bible studies, and many young people were introduced to Jesus Christ through those studies. Eventually the Bible studies grew into a full-fledged church—Lawndale Community Church—and Coach Gordon was the founding pastor. He knew that in a community with so many desperate needs, it was crucial for the church to listen to people and find ways to meet their needs.

One night a meeting was held in which people could voice the needs they wanted the church to become involved with. It was a wide-open brainstorming session, and many of the ideas were simply beyond the means of this newly formed inner-city church. But then someone came up with an interesting suggestion: Could the church provide people in the community with a safe place to do their laundry? It turned out that the gangs had taken over the Laundromats in the neighborhood, so the people in the community didn't feel safe when washing their clothes. Someone suggested installing a washer and dryer in the back of the church—but where would the appliances come from? "Let's pray about that," said Coach Gordon.

Two weeks later God answered their prayer. Some Christians in an upscale section of Chicago had decided to change the color scheme in their house—would the church like to have their washer and dryer? The appliances were in perfect running order. Wayne was amazed—God had met their need in a miraculous and unexpected way. From this experience, he learned what he has come to call "the Three *P*'s of Ministry." They are:

1. *People*—listen to their needs and concerns.

2. *Pray* about those needs and concerns.

3. *Partnership*—link up Christians who have a need with Christians who can meet that need.

From those small beginnings, the Lawndale Community Church has gone on to build a gym, a youth recreation room, a busy health clinic, and an economic outreach to the neighborhood called the Lawndale Christian Development Corporation. The LCDC works to create affordable housing, assist in economic development (such as small-business startups to provide jobs in the community) and help provide educational opportunities. Thanks to the church, more than seventy young people have gone from the 'hood to a college cap and gown—and most of those who have gotten their college degrees have returned to reinvest themselves in the community and in the lives of their neighbors. This is helping to revitalize the North Lawndale community. Above all, the church is leading people to Christ and seeing lives transformed by the Gospel.

All of this came about because one man was willing to simply say like the apostle Paul, "Lord, what do You want me to do? I'll do anything You say."

The people in the community talk openly about the love they have received from Wayne Gordon and the Lawndale Community Church. When Coral Ridge Ministries sent a television crew to Chicago to document what had taken place in that community, many people were eager to talk to us. "The church has helped me a lot," said one young man. "They have so much love and they just have their arms open, like Jesus, to all of us." And another young African-American told us, "Because of Christ, my life is different today. Without Him I'd still be out there on drugs."

It hasn't been easy for Coach Gordon and his family. In fact, there were times he felt he was trying to raise his family in an urban war zone. In his book *Real Hope in Chicago,*[1] you can read about the price he and his family paid for living in a dangerous inner-city neighborhood. He told us, "Our house has been broken into many times over the years. I've had so many cars stolen and broken into that it was just a joke. I think that at one time we had an eighteen-month stretch where every month somebody either stole my car or broke into my car. We've learned that material things are not as important to us as they used to be."

The result of such an unselfish attitude is that God has blessed Coach Gordon, making him a part of what many in the community are calling "the Lawndale miracle." As he told us, "the Lawndale miracle has been all about the body of Christ coming together, demonstrating the hope that comes through Jesus Christ and the miracle it is to see Him transform a life. Jesus is in the business of making old, dilapidated things new—that's 2 Corinthians 5:17. The Lawndale miracle is where God has taken a lot of old, dilapidated lives and a lot of old, dilapidated buildings in a community of need—and He has made them into new creations in Jesus Christ."

One submitted human being plus God is a majority in any community—even a drug-plagued, gang-infested, crime-ridden inner-city war zone like North Lawndale. Beautiful, fragrant gardens of Heaven are sprouting up and transforming an urban Hell—thanks to the power of one, plus God.

What in the world can one person do?

You may be thinking, *Well, the Lawndale miracle is a wonderful thing—for Lawndale. But I don't think God has called me to go to the inner city and start a new church. What can one person do—what can I do—in the place where God has placed me, right here, right now?* I'm glad you asked! Because I just happen to have a few ideas . . .

Be salt and light through your church.
- Get involved in your church's Evangelism Explosion program. If your church doesn't have an EE program already, talk to your pastor about starting one. Contact Evangelism Explosion International at 954-491-6100, or stop by the EE website at http://www.eeinternational.org/.

- In your EE team, in concert with church elders or deacons, monitor the church roll on a regular basis. Make sure that people who have stopped attending are quickly followed up, and that their physical, emotional, and spiritual needs are being met.

- Become involved in your church's other outreach ministries, such as "seeker-friendly" home Bible study groups and vacation Bible school, and ministries to minorities and refugees, to the poor and homeless, to hospital patients and shut-ins, to prisoners and their families, and to other needy people in your own community. (For more information, contact Prison Fellowship International, P.O. Box 17500, Washington, DC 20041-0500; telephone 703-478-0100; or Evangelicals for Social Action, 10 E. Lancaster Ave., Wynnewood, PA 19096-3495; telephone 610-645-9390.)

Be salt and light in your everyday life.
- Wear a cross, an ichthus (sign of the fish), a "What Would Jesus Do?" pin or bracelet, or some other symbol of your faith. You'd

be amazed at how many times such a seemingly small symbol can open a conversation about what Jesus means in your life.

- Always use mealtimes as a witness. Bow in prayer before your meal with family and friends, whether in the privacy of your home or in restaurants or other public places. Don't pray to be showy, but give genuine thanks to God for His blessings—and He can use that moment to open evangelistic doors and bring honor to Himself.

- Use every casual conversation with others as an opportunity to mention your faith, your values, your Lord, and the Bible. When people share a hurt or concern with you, use it as an opportunity to pray with that person and show your genuine Christlike concern for their lives.

- Send cards, notes, and e-mail messages of concern, encouragement, and blessing.

- Always practice Christlike grace and courtesy in your interactions with others. Never assume: No one knows I'm a Christian—it doesn't matter if I blow my top or chew this guy out. You are a witness for Christ—or against Him!—wherever you go, whatever you do, twenty-four hours a day, seven days a week. Never let your guard down—or you'll be letting your Lord down!

- Be a blessing to people wherever you go. Smile. Be friendly. Be interested in others. Be a good listener. Always have a positive word for others. Be quick to offer love, grace, acceptance, and encouragement at every opportunity.

- When you fail someone or sin against someone, always be quick to admit your fault and ask forgiveness. A humble and contrite heart is a rare grace in the world today, and when you are willing to say, "I was wrong, I'm sorry," people stand in amazement at the beauty of your mature and Christlike character. In this way, you can even turn your mistakes and sins into opportunities for witness!

- Speak out against immorality, sin, injustice, and evil. When you see someone being mistreated, stand up for that person. The courage to stand up against wrongdoing is a powerful witness for

Christ. Make it clear that you are taking a stand because of your love for Christ.

- When you hear someone taking the Lord's name in vain, speak up! You don't have to be rude, just firm. Say, "Please don't use the Lord's name that way. You are speaking about Someone who is very important to me."

Be salt and light in your workplace.
- Keep a Bible and Christian plaques, books, or other Christian decorations in your office. Make sure that you unmistakably mark yourself as a follower of Jesus Christ.

- Once you have marked yourself as a Christian, make sure that you live worthy of your calling. Practice 100 percent integrity, honesty, and fairness in all your business dealings. Offer affirmation and appreciation to others in your office. Be respectful toward the boss, and be kind and caring toward your fellow workers. Perform your chores cheerfully and with excellence as unto the Lord, and witness not only by your words but by your works.

- Use business lunches as opportunities not only to advance your business, but also to advance the cause of Christ. Don't be embarrassed about bowing your head and asking God's blessing on your food and conversation. Be open with colleagues and clients about what God is doing in your life.

- Invite coworkers to church and Bible studies. With your employer's permission, host a weekly lunchtime Bible study at the office. Organize a quarterly luncheon for businesspeople with a speaker who is able to spark broad-based interest—and who will present the Gospel without compromise.

Be salt and light in your neighborhood.
- Get to know all your neighbors up and down the block. Get acquainted with their hurts and needs—and find ways to meet those needs with the love of Christ. Practice Christian hospitality

and invite your neighbors over for coffee and dessert or a backyard barbecue—and always be ready to share the hope and faith you have in Christ!

- Be a servant. Once you truly know your neighbors, you'll be in a position to do the things that communicate the love of Christ and touch human hearts. When your neighbor is in need, go over without waiting to be asked and mow the lawn, wash the car, shovel the driveway, do the grocery shopping, clean house, baby-sit, prepare meals, do the washing and ironing, provide transportation, perform house repairs, or other acts of kindness. When your neighbor asks, "Why are you so nice to us?" you can say, "After all Jesus has done for me, I just want to help other people as much as I can." And that will give you an opening to share the Gospel.

- Offer to pray for your neighbors when they have a need, a problem, or a crisis. Don't just say, "I'll pray for you," and walk away. Put your arm around that person, bow your head, and pray on the spot. Then, if possible, become involved in helping to answer that prayer. Show your love and Christian caring over the long haul. Be available. Be a good friend and a good Christian neighbor.

- Invite neighborhood children to an after-school kids' club where they can hear Bible stories, sing songs, enjoy refreshments and activities, and hear the Gospel. (For more information, contact Child Evangelism Fellowship, P.O. Box 348, Warrenton, MO 63383-0348; telephone 314-456-4321.)

- Deliver a plate of homebaked cookies or a loaf of freshly-baked bread to a neighbor for no particular reason.

- When newcomers move into the neighborhood, introduce yourself, lend a hand with their moving chores, give them a plate of snacks, and ask if they will be looking for a church to attend. If they don't have a church home, invite them to your church.

- In your heart and in your prayers, claim your neighborhood for Christ—then consider ways you can have an outreach, such as: a neighborhood Bible study, a neighborhood block party or yard sale, a women's Bible study, and Super Bowl or NBA play-off parties. At these relaxed, informal settings, find ways to engage your neighbors in conversations about themselves, their attitudes, their beliefs, their needs, their hurts—and always be ready to give them the Good News of Jesus Christ. Build relationships that can become bridges to God.

- Start a mothers' support group (with childcare provided). Promote family values while sharing the Gospel and caring for mothers of all kinds—married, single, divorced, widowed, working, stay-at-home.

- When you witness to others, do as Jesus did with the Samaritan woman at the well: Draw them out. Have dialogues with them— not monologues. Listen carefully to the other person—and to the leading of the Holy Spirit within you. When you speak, always communicate love and caring as well as truth.

- Beware of letting yourself off with impersonal "hit-and-run" evangelism techniques. I'm not saying it's wrong to invite a person to church or an evangelistic meeting, or to drop off a Christian book, tape, or personal note. But none of these approaches are as personal and powerful as actually sitting down with someone for coffee or tea and saying, "I care about you. I know you have a need, and I know that only Jesus can fill it. Do you know whether you would go to Heaven if you died right now? Would you like to have that assurance? Here's how I met Jesus. Here's what God's Word says about your need for Him. Why don't we pray about that together right now?" When in doubt, always use the more personal approach.

- Plan a retreat, such as to a Christian family camp, and invite a non-Christian family to go with you. Plan to have plenty of time for fellowship and relaxed sharing. Pray for that family and for opportunities to share Christ during the retreat.

- Organize a weekly community group around a common interest (such as effective parenting, making crafts, or creative writing) and provide a regular "friendship time" that can be used for building relationships, sharing, and talking about your faith.

- Join with other Christians to host a monthly open house at different Christian homes in the neighborhood. Offer refreshments and good music, possibly a speaker or a video presentation (for example, a James Dobson Focus on the Family film). Keep the atmosphere relaxed and convivial, with plenty of time for one-on-one relationship building and sharing of convictions and personal stories.

Be salt and light by meeting social needs.

- Start an evangelistic soup kitchen, food pantry, meals-on-wheels, or visitation outreach to nursing homes, hospitals, and retirement villages.

- Be a foster parent or adoptive parent. Pray about the possibility of adopting a child from another country or a hard-to-place child (such as an older child, a child with emotional problems, or a child with physical handicaps).

- Open your home to exchange students from other countries and other cultures.

- Offer your services as an after-school tutor to the local high school or middle school. Use those opportunities to build discipling and mentoring relationships with young people.

Be salt and light through your political involvement.

- Become politically aware—and involved. Get to know the candidates and parties and what they stand for, especially with regard to moral issues, abortion, education, and religious freedom. Study the biblical principles found in such passages as Mark 12:13–17; 1 Timothy 2:1–4; and Acts 5:29. In these passages, Christians are instructed in how to "render unto Caesar" and "render unto God." In the 1 Timothy passage, Paul says that we should pray for our government leaders so that "we may lead a quiet and peaceable life in all godliness and reverence," so that our nation and our communities may be evangelized without hindrance or restraint.

- Combine political action with genuine service to human need. In 1997, when Promise Keepers held a massive rally in Washington, D.C., they organized an effort to go into the city's run-down public school buildings to paint, patch, and repair. By doing so, they demonstrated to the city and the nation that Christians want to serve just as their Lord came to serve. D.C. schools maintenance chief Charles Williams estimated that the school district received nearly $600,000 worth of skilled labor from the Promise Keepers group.

Be salt and light through using your talents and abilities.
- Has God gifted you with a special ability in the arts or entertainment field? Then use it to be salt and light in the world! Christian artists, writers, poets, musicians, actors, stand-up comics, jugglers, illusionists, and ventriloquists can have a tremendous impact on audiences and society, demonstrating God's creativity through their own God-given, inspired, baptized abilities and imaginations! This is nothing new, of course; in Old Testament times, God used faithful artists to adorn His temples and faithful musicians to lead His people in battle. Today, Christian artists and entertainers must use their abilities not only within the Church but also to carry the spiritual battle into the world. When they do so, they are fulfilling God's highest purpose for their lives!

Be salt and light through seasonal events.
- Plan a neighborhood or community-wide Sweetheart Banquet close to Valentine's Day. Make it open to non-Christians and arrange to have several Christian couples share testimonies of how Jesus Christ has made a difference in their marriage and family life.

- Invite neighborhood friends and children to share your Easter celebration. In addition to the traditional Easter egg activities, be sure to make it clear that your family views this special day as Resurrection

Sunday. Share openly with your neighbors what the death and resurrection of Jesus Christ mean to you and your family.

- Use Mother's Day and Father's Day as an opportunity to reach out to those in your neighborhood and your community who do not have family close by. Celebrate them, honor them—and be sure to tell them about the love of Jesus Christ.

- Create an alternative to Halloween, such as an "All Saints' Party." Replace witches and demons with wholesome fun, games, pizza and ice cream, treasure hunts, singing—and a testimony to your neighborhood that yours is a godly, Christian home.

- Host a Thanksgiving celebration for your neighbors that is focused around God and His blessings in our lives—especially the blessings of salvation through faith in Jesus Christ.

- Turn Christmastime into an evangelistic opportunity in your neighborhood, with caroling, a Christmas open house for the entire neighborhood, a meal, and a Gospel presentation. Christmas is a perfect open-door opportunity for witnessing. After all, what could be more natural than a time of sharing with friends and neighbors what the birthday of the Savior means to you!

Ways for kids and students to be salt and light
- Wear T-shirts with Christian slogans and Bible verses; wear Christian necklaces, bracelets, and buttons; write or stick Christian messages on your backpacks, binders, folders, and so forth. Be a walking statement of your faith and values.

- Find ways to witness to your classmates and fellow students about Jesus Christ in the papers, oral presentations, and assignments you do at school.

- Take your Bible to school and bow your head in prayer before lunch. Don't be intimidated by those who would say it's "unconstitutional" or that it "violates separation of church and state" to demonstrate your faith at school. The truth is, it's a violation of the First Amendment for anyone to prevent you from doing so!

- Share contemporary Christian music CDs with your friends. Tell them where to tune in to positive, contemporary Christian stations in your area.

- Invite friends to your church and youth group.

- Always be prepared to share the Gospel, boldly and directly. God's Word tells us, "Always be ready to give a defense to everyone who asks you a reason for the hope that is in you" (1 Peter 3:15). So have your own Christian testimony prepared in your mind and have Bible verses memorized so that you can share Christ with others at a moment's notice. Get involved with Evangelism Explosion for Youth so that you are well prepared to share the Gospel.

- Pray for God to send opportunities your way.

These are just a few ideas for ways one individual can be salt and light in his or her own little corner of the world. I trust that one or more of these ideas may even spark some new ideas and possibilities in your own mind. We serve a creative God, and I believe He has some creative ways in mind for you to serve Him and change your corner of the world!

The significance of one

The power of one is really the power of *every*one.

One of the reasons there is so much power in the decision of a single person to submit himself to the will of the Lord Jesus Christ is that we know we are not alone. I know that if I say to Him, "Lord, what do You want me to do?" then there are certainly others whom He has called, and who are also responding, "Lord, what do You want me to do?" I am not alone and neither are you—even if we sometimes feel like we are. God is raising up an army of men and women, each of whom is only one person—but collectively, we are the irresistible force of the body of Christ. And Christ Himself has said that the gates of Hell cannot prevail against us.

Alexander Solzhenitsyn, in a book called *From Under the Rubble*, said that the shackles of tyranny and slavery could be thrown off around the world if every single person would simply take one positive moral step. I believe he is right—and I am convinced that it is incumbent upon you and me to take that positive moral step. We must do it now—because tomorrow may be too late. As I look around at the moral state of our nation, I am concerned—deeply concerned.

I compare the days in which we live with the days I read about in the Bible, and I am reminded that the Old Testament prophets warned the people, "The Assyrians are coming!" The people laughed and said, "Go to Judah and tell them that. We don't want to hear that in Israel." The prophets of Judah said, "The Babylonians are coming!" And the people said, "We don't want to hear that. Go away." They threw Jeremiah in a well to shut him up. They didn't want to hear about it. But God had given to those prophets a vision of the way things really were and what was really coming. The people didn't listen because they believed *It can't happen here! God would never let that happen to us!*

But it happened.

It happened in Israel. It happened in Judah. And the Bible says that a time is coming in our own world when people will be saying, "Peace, peace"—and then sudden destruction will come upon them. It amazes me to see the blindness of people who just go on about their lives as if they have forever. My friend, we do not have forever. We have today, and we dare not squander it. We must make the most of it for the sake of Jesus Christ. That is our mandate. That is our purpose.

What stands between America and destruction? Friend in Christ, I submit to you that you and I are all that stand in the way. The moral choices we make, the virtuous and godly stands we take, will determine the fate of our society. Remember the words of Alexis de Tocqueville: "America is great because America is good, and if America ever ceases to be good, America will cease to be great." When I think of those words, and then look around at the society we have become—I tremble. I can't help but remember the words of Ruth Bell Graham: "If America doesn't repent, and if God doesn't punish America, He is going to have to apologize to Sodom and Gomorrah."

And God does not apologize.

I am often asked, "Do you believe it's too late for America? Do you believe America is so awash in sin, evil, and immorality that her fate is sealed?" I don't know, but I am sure of this: We don't have much time to decide the matter one way or another. As a nation, as a community of responsible individuals, we have to make a choice—either to serve God or reject Him. I do not like to be a Jeremiah or a prophet of gloom and doom. In fact, I am an optimist at heart, and I believe that God does have a great future for America—*if* America will return to the great purpose for which it was founded. But I also know that the world got along for thousands of years without America, and it can get along without America again. God's eternal plan doesn't hinge on the existence of this nation. So if America were to be destroyed from without or collapsed from within, it would not be the end of the world.

But it would certainly be the end of us!

There is only one force on this planet that is going to change the direction of this nation: the power of the Gospel of Jesus Christ. That is why I am committed to this one great purpose—the goal of changing the course of history, of bringing about the kingdom of God, of transforming the world—

One human heart at a time.

Now, perhaps, you begin to see the *power* and *significance* of one. In God's eternal plan, no one is expendable. No one can say, "I'm not important. My contribution doesn't matter." You are *crucial*, you are *significant*, you are *irreplaceable*. You have a significant part to play in transforming the world for Jesus Christ. Can one person really make a difference in the world? Let me tell you a true story from American history.

"I'm only a [fill in the blank]"

In the early 1800s, just a few decades after the successful conclusion of the American Revolution, the scent of war was in the air—a second war against Great Britain. The nation was almost evenly divided between those who wanted to go to war with the mother country and those who wanted to find some way to avoid it. In the end, the matter was decided by a single Rhode Island farmer and his pig.

You doubt me? Well, read on! This is absolutely true.

In the year 1811, in a small rural district in Rhode Island, a farmer's pig became stuck in a fence. It was so solidly stuck, he couldn't get the porker out. The farmer was almost ready to break its legs and kill it rather than allow it to suffer in that condition. Finally, he was able to free the pig and return it to the pen.

Then he went to town to vote. It was an election day, and the district was electing representatives for the state legislature. But by the time the man arrived in town, the polls had closed and it was too late to vote. The farmer had intended to vote for a candidate who was opposed to war with Britain, but because his pig got stuck in a fence, a rival, pro-war candidate was elected by a single vote. The legislature then elected a senator to go to Washington—and again, this U.S. senator was elected by a single vote (in those days senators were not elected by popular vote as they are today, but by the state legislatures). The newly elected senator was in favor of war.

When this senator went to Washington, a debate was held in the Congress about whether America should go to war with England. The Senate decided—again by a single vote!—to take America to war.

And so the War of 1812 began—

A war that would have been averted if a Rhode Island farmer hadn't stopped to free his stuck pig!

We tend to think, *I'm just one person—what can I do?* Friend in Christ, don't ever minimize the contribution one person can make to God's eternal plan. If only we would recognize the power of one. If only we would be aware from day to day, from moment to moment, of the awesome fact that one Christian plus God equals a majority.

We should never be intimidated by the fact that "I'm only one person." Or, "I'm only a farmer." Or, "I'm only a student." Or, "I'm only a layperson." Or, "I'm only a housewife." Or, "I'm only a [fill in the blank with whatever you are]." God has a purpose for you, no matter what you "only" are! He "only" wants to use you as part of His plan to roll back the forces of evil and unbelief, and to enthrone Christ over the nation. He *can* and He *will* use you—

If only you will ask Him, "Lord, what do You want me to do?"

7

GOD'S PURPOSE FOR
YOUR MARRIAGE

*So God created man in His own image; in the image of God He
created him; male and female He created them. Then God blessed
them, and God said to them, "Be fruitful and multiply; fill the
earth and subdue it . . ."*

(GEN. 1:27–28)

Bob and Rosemary Barnes travel the country, conducting Christian
seminars designed to help couples build stronger, more lasting marriage
relationships. They have authored several books on marriage, including
*Rock-Solid Marriage: Building a Permanent Relationship in a Throw-Away
World* and *We Need to Talk: Opening Doors of Communication with Your
Mate.* Though they have shown thousands of couples the way to a better marriage, their own marriage was once in serious jeopardy—

And Bob didn't even know it!

"We were conducting a seminar once," Bob recalls, "and during the
question-and-answer session, someone asked, 'What was your first year of
marriage like?' Well, I tend to be a little more reckless and bold in answering, while Rosemary is more thoughtful—so I foolishly answered the
question first. I said, 'Well, our first year of marriage was just fine.' But
when Rosemary answered, she said, 'My first year of marriage was the
worst year of my life!' And the audience burst out laughing and thought
she was kidding. But I looked at her and realized, *No! She's serious!*

"As we were in the car, driving away from the seminar, after a long silence I said to her, 'You were serious about that, weren't you?' She said, 'Oh yeah. It was the worst year of my life.' I said, 'Well, why didn't you tell me?' She said, 'I tried to tell you. I tried to tell you all along, but you were so busy going off in your own direction, you couldn't hear me. You just *got* married—and that was enough for you. But I wanted to *be* married.'"

Rosemary remembers those days well. "Bob was very involved in building his career," she says, "and I was very involved in my teaching, and we didn't have the communication we should have had."

"In those early days of our marriage," Bob adds, "I didn't know we had to communicate just for the sake of communication, in order to blend. And we could not have been more opposite. In our approach to everything in life, we were like puzzle pieces that didn't fit together."

Yet despite their differences and contrasts—or perhaps even *because* of those differences and contrasts!—God had a purpose and a design for Bob and Rosemary's marriage. His plan was to use their imperfect marriage and personality traits to demonstrate His perfect plan for bringing a man and a woman together in the sacrament He created at the very beginning when He said, "It is not good that man should be alone; I will make him a helper comparable to him" (Gen. 2:18).

In the trenches of everyday living, God has taught Bob and Rosemary Barnes how to overcome the hurdles of life, bridge the differences and contrasts between them, and build a successful marriage that fulfills the two great mandates God has given us—the Cultural Mandate and the Great Commission. God wants to use the love between a Christian husband and a Christian wife to show the world what His love is like. He wants to show the world how He has reconciled the world to Himself by showing how a Christian man and woman bridge the gulfs and the contrasts between them to truly become one in Christ.

When Christian husbands and wives truly live out their faith in the day-to-day struggles and joys of married life, they send a powerful message to a watching world—a world littered with disposable marriages, shattered families, and casual sex. Healthy Christian marriages are a powerful witness of the protective, healing, forgiving, restoring, reconciling love of Christ. When Christian couples live and love as God intended, other people will want what they have. Maintaining a healthy, godly marriage is one of the most powerful ways in which you and I can be salt and light in a corrupt and darkening world.

I believe that when you begin to catch a glimpse of God's eternal purpose for your marriage, it will totally transform the way you approach your mate, the way you approach problems and issues in your marriage, and the way you live together and love each other.

Submission and love

Once, when I was doing a sermon series on the book of Ephesians, I preached on Ephesians 5:22 ("Wives, submit to your own husbands, as to the Lord"). The husbands in the congregation seemed to be all in favor of that sermon! But looking in their bulletins, those husbands noticed that the following Sunday's message would be on Ephesians 5:25 ("Husbands, love your wives, just as Christ also loved the church and gave Himself for her"). One of the men said on his way out the door, "Somehow I've got to figure out a way to get my wife out of town before next Sunday!" No doubt, many men in the congregation shared his apprehension!

After the sermon to husbands, I was told of another comment—this one by a little boy to his parents as they were going to the car after church. "Gee, Dad," said the boy, "you've got the easy job. Mom has to submit to you, and all you have to do is love her! That's easy!"

Well, is it? Who really has the "easy job" in a Christian marriage? It may seem that the Bible places the man in an envious perch from which he can look down in imperious sovereignty upon his submissive wife. But wait! Let's think about that for a moment! Let's examine Ephesians 5:22–29, which is the apostle Paul's handbook for a healthy Christian marriage:

> Wives, submit to your own husbands, as to the Lord. For the husband is head of the wife, as also Christ is head of the church; and He is the Savior of the body. Therefore, just as the church is subject to Christ, so let the wives be to their own husbands in everything.

Husbands, love your wives, just as Christ also loved the church and gave Himself for her, that He might sanctify and cleanse her with the washing of water by the word, that He might present her to Himself a glorious church, not having spot or wrinkle or any such thing, but that she should be holy and without blemish.

So husbands ought to love their own wives as their own bodies; he who loves his wife loves himself. For no one ever hated his own flesh, but nourishes and cherishes it, just as the Lord does the church.

Here we are told that the Christian wife is to submit herself to her husband as the Church submits itself to Christ. We are also told that a Christian husband is to love his wife as Christ loves the Church. Question: Who has the easier part in the relationship between Jesus Christ and His Church? Is it Christ? Or is it the Church?

I don't think there's any question! It is far easier for us as His Church to submit ourselves to Christ than it was for Christ to give Himself in love for us! It is a great and sacred task for wives to submit to their husbands and for husbands to love their wives as Christ loved the Church— and when we carry out our roles as God intended, we demonstrate to the world the beautiful love relationship between God and His Church. What a powerful witness that can be!

Now, what does this mean, for wives to submit to husbands and for husbands to love their wives? In our culture, which is drenched in radical feminist propaganda and marred by male selfishness and egotism, neither of these biblical commands is readily received. The idea of submission goes against the grain of "liberated" womanhood in our culture today. And the true import of what it means to really love one's wife— which involves a high degree of responsibility, fidelity, involvement, sensitivity, and listening—goes against the grain of today's male culture.

When men and women hear that the Bible calls women to be submissive, men tend to react with misplaced jubilation, and women tend to react with misplaced horror. Both envision a kind of marital tyranny in which the husband keeps his wife in a yoke of involuntary servitude. If that is the image you derive from these words in Ephesians, you have a distorted impression. The Bible doesn't remotely suggest that Christian marriage involves husbands dominating their wives in a dictatorial fashion. Instead, the Bible tells us that the husband has a solemn and sacred responsibility before God to love his wife. It is not the husband's job to *make* his wife submit, but to love her. It is not the wife's responsibility to "knuckle under," but to willingly submit to her husband's headship as unto Christ.

This is a mutual relationship, and there is a beautiful symmetry involved in the different roles of husband and wife. The relationship becomes unhealthy and unrighteous when this symmetry is disturbed, when either the husband tries to lord it over his wife as a dictator or when the wife undermines or rebels against the husband's role of responsibility.

The first problem that so many husbands get into is that they are careless in reading the Scriptures and understanding the responsibility they have been given—because that's what the husband's authority is all about: not power, not prerogative, but *responsibility*. Too many men read, "For the husband is head of the wife . . ." and they stop there—failing to read the next few words: "as also Christ is head of the church; and He is the Savior of the body." What is the head of a body for? To abuse and tyrannize and terrorize the body? No! To protect and serve and honor the body, and to keep the body out of trouble! The head keeps the hand from burning itself and the foot from stepping on a nail. As a man in Christ, you are the head of the body, and it is your responsibility to love and care for the body—that is, you are to love and care for your wife.

Does God exercise Napoleon-like power and tyranny over us as Christians? He would certainly have the right and power to do so—but that is not how He treats us. He guides us gently and reasonably, and He loves us unconditionally. He is patient with us, encourages us, and honors us. He doesn't insult or berate us but treats us with respect, entrusting us to carry out His program under His benevolent authority. As Christian husbands, we should learn a lesson from His example.

Husbands should also remember that while the wife is under the headship of the husband, the husband is under the headship of Christ.

It is the will of Christ, not the will of the husband, that is sovereign in a Christian home. As men of God, Christian husbands are to seek to fulfill God's purpose for their lives and their families by setting a Christlike example and by living every moment in obedience to the Cultural Mandate and the Great Commission. You cannot be a tyrant and an example of God's character at the same time.

Many Christian husbands mistake material things for love. They read the words, "Husbands, love your wives," and they say, "Of course I love her! Don't I go to work every day? Don't I bring home a paycheck? Doesn't she have food on the table and a roof over her head?" That's not love. The basic provision of material necessities is your basic duty as a man—even non-Christians do that. Many people are confused about the role of *persons* versus the role of *things* in their lives. While God made us to love people and use things, all too many people in this world seem to love things and use people! That is a perversion of God's plan for our lives and our marriage relationships.

Let's get our focus off things and onto what people really need in a marriage relationship. A Christian husband's duty to love goes far beyond mere material provision. A husband is more than a business suit and a paycheck. He is a protector, a lover, a partner, a confidant, a listener, a shoulder to cry on, an encourager, an ally, a friend. When was the last time you said, "I love you. I'm so glad I married you. How could I ever live without you?" When was the last time you gave your wife the gift of your undivided attention, looking into her eyes and really listening to what she says and what she feels? When was the last time you treated your wife not as a cook or a maid, but as your *partner,* as a *person?*

Women, too, often fall into the trap of focusing on things instead of people. Because of their natural nesting instinct and their concern for the home and their responsibility to care for it, many women fail to see that their primary responsibility is toward the people in the home—not toward the house itself. When your husband walks in the door and tracks mud on the carpet, what is your first concern—the trials and struggles and problems that got his shoes muddy, or the footprints themselves? Do you ask him what happened during the day that got his shoes so scuffed and muddied—or do you blast him for messing up your carpet? Is your focus on the relationship with your husband—or on things? Many a couple, including Christian couples, have become so fixated on things, they have acquired beautiful, gleaming houses that are emotionally and spiritually as dead as tombs because no love lives in them anymore.

Christian wife, remember why you are to yield yourself to your husband—not for his sake but for Christ's sake. Just as your husband is under the authority of Christ and loves you for the sake of Christ, so you should yield to him for the sake of Christ. When your husband fails to be everything you would like him to be, don't be bitter. Pray for him, honor him, and encourage him, always remembering that God has placed him in that role for your protection, provision, and edification. When you adopt the role God designed for you, and your husband adopts the role God designed for him, you will experience a foretaste of glory above.

What a contrast true Christian marriage is to the marriages of this world, where the husband is either weak and ineffectual, dominated by an angry, embittered wife—or where a thundering tyrant is locked in a death-struggle with a rebellious wife! Such a home is a foretaste of Hell! If we are obedient to God's purpose and plan for marriage, we will make our homes the paradise God wanted them to be from the moment of creation.

The husband is the "house-band"

The word *husband* was originally a compound word in Old English: "house-band." God designed the role of husband to be a band of protection around the house, around the family, to support, defend, and provide for the family. It is tragic that in our own society the roles of husband and wife are no longer complementary but competitive. The husband has been robbed to a great degree of his role as a "house-band." In all too many marriages, the wife no longer views her husband as a defender and friend, but as a rival. There are a number of reasons for today's increasing competition between husbands and wives—and all of them are unhealthy and violate God's plan for marriage:

1. The rise of materialism and selfishness. Many couples today feel they cannot be happy and fulfilled unless they have that larger house, that extra SUV in the driveway, that boat on the lake. And to acquire these things, many mothers are going off to work, in competition with fathers. As a result, all too many children today are growing up surrounded with *things* but without the nurturing enclosure of *family*. They grow up in daycare centers. They come home from school to an empty house. When Mom and Dad are home, the parents have no time or energy to give to their children or to each other. So the family is rich in *things* but poor in *relationships*.

Many working mothers have discovered that once they added up the cost of being employed—daycare costs, new wardrobe, transportation, restaurant meals, a higher tax bracket—they were really better off staying home and being full-time wives and mothers. And they found that they were happier and more fulfilled as full-time mothers because they were living out God's plan for Christian families.

2. The rise of feminism and "political correctness." The liberal "politically correct" agenda of radical feminism (which is clearly "biblically incorrect") says to women, "You have no value as a wife, mother, and homemaker. You only have value if you are competing with men in the marketplace and the workplace." Today many women are made to feel guilty if they are not shoving their children into an anonymous day-care center and going to an office to fight for a paycheck. In truth, a woman should feel honored to carry out the role of wife and mother.

There are situations, of course, that make it impossible for a woman to be a full-time wife and mother. Sometimes divorce or the death of a spouse is unavoidable, and a woman must work outside the home to provide for herself and her children. But in all too many cases, women make a choice that is dictated by the culture or by personal ambition, not necessity. The Bible tells us that we are not to allow the ideologies and -isms of this world (such as radical feminism) to squeeze us into its mold. We are to mold ourselves after the will of God, not the will of some worldly political agenda.

3. The rise of the welfare state and the middle-class tax burden. Gary Bauer, president of the Family Research Council, expressed this concern in a speech before the Heritage Foundation:

It is getting harder, not easier, for working families to make ends meet
. . . We have created ten million-plus new jobs, but only eight million
more workers are now employed. Every three workers are holding
down four jobs. One income used to provide for a family. Then it
took two. Now, increasingly, it takes three!

A generation ago, most middle-class families lived comfortably on a
single salary. Why is that no longer possible? To a large degree, the
answer is *taxes*.

Every wage earner spends a certain portion of each working year just
to pay his taxes. In the early 1900s, the average wage earner spent the
month of January earning the money to pay the tax man; from February
1 on, he got to keep everything he made for the benefit of his family. By
1925, taxes had increased to the point where a wage earner worked for
the government until February 6. By 1940, the spending programs of
the New Deal had extended the tax bite to March 8. By the end of
World War II, wage earners were in bondage to Uncle Sam until April
1. By 1965, wage earners worked until April 14 to pay the government.
Under Jimmy Carter, taxpayers worked for the government until May 5;
the Reagan tax cuts moved that date back into late April. Today, as
America enters the new millennium, Americans work for Uncle Sam
until May 10. In fact, the nonpartisan Tax Foundation says that
American families now spend more on federal, state, and local taxes than
on food, shelter, clothing, and transportation *combined*.

This crushing financial burden on American families forces moms
into the workplaces, and often forces dads into a second job. The tax
policies of our government are literally depriving our children of their
parents, and depriving husbands and wives of precious time together to
build relationships. This should not be.

4. The rise of the "self-fulfillment" movement. There was a time when
a man would do whatever it took to provide for his family—go down
into the coal mines, work in the fields, or dig ditches. Today many men
would rather sit idle and let their wives go to work than work in a job
that is not "fulfilling." I submit to you that if Jesus, the Lord of creation,
was not too proud to take the lowly form of a servant in order to love

His bride, the Church, then we men should not be too proud to serve our families in any way we must in order to provide the necessities of life. Although there are many reasons why women either choose or are forced to compete with their husbands to provide a family paycheck, one of the most tragic and needless reasons of all is men who fail to meet their basic responsibility.

I am not saying that women have no right to be in the workplace if they so choose. But we all need to realize what it means to make a choice. No one can have it all. When you say yes to one thing, you must say no to another. You cannot be both a CEO and a supermom. There are only so many hours in a day and so much energy one person can expend. If you as a woman choose the business world, that is your choice—but don't bring children into the world with the intent of hiring people to parent them for you. If single parenthood is forced upon you by unavoidable circumstances, then you must do the best you can. But if you have a choice, and the choice is motherhood, devote yourself to that role 100 percent. Commit yourself to your God-given purpose of raising your children to grow up into the image of God. Train them, love them, nurture them, and be available to them.

And Christian husband—commit yourself to being the "houseband" of your family. Be the defender-protector of your wife and family, as God intended you to be. Be sure to love and honor your wife, because the way you treat your wife is a test of the reality of your Christian faith. The Bible tells us that if we do not love our neighbor, whom we have seen, how can we love God, whom we have not seen? And who is your closest neighbor? Your wife! The most important test of your faith takes place every day, right in your own home.

Make love your aim

If you attend a wedding ceremony these days, you might be surprised at the vows that are exchanged. In some cases, couples have been known to alter the wording from, "I promise to love, honor, and cherish as long as we both shall live" to ". . . as long as we both shall *love.*" In other words, there is an explicit expectation that this union will only last as long as the emotions last. Once the feeling is over, the marriage becomes disposable, like a used Kleenex. People seem to think, *When I get tired of this marriage, I can always get out of it and find true (if temporary) love again.*

Former education secretary William Bennett tells of the time while he was teaching at Boston University that he attended the wedding of two students. The couple vowed to stay together "so long as love shall last." Hearing this nearly meaningless "vow," Bennett seized upon the perfect wedding gift to symbolize the disposable nature of this couple's pseudocommitment: He gave the newlyweds a box of paper plates!

The increasingly widespread attitude toward love and marriage expressed by the couple in Bennett's story typifies the cultural decay in our society. It is the chief reason why so many children live in one-parent homes, so that the only daddy they know is a man they visit every other weekend—a virtual stranger who sends child support checks in the mail. It is one of the reasons for the soaring crime rates we endure today. Statistics show that 70 percent of long-term prison inmates (including 72 percent of adolescent murderers and 60 percent of all rapists) come from fatherless homes. Stable, intact families are more prosperous and less likely to use social services such as welfare. So we all have a stake in seeing that the children in our society be raised in whole, healthy, two-parent families where Mom and Dad are committed to each other for life.

Certainly, there are situations where divorce becomes a reluctant necessity—for example, where one partner exhibits a pattern of adultery, addiction, or violence that threatens the other partner or the children. But I daresay the vast majority of divorces in our society occur for reasons that can only be termed trivial: "I'm bored." "I don't feel excited in the relationship anymore." "There's no magic in our marriage." "Money is tight and I'm stressed out." "I need to go find myself." "I don't feel fulfilled."

Today the United States (where according to a Gallup poll, 40 percent of Americans attend church on a weekly basis) has the highest divorce rate in the world. In fact, the U.S. divorce rate is three times that of Japan and twice that of Europe (where only 10 percent of the people are regular church attenders!). In 1986, a community-wide group of pastors in Modesto, California, decided to put the brakes on this marriage-go-round that sends nearly half of all marriages crashing in divorce.

Noting that 75 percent of all marriages are performed by clergy, these pastors were troubled by the nearly 50 percent divorce rate. As a result, they drew up a community marriage policy for Modesto, which each minister signed. Its goal:

> to radically reduce the divorce rate among those married in area churches. It is the responsibility of pastors to set minimum requirements to raise the quality of the commitment in those we marry. We believe that couples who seriously participate in premarital testing and counseling will have a better understanding of what the marriage commitment involves.

The pastors formed an organization called Marriage Savers, which has since spread nationwide. Marriage Savers requires its member churches to take engaged couples through a four-month premarital course (a "prenuptial boot camp"), including a premarital inventory to help them assess the maturity of their commitment and relationship. The course also places the couple in a mentoring relationship with a mature married couple to give them guidance, counsel, and a mature perspective on what the marriage covenant is all about.

The results of the Marriage Savers program have been nothing short of astonishing. During Marriage Savers' first decade in Modesto, the number of divorces fell from 1,923 in 1986 to only 1,606 in 1995—despite the fact that the county's population grew from 303,000 to 420,000. If the number of divorces had grown with the county population, there should have been 2,634 divorces in 1995—so the numbers indicate that Marriage Savers saved 1,000 marriages in that year alone!

Why is Marriage Savers so successful? I believe one of the key reasons is that Marriage Savers helps young couples distinguish between being "in love" and real love, *authentic* love as defined in the Bible. One of the great tragedies of our culture is the fact that most people have bought into the mythical notion that "love is all you need," that "love conquers all," that "love makes the world go 'round." And when most people use the word *love,* they really mean romantic attraction—a mysterious, ecstatic feeling that descends upon a couple like an ethereal bird of paradise, hovering and flapping wings of enchantment, causing their hearts to flutter. This kind of "love" comes without warning—and all too soon, it flies away.

What people today call "love" is really nothing more than infatuation. The word *infatuation* comes from the same Latin root word from which we get the English word *fatuous*. If you're not familiar with the word *fatuous*, let me open my thesaurus for you: It means "foolish, silly, idiotic, and dim-witted." The ancient Latins understood that infatuation isn't love— it is mere foolish attraction. Infatuation dulls the thinking and makes us do silly things. Those who base their lives and their homes upon the foolishness of infatuation, then compound their foolishness by calling it "love," will end up regretting their foolishness for years to come.

Feelings of attraction and infatuation are powerful and exciting— but you can't build a lasting, healthy marriage on mere emotion. In order to build a marriage to last a lifetime, you need to have something stronger, more reliable, and more durable than being "in love." You need *real* love, *authentic* love, Christlike love. And where do you find such love? You find it in the Bible:

> Love suffers long and is kind; love does not envy; love does not parade itself, is not puffed up; does not behave rudely, does not seek its own, is not provoked, thinks no evil; does not rejoice in iniquity, but rejoices in the truth; bears all things, believes all things, hopes all things, endures all things. Love never fails. (1 Cor. 13:4–8)

These are the most instructive, insightful, and powerful words in all of literature on the subject of love. But did you notice something amazing in those words? Nowhere in that passage can you find even a hint of anything mysterious, ethereal, or emotional! It deals with very down-to-earth, straightforward, action-oriented matters—not flights of fancy, romance, or ecstasy. In fact, this entire passage is rooted not in feelings, but in decisions, choices, and actions. It is rooted not in the emotions, but in the will. Every attitude and action we find in 1 Corinthians 13 is something we can choose, something we can do—not a feeling that merely comes and goes.

Real love is a *decision*, not a feeling. Love is a choice we make, regardless of feelings—and, in fact, often in contrast to our feelings. There are times in a marriage where, in order to be true to our marriage vows, we must deny feelings and choose to love by our actions.

At times in your marriage, you may *feel* angry and spiteful and resentful toward your spouse—but authentic love suffers long and is kind; it does not behave rudely; it is not provoked. At times in your marriage, you may *feel* that you want out, you may even *feel* attracted to another person and tempted toward the sin of adultery—but authentic love does not rejoice in iniquity, but rejoices in the truth; love never fails.

Brother in Christ, is that how you love your wife? And sister in Christ, is that how you love your husband?

This authentic kind of love is disregarded and completely unrecognized by those hopeless romantics who vainly seek the experience of being "in love"—that sweet mystery of life, that bird of paradise, that Cupid's arrow. God's love has nothing in common with what people today mistakenly call "love." When the Bible says that God loves us, it doesn't mean that God gets all gooey inside when He thinks about us. *When God looks down at me, I'm sure He doesn't have heart palpitations and warm fuzzies!* God made a decision to love a world that had sunk to its eyeballs in the quagmire of sin. God made a choice to love the most unlovable, unlovely creatures imaginable—human beings! He chose to send His Son for the sake of a race of murderous, thieving, lying, lusting, cheating, vain, arrogant sinners.

God hates sin. But, fortunately for you and me, He loves sinners. That's the Good News. He saw us, steeped in evil, mired in sin, and He made a decision to do good to us in whom nothing good dwelt. That is the very same love that is described in 1 Corinthians 13—and it is the very same love that we as Christians are to practice every day of our married lives. Not a feeling—a choice. And sometimes a very tough choice.

I sometimes liken love to the fragrance of a rose. If I said to you, "A rose is a delightful fragrance," you could say, "No, that's not quite right. A rose is a flower, and it produces a fragrance—but the fragrance isn't the flower. Don't confuse the flower with the fragrance."

In the same way, I say to you: Don't confuse *real* love with the *fragrance* of love. You see, one of the by-products of authentic Christlike love is that it produces a fragrance, which is the *emotion* of love. When we make loving decisions and do loving acts, we cause loving feelings to grow.

Many people, unfortunately, focus on the emotion of love rather than on love itself. They confuse the fragrance for the flower. They say, "I don't detect the fragrance, so there is no love here. We must have fallen out of love." Yet the reason they don't detect the fragrance is that they have neglected the flower. When they got married, they planted a rose in their garden and they went out each day to smell the fragrance. Over the years, however, they trampled the rose with neglect, unforgiveness, pettiness, selfishness, and cutting remarks. They stomped the rose into the mud—then they sniffed the air and said, "The fragrance is gone!"

Now, a rose is not a particularly mysterious thing—but it is a delicate thing. It needs to be handled with care. Treat it carelessly and you'll soon wonder where the fragrance went. So when people say, "The love is gone. We fell out of love. I don't feel any love for my spouse anymore," they are talking about the missing fragrance. The rose is still there, waiting to be lifted out of the mud of neglect and abuse—but we must make the choice to lift it up. If we stubbornly leave it there, we have no one but ourselves to blame.

Let me be quite candid: I know for a fact that there are people who have accepted Christ as Savior and Lord, yet they have not experienced the joy of authentic love in their homes. Why? Because they have not yielded themselves completely to God. They are still trying to live with one foot in the world. I am utterly convinced that the miserable home life so rampant in our neighborhoods and our world today—even in the Church—is simply the price people pay for living unyielded lives. Homes that are a little bit of Hell on earth are the dividend the devil pays for our infidelity to God.

God's purpose for your sex life

Just as God has an eternal purpose for your marriage, He also has an eternal purpose for the expression of your sexuality within marriage. In fact, we see that the sexual relationship in marriage is a central component of the Cultural Mandate, for there, in Genesis 1:27–28, we read:

So God created man in His own image; in the image of God He created him; male and female He created them. Then God blessed them,
and God said to them, "Be fruitful and multiply; fill the earth and
subdue it . . ."

Up to this point in our discussion of God's purpose for our lives, we
have been viewing God's command, "Be fruitful and multiply," in its
spiritual sense, in the sense of evangelism and witnessing. We are to
"reproduce" for God by sharing His Gospel, so that more and more
people will receive Jesus Christ as Lord and Savior, be reborn as God's
children, and become refashioned into the image of God. This principle
is at the heart of both the Cultural Mandate and the Great Commission.

But, of course, this command also has a physical sense. Before sin
entered the world, defacing the image of God that was stamped upon
the human race at creation, God commanded human beings to "be
fruitful and multiply" in a physical way. In other words, He commanded men and women to have sex.

Does that shock you? It shouldn't. If that statement shocks you, it is
because our society has developed some very distorted and unhealthy
views toward sex, characterized by extremes in two directions. Some
people in our culture are obsessed with sex, indulging in all sorts of illicit and self-destructive sexual practices, from fornication to adultery to
homosexuality to various other forms of perversion. On the other
extreme, we have people who are sexually repressed—they don't consider it a fit subject to discuss or even think about. To them, even sex within marriage is a dirty, shameful matter—at best, something to endure
rarely, reluctantly, and only for the sake of procreation. I submit to you
that neither of these extremes is a healthy or godly view of sex.

God is in favor of sex. He thinks sex is a great idea. He invented it.
The whole concept of sex arose in His mind.

To look at our culture, at either the XXX-rated obscenity that satu-
rates our culture or the priggishness and prudishness that characterizes
the opposite extreme, you would conclude that most people assume that
the devil created sex! No, the devil cannot create—he can only pervert
and distort something that was originally good. Sex is God's creation,

and when He created it He blessed it and saw that it was good. God made us to be sexual beings, and He blessed us and said to us, "Enjoy your sexuality, My children; be fruitful and multiply." He gave us this command right in the middle of the Cultural Mandate, so this is clearly a very important subject in the Word of God and in the mind of God.

The problem, obviously, is that there are a great many people today who have taken a good thing—God's gift of sex—and because of the depraved nature of mankind, they have twisted it and distorted it and perverted it. Some have exploited sex for money, and others have made it into something shameful and disgraceful because of the way they have misused it.

By way of example, let me ask you this: What is your favorite food? Is it a tender filet mignon smothered in mushrooms? Fresh Maine lobster drizzled with butter? Peking duck? Flaming kabob on a sword? A Big Mac with fries? All of these are good things that God has given us to enjoy. But suppose you happened to find your favorite food sitting atop a pile of garbage in a Dumpster, surrounded by buzzing flies. It's the same food whether it's in the Dumpster or served by candlelight with cloth napkins. But would it still make your mouth water—or would it make your stomach turn?

The same is true of God's gift of sex. In its proper place, as God intended, sex is one of the most beautiful and satisfying of all human experiences. In the wrong place, outside of the protective enclosure of a marriage covenant between a man and wife, sex becomes nauseating; it produces shame, destroys respect and relationships, spreads disease, creates unplanned pregnancies and abortions, and robs children of fathers.

Danielle from California writes this letter, which was read on a national radio talk show:

> I'm twenty-six years old, and I have two beautiful daughters, ages five and ten. If you do the math, you can readily see that, yes, my first child was born when I was sixteen. She was conceived when I was fifteen. My father is a Christian pastor, and he refused to allow me to have an abortion. So I raised my daughter with the help of my parents.

The eighteen-year-old boy who fathered my child did not participate at all during the first three years of my daughter's life except (reluctantly) with money. My mother took me down to the D.A.'s office, and we got a court order to garnish his wages for child support.

If it weren't for the godly emotional, spiritual, and financial support of my parents, I don't know where I would have ended up or what I would have done. My dad made it clear that after the birth of my first child, I was not to be on birth control. He said, "You don't give an eight-year-old the car keys, then forbid him to drive the car. And you don't give birth control pills to a teenager, then forbid her to have sex."

My parents did not allow the boy who fathered the baby to be in the delivery room, because the child was conceived in sin. Also, my parents did not allow me to have a baby shower, because showers are only for married couples. A few years later when the baby's father and I married, I did not show up in virgin white or anything close to white because that would have been a lie. It was hard living under all the restrictions my parents placed on me, but today I thank God for my parents and their godly standards.

I did eventually graduate from high school and am now pursuing a college degree. After taking a serious detour through immorality, I have gotten my life back on track—thanks to my parents' support and their tough enforcement of Christian moral standards. People sin and make mistakes, and hopefully we learn from those errors and don't make them again. With the help of my parents and the grace of God, I have grown up a lot in the past few years.

I ended up marrying my daughter's father, and he has grown up a lot as well. He has turned into a responsible husband, my best friend, and a loving father—all as a result of our faith in God. A couple of years into our marriage we had a second child. I'm determined to raise my two daughters to have Christian morals and to avoid the bad choices I made.

I'll always be grateful that God gave me parents who loved me enough to beat me over the head (not literally, though sometimes I thought so!) with the Bible.

—DANIELLE

I, too, am grateful for Danielle's godly parents who loved her enough to enforce an uncompromising, biblical moral standard in her life. There are all too few parents like Danielle's anymore. There are all too few Christians who are willing to take an uncompromising stand on biblical morality—and our society and our children are paying the price of that moral cowardice. Those who are willing to take such a stand are all the more conspicuous for their godliness and courage in this wicked and perverse age.

God has a vitally important purpose in mind for marriage, for human sexuality within marriage, and for the human love relationship that takes place within a family. He intends to use Christian marriage as a means of expressing to the world the true beauty and richness of His own character and love toward the family of humanity. But that can only happen when we, as His followers, are willing to courageously live out His truth, uncaring of the fact that the world may think us comical, peculiar, and hopelessly out-of-date.

We have no reason to be ashamed of sex or embarrassed about our stance on sexual morality. Genesis tells us that the man and the woman were naked, and they were not ashamed. Today a man and a woman can still be naked and unashamed within the protective enclosure of a covenantal marriage. It is only sex outside of marriage that is worthy of shame, and which always produces bitter fruit in the lives of those who practice it. Sex is never a so-so thing. It is either ecstasy or tragedy. It is either the richest and most profound of human satisfactions—or it is the ugliest, most degrading experience in life. The sole factor that determines whether our sex life reaches the pinnacle or plumbs the depths is whether we express our sexuality in the way God intended.

God's Word is certainly not bashful or embarrassed when it speaks of sex. The entire book of the Song of Solomon is a beautiful picture of married love as well as a symbol of the relationship between Christ and

His Church. And Proverbs 5 is both a warning against the sin of adultery and an ode to the joys of marital sex. There we read, "And rejoice with the wife of your youth . . . Let her breasts satisfy you at all times; and always be enraptured with her love" (Prov. 5:18–19).

Without question, God has looked upon this beautiful gift He has made—the gift of sex and sexuality—and He saw that it was very good. When we misuse and abuse this gift, we bring shame upon ourselves and disgrace upon the name of God. But when we use this gift as the Maker intended, according to His purpose and His plan, we bring honor to His name and we fulfill His purpose for our lives.

Five keys to a healthy marriage

When our Coral Ridge television ministry interviewed Bob and Rosemary Barnes, they shared with us five keys to a healthy marriage, based upon the principles laid out for us by the apostle Paul in Ephesians 5:

Principle 1: Communicate with each other—and listen to each other. This is an important part of the job of loving one another. Communicating feelings and listening to needs come much more naturally to women than to men—so men have to work at their communication skills. We men have to be more conscious and deliberate about talking openly, listening carefully, and really hearing what our wives are saying. Remember the first year of Bob and Rosemary's marriage? Bob thought everything was great, and Rosemary thought it was the worst year of her life! How much pain and conflict we could spare each other in our marriages if we would only *communicate*—and *listen!*

Principle 2: Communicate with God. "You can't have a healthy Christian marriage," said Rosemary, "without committing the relationship to fervent prayer. Asking the Lord to do a work in my life as a wife and in my husband's life—that's the foundation for any relationship working well. God wants the marriage relationship to not only work and function, but also to be an ecstatic experience between the husband and wife. So we know that when we are praying for the relationship, we are praying God's heart, we are praying in His will."

"For seven or eight years," said Bob, "when our marriage was going through difficulties, Rosemary prayed in an interesting way. Her prayer was, 'Lord, make me to be whatever I need to be so that You can make Bob the man You want him to be.' Wow! I mean, her prayer should have been, 'Lord, change Bob now! He's such a jerk!' But that wasn't her prayer. She prayed for God to shape her life—and as a result of God making her to be such a godly woman, my eyes were opened and my heart was changed. I give credit to the fact that Rosemary's commitment was first and foremost to the Lord."

Prayer is such a crucial—and frequently overlooked!—aspect of marriage. All too often, people try to change a marriage partner with anger rather than prayer. A woman might pray, "Lord, please change my husband, please soften his heart," then the next moment she'll be attacking him and yelling at him, not even realizing that her own angry words are completely negating the effect of her prayer! When we pray, we must commit *ourselves* to changing as well as praying for our mate to change. Our goal must be healing the relationship, not just winning an argument—and our behavior must work in concert with our prayers.

Principle 3: Seek out godly mentors. "Having an older, godly woman to mentor you," said Rosemary, "can be very helpful, especially in the early years of marriage. I think we are sometimes set adrift in those early years of the relationship. We think everything is going to be wonderful just because we love each other. But romance is not enough to solve the problems and ease the adjustments that have to be made early in a marriage. Our expectations are so high that when reality sets in, we can easily find ourselves disillusioned and discouraged. But if we have somebody we can go to and say, 'I'm struggling at this point in my marriage,' that person can give us godly counsel and the benefit of having already been there."

Principle 4: Focus on changing yourself, not your spouse. When problems arise in a marriage, our tendency is to blame the other person rather than to look in the mirror. "We tend to think, *If only he would be this way, if only I could get him to change,*" said Rosemary. "I found in my own marriage that I needed to switch the focus back onto me. You know, I cannot change another human being. Only God can do that. So if my focus is on me and on being everything I can be as a wife, then at least I am solving my half of the problem while praying for God to solve the other half. Instead of putting angry, negative energy into the relationship, which only worsens the problem, we are focusing positive energy—prayer and healthy self-examination—on the relationship. And that's how the healing begins."

Principle 5: Spend time alone together. In other words, keep the honeymoon going. Don't let your marriage get into a rut.

"Once, before we had children," Bob Barnes recalled, "Rosemary and I were sitting in the bedroom talking. It was 10:15 at night. Rosemary was in a negligee and I was in my underwear, and she said, 'Boy, I would love to have a chocolate milk shake right now.' I said, 'Well, let's go get one.' She said, 'Oh, I don't want to get dressed just for a milk shake. It was just a thought.' I said, 'You know, Rosemary, they just opened a Burger King with the drive-through not far from our house. We have a new car with tinted windows, and we can get in the car in the garage, and we'll go get you that milk shake!'

"Well, she was horrified at the thought of going out in her nightgown. She grew up twelve years on the mission field, and it was pretty daring to just unbutton her top button! A half hour later, I talked her into it. She said she wasn't going to have a good time but she agreed to go. So we got in the car and went through the drive-through and ordered our milk shakes. When I buzzed down the car window, she said, 'Roll it up! Roll it up!' Well, we got our milk shakes and we pulled out and I was feeling kind of spunky—but of course Rosemary was sitting there with her milk shake, staring straight ahead. So I said, 'Let's take a little drive to the beach!'

"Well, we hadn't gone two blocks and I looked in my rearview mirror and—you guessed it! There he was, red lights flashing! I can laugh about it now, but nobody was laughing at the time—least of all Rosemary! And me? I didn't know who I wanted to face least—the policeman or my wife! So I pulled over, and I realized, first of all, that the policeman was waiting for me to get out of my car; and second, I realized that my underwear didn't have a pocket in the back for a wallet—I didn't have my driver's license!

"Fortunately, the officer was a compassionate man. Instead of hauling us in to the police station, he followed us home so that I could produce my driver's license. Needless to say, I slept on the couch for the next month!"

Bob and Rosemary Barnes don't recommend this particular approach to spicing up your marriage—and neither do I! But this much is true: It is important to keep your marriage relationship fresh, exuberant, spontaneous, and alive. How you choose to do that—well, I leave that up to you.

"God doesn't want any of us to fail in marriage," concluded Bob Barnes. "He has supplied us with His plan for marriage so that we can make our marriage relationships successful." And through the health, vitality, and joy of successful Christian marriages, the world learns a little bit more about this loving, reconciling, creative God we serve. In a world where marriage is devalued and under fire, we prove that it is possible for *real* love—God's *agape* love—to last a lifetime.

One final postscript on 1 Corinthians 13: There is a phrase at the beginning of chapter 14 that many Bible commentators believe should actually be the last phrase in chapter 13, completing Paul's thoughts on the subject of love. In 14:1, he writes, "Pursue love." That word *pursue* is the same word Paul used when he talked about his preconversion life when he used to pursue Christians to persecute them. It is a strong, dynamic, energetic word that suggests a fervent searching, reaching, striving, and aiming for something. Another way to translate that phrase would be, "Make love your aim."

So the final question I would ask you on the subject of love and marriage, on the issue of God's purpose for your marriage, is this: Will you make love your aim? Will you make authentic, Christlike love the aim of your marriage and your home? Will you determine to work and pray to the end that the love of Jesus Christ would fill your heart and overflow into your home? Jesus, the One who can make all things new, is waiting to give you a new beginning in your home. The choice is yours.

So pursue love. Make love your aim in your family. When you do, God will use your home as a lighthouse, reflecting the light of the world—the light of God's love—out into your neighborhood and into your world. God will use your home as a testament to what His love can do in a human heart, in a Christian home. Truly, the Lord can make any home a bit of Heaven on earth—and when that happens, the people around you will ask, "Where can I find this love you have?"

And what a joy it will be for you to lead them to the Source!

8

GOD'S PURPOSE FOR
YOUR CHILDREN

*And these words which I command you today shall be in your
heart. You shall teach them diligently to your children, and shall
talk of them when you sit in your house, when you walk by the
way, when you lie down, and when you rise up.*

(DEUT. 6:6–7)

They were the perfect Christian family.

Lowell Lundstrom and his wife, Connie, had begun a ministry of touring, singing, preaching, and evangelizing right out of Bible college. Their *Message for America* radio program aired on 150 stations across the country, and their prime-time Christmas specials had been seen by millions of TV viewers. Lowell, Connie, and their four children traveled the country by bus, often for 300 days a year, taking their evangelistic crusades to cities throughout the U.S. and Canada. Literally thousands of people had come to Christ through their ministry. "All four of our children grew up sleeping in guitar cases backstage," Lowell says today, "while Connie and I were on the stage, preaching and winning the lost."

But while they were winning the lost, Lowell and Connie didn't realize they were losing their own child—their second oldest, Lisa. Lowell recalled, "Lisa was sandwiched between her older sister Londa and her younger brother, Lowell Jr., who was quite a little star in his own right. Though Lisa was a talented singer, she didn't enjoy performing in front of audiences like her brother and sister did."

"My sister Londa was very talented musically," Lisa remembered. "She sang beautifully, played the piano, and the audience loved her. And my little brother sang in a cowboy outfit, and he was really cute, and the crowds would go crazy for him. But I just sort of floated through it. I didn't enjoy music, so the audience would only respond politely—and for me that lack of applause was deafening. My dad felt that the whole family was called to be musical. He told me early on that part of what gave me worth was the fact that I would perform on the stage. When I started to reject being musical, I felt a sense of judgment from my father."

"I failed to see how hurt Lisa was," said Lowell. "This hurt and pressure inside created a root of bitterness in her spirit. She was never a behavior problem. She was always faithful in her duties. But inside she was getting ready to explode. I tried to reassure her that she had value, that I loved her very much, but somehow it never seemed to register. We continued touring and performing almost every night. I was doing God's work, carrying out the Great Commission, trying to rescue the lost—and completely unaware that my own precious daughter was slipping away from our family and from God."

One day Lisa told her dad that she had decided to pursue a career in interior decorating. Lowell was shocked. He recalled, "I responded, 'How do you get people saved by decorating rooms and hanging drapes?' I didn't understand what she was trying to tell me."

"I felt that I couldn't meet the standard my parents wanted for me," says Lisa. "I kept telling myself, 'I'm not talented, I'm not of any worth, my parents don't love me, God doesn't love me, and I'm ugly.' I realize now that long before people do worthless things on the outside, they usually have an inner feeling of worthlessness inside. I was looking for a way out of that pain."

The "way out" that Lisa chose completely shattered the hearts of her parents and nearly destroyed her own life.

"One day I received a phone call from the police," Lowell recalled— and the pain of that memory still strains his face. "The officer said,

'Reverend Lundstrom, I'd like you to come down to the station. Your seventeen-year-old daughter has just been arrested.' I couldn't believe it! 'Arrested? On what charge?' He said, 'Prostitution. Your daughter propositioned a vice officer.' Lisa, a prostitute? Impossible! Connie and I had dedicated Lisa to the Lord when she was a baby. We had raised her on Bible stories, prayer, and Gospel songs. This couldn't be happening."

But it was happening. When Lowell Lundstrom arrived at the police station and saw the mug shot, he couldn't deny the truth. It was Lisa.

"Please pray for Lisa"

During the next few years, Lisa dropped out of sight, and the Lundstroms didn't hear from their daughter for months at a time. They had no idea where Lisa was or even whether she was alive. Each day Lowell awoke with an agonizing sense that he had failed as a father and that he had been rejected and forsaken by his daughter. Some of his friends began to distance themselves—and he even felt that God had failed him. Despite his pain and doubts, Lowell continued to travel, sing, and preach as he had for more than two decades, faithfully sharing the message of salvation some three hundred nights a year. Scores of people continued to respond to the Gospel—yet the one person whose soul he agonized over was lost to him.

Why did she give herself over to such a lifestyle? "For the first time," Lisa recalled, "I was applauded, even if it was for all the wrong reasons. People told me I was beautiful, I was special, so to me it was like oxygen after feeling suffocated for so long. I became very successful. I went from working for escort services and call girl services to owning several services of my own. But it was also a very disillusioning, empty experience. I would see the so-called 'rich and beautiful people,' and they were leading ugly and miserable lives."

Throughout the agony of separation from his daughter, Lowell prayed continually for Lisa. "I knew that Jesus was the only One in the universe who could find my precious girl," he said, looking back on that time of torment. "I had to cast myself upon His mercy. I closed every evangelistic meeting with an appeal to the audience: 'Please pray for Lisa.' I didn't talk about where she was or what she was doing, but I wanted believers to join me in praying that God would reach her and restore her."

"We were absolutely crushed," recalled Connie. "We couldn't believe this was happening to our family. Worst of all, I started to blame Lowell, and he started to blame me."

"Connie blamed me," said Lowell, "saying I was too hard with Lisa. Then I would blame her for being too easy with Lisa. I would replay scenes from Lisa's childhood in my mind over and over again. I tormented myself with thoughts of *I could have—, I should have—, If only—*. To make matters worse, as I was struggling with feelings of self-condemnation, some of my ministry staff quit. One told me I should quit preaching and get out of the ministry, that I wasn't fit for the pulpit if my daughter was living such a lifestyle."

One night while driving to the next crusade destination, Lowell became so overcome with grief that he pulled the car over, sobbing uncontrollably. A patrolman stopped, tapped on the car window, and asked if he was all right. "I'll be okay," Lowell replied. "It's just a bad case of a broken heart."

"I didn't know where Lisa was," he said. "So in every city I visited, I picked up a newspaper and read the obituary columns, thinking, *I hope I don't find her body here. I hope I don't find her murdered in this town.*

Lowell Lundstrom had good reason to worry, because his daughter eventually ended up in the hands of a serial killer. "If you knock on enough doors," Lisa recalls with a shudder, "odds are, you're going to end up with someone who is crazy." The man she called had already murdered eighteen women, and he had planned to add Lisa to his list. Putting a knife to her throat, he forced her to stretch out on a plastic garbage bag while he ran knives up and down her body. "I didn't wonder *if* he would kill me," said Lisa. "I wondered how painful and how lingering it would be." Her ordeal lasted four hours. During that time Lisa silently prayed, "Oh God, don't let me die like this! Don't let my family find out I died this way!"

Miraculously, God answered her prayer. Without explanation, the killer decided to set her free—then he turned a gun on himself and committed suicide.

You might think this experience would have scared Lisa out of the sex business—but she went back to prostitution. "I didn't think I could go back to my family and the Church," she recalled. "I thought the Christian community would judge me. I didn't yet realize that the important thing is not returning to the Church—it's returning to God, it's giving your life to Jesus. He will always accept you without judgment. Once you've given your life to Him, then you go to church to know more about Him. I didn't think I could do that."

The separation from Lisa stretched out to seven, eight, nine years and more, yet the Lundstroms never gave up hope. They continued their evangelistic ministry, coping with their pain and worry through prayer and by reaching out to other hurting families in their crusades. Eventually, hope began to fade and a sense of despair set in. "I was ready to throw in the towel and quit the ministry," Lowell recalled, "when the Holy Spirit spoke to me firmly and said, 'What did God do wrong that caused the devil to go bad?' I said, 'Whoa! That's right!' I was not perfect, I had made my failures as a parent, but there was also an element of Lisa's own will involved in this situation. I could not accept total blame for Lisa's choices. This realization, along with Connie's prayers and encouragement, helped me to keep going in the ministry. Connie refused to give up."

His determination reignited, Lowell redoubled his efforts to reach out to people with hurts like his own—and to reach prodigal children who might be in his audience. "I determined I would reach every prodigal young person I came in contact with," he said, "trusting that God would one day reach my own unreachable daughter. I began to view every troubled teenager as some other parent's Lisa."

Finally, after eight years, Lisa came home one Christmas. It was a wonderful celebration, with laughter and memories of Christmases past. Yet, though it had been a good visit, when Christmas was over, Lisa got in her car and left. "The day she drove away," said Lowell, "we were devastated. Connie sat down on the front steps and cried so hard I thought she would die. The sense of horrible loss just opened up for us all over again."

"Things were catching up with me," Lisa recalled. "It was the fall of my season of living in the world. I believe that sin has a season, and I was living in the fall—things were falling apart. AIDS was in the newspapers. Everywhere I looked it was AIDS this, AIDS that. While this was happening, the Gulf War took place in Iraq. I had been raised hearing Bible prophecy, and events like the Gulf War were predicted for the end of the age. I knew that if Jesus came back at that moment, I would go to Hell. So I got very scared and I decided to take a month off to visit my sister. I knew there would be an open door and no judgment with her.

"My sister had given birth to my little nephew. I held that little baby in my arms and I looked at myself through his eyes and started to think, *How do I want him to see his Aunt Lisa?* As I held my little nephew, I started to think of another little baby. And I realized that little baby— the baby Jesus—had come and died on a cross for my sins. I didn't feel I was giving God much, but as I held my little nephew in my arms and thought of Jesus' love for me, I said, 'Jesus, if You do something with this mess, this wreck of a life I have created for myself, I will give it all to You.' And when I gave my life to God that day, a huge weight was lifted from my shoulders. My next step was to go and reconcile with my family. I called my dad and said, 'I think it's time for me to come home.'"

"I'll never forget the day I got the call from Lisa," said Lowell. "She had been gone for nine-and-a-half years. The call reached me while we were on tour in Canada. I just dropped everything, rented a moving van, and drove two thousand miles nonstop to pick her up. The day I put my arms around her and welcomed her back into our family was like Christmas—and every day's been Christmas ever since."

"It's all an incredible miracle," says Lisa. "It's a miracle that I'm HIV-negative and GOD-positive. It's a miracle that our family has been restored."

Today Lisa is completely reconciled with her family. She and her father are even involved in ministry together, cohosting the nationally syndicated radio hour *Lowell Live* on the USA Radio Network. Today God uses Lisa in a tremendous way as she tells her story and shares the Gospel with thousands of young people in crusades, youth conventions, drug abuse support groups, women's shelters, youth shelters, and conventions.

"Train up a child in the way he should go . . ."

"As the twig is bent, so grows the tree," says the familiar aphorism. Of course, many influences can bend the twig as it grows toward mature treehood. Though our children are exposed to these influences during their formative years—teachers, peers, the media, and more—parents are the first and foremost influences in a child's life. It is our job as parents to train our children to know and fulfill God's purpose for their lives—to keep the twig of their lives growing straight and tall.

"Train up a child in the way he should go," says Proverbs 22:6, "and when he is old he will not depart from it." These words are as true today as when they were written. Does this mean that a child in a Christian home will never stray? Clearly not. The experience of the Lundstrom family proves otherwise. Lisa Lundstrom did stray during her youth— but when she was older, she returned to the way she should go! I believe she returned because scores of people were praying for her, because God had a purpose for her life, and because the Lundstroms had laid a foundation for her life when they were training her in her childhood.

Every child is an individual human being with his own will. Every child must choose Christ for himself or herself—we parents cannot make that choice for our children. All we can do is train them, love them, and pray for them. The rest is up to our children—and, of course, ultimately to the sovereign will of God.

How, then, do we train our children in the way they should go? How do we train them to know God's purpose for their lives—and to live in obedience to that purpose? That threefold purpose, you recall, is found in the Cultural Mandate of Genesis 1:26–28:

1. To be refashioned into the image of God
2. To be spiritually fruitful and multiply; to witness and share the Gospel of Jesus Christ with others
3. To take part in God's plan for us to subdue the earth and exercise dominion in His name

I suggest eight steps to godly parenting, eight steps that you should follow daily in order to train your child in God's way and purpose for his or her life:

Step 1: Get married

Get married! That may sound absurdly basic to you—in fact, I hope it does! A generation ago, I would never have bothered to offer such basic advice. Today, however, our culture and even many Christians have become so infected with worldly thinking that I dare not take it for granted that marriage is a given. In many of our larger cities today, as many as 80 percent of children are born to parents who never got married. Barbara Dafoe Whitehead, author of a crucially important book called *The Divorce Culture: Rethinking Our Commitments to Marriage and Family*, observes,

> Divorce and out-of-wedlock childbirth are transforming the lives of American children. In the postwar generation more than 80 percent of children grew up in a family with two biological parents who were married to each other. By 1980 only 50 percent could expect to spend their entire childhood in an intact family. If current trends continue, less than half of all children born today will live continuously with their own mother and father throughout childhood. Most American children will spend several years in a single-mother family. Some will eventually live in stepparent families, but because stepfamilies are more likely to break up than intact (by which I mean two-biological-parent) families, an increasing number of children will experience family breakup two or even three times during childhood.[1]

These are alarming and disastrous trends in the lives of our children. That is why I'm beginning with the basics: If you want to be a good Christian parent, first get married!

"Why?" some may ask. "What is so important about a piece of paper called a marriage license? Can't two people build a good and stable home for their children purely on the basis of their love for each other?" The answer is no. Supermodel Kim Alexis, in her book *A Model for a Better Future*, explains why:

> Marriage isn't just a "piece of paper," as people so often say these days. Marriage is proof of commitment. The person who says "Our love doesn't need a piece of paper to prove it's real" is a person who already has the back door open and his sneakers laced up. Don't be fooled. Hold out for that all-important "piece of paper." It spells *commitment*.[2]

You may remember a few years back when television's Murphy Brown (played by Candice Bergen) made a nationwide stir by deliberately having a baby out of wedlock. The night this episode aired, CBS posted a massive 35 percent share of the audience, attracting thirty-four million viewers. For this comedy-drama assault on traditional morality, actress Candice Bergen was celebrated on magazine covers and was honored with an Emmy award and an honorary degree by the University of Pennsylvania. When then-Vice President Dan Quayle suggested in a speech that having babies out of wedlock was both immoral and harmful to children, he was widely jeered and condemned in the media.

But as Barbara Dafoe Whitehead convincingly demonstrated in the April 1993 issue of the *Atlantic Monthly*, Dan Quayle was right. In fact, that was the title of her article! In "Dan Quayle Was Right," she cites these facts:

> According to a growing body of social-scientific evidence, children in families disrupted by divorce and out-of-wedlock birth do worse than children in intact families on several measures of well-being. Children in single-parent families are six times as likely to be poor. They are also likely to stay poor longer. Twenty-two percent of children in one-parent families will experience poverty during childhood for seven years or more, as compared with only two percent of children in two-parent families. A 1988 survey by the National Center for Health Statistics found that children in single-parent families are two to three times as likely as children in two-parent families to have emotional

and behavioral problems. They are also more likely to drop out of high school, to get pregnant as teenagers, to abuse drugs, and to be in trouble with the law.[3]

Despite all of these tragic facts, it is not fashionable, it is not "politically correct" (from the point of view of decadent liberalism) to say that having children out of wedlock is destructive or wrong or immoral. What used to be called "living in sin" is now simply a "lifestyle choice." Wouldn't it be refreshing if society were to once again call a spade a spade? Wouldn't it be refreshingly honest and candid, whenever we hear about unmarried couples living together, if we were to simply say, "Oh, that's not a lifestyle choice. That's sin. That's fornication. That's wrong."

Today it seems that the only sin anyone condemns is the sin of being "judgmental." We can't say, "That's fornication," because that would make fornicators feel criticized and judged. We can't say, "That's adultery," because that would hurt the feelings of adulterers. Friend in Christ, the root word of *judgmental* is *judgment*. Clearly, our society has lost all sense of judgment, of discernment, of the ability to tell right from wrong. It's up to us as Christians to restore good judgment, common decency, and common sense to our society. The rampant disregard and disrespect toward marriage in our society today is hurting too many children and dragging our society toward an uncivilized and chaotic state.

So the first thing we must say to those who would be parents is, "First, get married."

Step 2: Stay married

The second thing we must say to those who would be parents is "Stay married." Again, this might seem to be an obvious statement to some, but remember that nearly half of all American marriages end in divorce—so I'm assuming there's a fifty-fifty chance that *you* need to hear this! Divorce is horribly destructive to children, as Barbara Dafoe Whitehead makes clear in her *Atlantic Monthly* piece:

> Contrary to popular belief, many children do not "bounce back" after divorce or remarriage. Difficulties that are associated with family

breakup often persist into adulthood. Children who grow up in single-parent or stepparent families are less successful as adults, particularly in the two domains of life—love and work—that are most essential to happiness. Needless to say, not all children experience such negative effects. However, research shows that many children from disrupted families have a harder time achieving intimacy in a relationship, forming a stable marriage, or even holding a steady job.[4]

Let me say very clearly that there are two biblical grounds for divorce: the breaking of the marriage covenant by adultery and the breaking of the marriage covenant by desertion of a believer by an unbeliever. I would add to those specific grounds that are listed in Scripture the grounds of self-defense: A spouse who commits acts of domestic violence against a marriage partner or against children has also broken the marriage covenant. No one should remain in a marriage at the risk of life and limb, or the risk of the children's safety.

Beyond these, there are no grounds for divorce. Beyond these grounds there is only sin.

Step 3: Give your child a godly education

Unfortunately, all too many parents today—including Christian parents—are abdicating their God-ordained responsibility. They are entrusting the training of their children to the state via our public school system, little realizing the anti-Christian ideas and attitudes that are being instilled in them. Most parents are unaware, for example, that public education is actually a fairly recent innovation in our society. From the time the Pilgrims landed in the early 1600s until the mid-nineteenth century, all education in America was private religious education. Public education has really only been around for about 150 years, and there is no right to (or even reference to) public education in the Constitution.

Because public education is funded by the state, militant atheists have seized upon the "separation of church and state" rationale as a pretext for removing every last trace and vestige of God from the public schools. Though schools were originally founded in America so that children could learn to read the Bible for themselves, the Bible can no longer be read nor can prayers be heard in public schools. Teachers fear to say anything about God, lest they be sued or fired. School administrators often squelch constitutionally protected religious expression in schools out of the mistaken notion that even children themselves are not allowed to bring God onto the schoolyard with them.

Today's secularized educational system would have horrified educators of a century ago. When the public school movement began, no one foresaw a time when schools would completely kick God off the campus, replacing Him with a completely atheistic worldview. But our children now sit in godless classrooms, absorbing a godless worldview by academic osmosis. They are being taught to see the world as a place where God has been silently, quietly, and ruthlessly banished.

Chaos reigns in the hearts and minds of many students today. They have been inculcated with the existentialist worldview that says that life is meaningless and absurd. There is no absolute truth, no absolute morality. All that matters is the pleasure of the moment. If you derive pleasure from doing good or from stomping an old lady to death, it does not matter. These are equivalent options in a meaningless and absurd world.

Is it any wonder that we have seen such a rise in random violence, suicide, brutality, and sadism in our time? It is just the meaningless violence of a meaningless world. Many people wonder why there is so much chaos in the world today without making the logical linkage to the chaotic, amoral presuppositions being taught to our students, on both a conscious and unconscious level, year after year. They ignore the content that is being soaked into their child's brain until one day that child decides to put a gun to his own head and blow those brains away.

According to Barbara Dafoe Whitehead, the teen suicide rate from 1970 to 1990 has *more than tripled*—an astonishing increase! Suicide is the second leading cause of death among adolescents ages fifteen to nineteen, and 8 percent of all high school students have made at least one suicide attempt in their lifetime. Never before in the history of mankind have so many young people taken their own lives. How do we explain this? There are undoubtedly a number of factors, but I see a clear correlation between the increase in teen suicides and the increasingly godless, meaningless, absurdist worldview that is being inflicted on our children at all levels in the public schools.

So many times in recent years, a parent has come to me, tearfully asking, "What did we do wrong? We sent our child to one of the finest universities in the nation, and after all those years of Sunday school, youth group, and church, after growing up in a Christian home—our child has come back an atheist in one year! What did we do wrong?" My heart goes out to these parents—yet the answer seems obvious: They sent their child to a godless university filled with godless professors with impressive degrees and devilishly clever skills of persuasion and an atheistic agenda—and they tore that young mind apart! They ran circles around that young mind and turned his or her thinking inside out!

"Oh, but he had to go to a prestigious school," the parent explains, "because, you see, he will land a much better career after going there! He'll make more money later! He'll be more successful!" Successful?! How do you define *success?* What does it profit your child if he gains the whole world but loses his eternal soul?

Parents have come to me saying, "I sent my daughter to the finest school, and what happened? She got pregnant! How did this happen?" Again, the amorality and immorality that saturate our public education system and our universities are taking a tremendous toll on our young people.

I remember in the 1970s, when the feminist movement was pushing hard for an Equal Rights Amendment to the Constitution, one of the arguments against the ERA was that it would lead to unisex bathrooms. "Oh, that's silly! That's just a bunch of crazy scare talk from some alarmist, right-wing nuts!" the pro-ERA bunch retorted. "Nobody in their right mind thinks the Equal Rights Amendment would ever produce anything as absurd as unisex bathrooms!" Well, there is still no ERA—but we got the unisex bathrooms anyway! On virtually every secular university campus in America, students live in coed dorms with coed bathrooms—that's right, boys and girls with raging hormones all together in the same bathroom! What's more, many universities *enforce* immorality by *requiring* freshman and sophomore students to live in coed dorms, even if it violates their religious beliefs!

Wendy Shalit, the thoughtful young author of *A Return to Modesty: Discovering the Lost Virtue,* says that the idea for her book came while she was campaigning against coed bathrooms at Williams College in Massachusetts. In an interview on ABC's *Good Morning America* on Valentine's Day, 1999, she said, "When the dorms are coed, and even the bathrooms are coed, and we're all thrown together—you know, there's no right of exit from the culture of immodesty. When everything is integrated, there's no mystery, there's no respect, there's no separation, and there's no reverence between the sexes."

Sexual immorality and amorality are not only being thrown at our kids at the university level but also at earlier, more impressionable stages of their development. Many parents are shocked to discover what their children are being taught in sex education classes in the public schools. Now there is nothing at all wrong with teaching a child the truth about sex, but there is something very much wrong with giving children erroneous information that pushes them toward sexual activity.

In the public school sex ed classes, the issue of morality—of right and wrong—is never even hinted at. Words such as *fornication* are never spoken, because that would be "judgmental." What does God think of children having sex? Who knows? He's been banned from the classroom! So all children are told anymore is, "If you are going to have sex, make sure you do it safely." And what is "safe sex," according to today's sex ed indoctrinators? Condoms! Thin latex sheaths that are known to have a 20 percent failure rate! Condoms offer only a limited amount of protection against pregnancy and against the virus that causes AIDS, and little or no protection against genital herpes and other sexually transmitted diseases. Little wonder, then, that cases of genital herpes have risen 500 percent among teenagers since the 1970s! What is "safe" about that kind of sex?

And if you think Christian teens are immune from temptation—think again! According to a survey conducted by the Josh McDowell Ministry, 43 percent of 1,400 churchgoing young people surveyed admitted that they had engaged in sexual intercourse by the age of eighteen! Is the problem that children don't have enough sex education and information? Hardly! Today's teens know more about how to have sex, how to use contraceptives, where to get abortions than any other generation in history. What is lacking is not information—it is moral character and spiritual wisdom. And it is not their fault that they lack these qualities; it is *ours*. Because it is our job as parents to see that our children are trained in wisdom and virtue—not just in reading, writing, and how to point and click a computer. "Train up a child in the way he should go," says the Word of God, "and when he is old, he will not depart from it."

By handing our children over to the state for instruction in a "values-free," amoral environment, we have allowed them to be given information without a moral and spiritual context in which to process that information. I am not in favor of keeping young people ignorant about sex—they should have the facts, including the truth that there is no such thing as "safe sex"; that losing your virginity outside of marriage is harmful to your soul, your psyche, your spirit, and your self-respect; that people are more than mere rutting, copulating animals, that we are eternal souls, and that healthy sex within a covenantal marriage is worth waiting for; that there is more to life than materialism, animal drives, and sexual indulgence.

As a parent, you may be shocked to discover that there are liberal social engineers in our society who believe that they have a right to control the minds of your children—that they have more rights over your children than you do! This frightening fact was illustrated by an incident in late 1998 in the quiet, conservative community of Bakersfield, California. An eighth-grade science teacher in the rural Rio Bravo-Greeley Union School District began openly discussing his homosexual lifestyle with his students—a subject that was completely unrelated to the science curriculum he was paid to teach. In response, a number of parents requested that their students be moved to other classes. They didn't picket the school or call the teacher names or try to have him fired—they just wanted their children removed from under his influence. You and I would consider that a reasonable request.

The teacher, however, filed a complaint with the school board, the state labor commissioner's office, the California Teachers Association, and the LAMBDA Legal Defense Fund (a gay rights organization). In his complaint, he demanded that the children be returned to his class. The story was covered in a highly biased fashion on NBC's *Dateline*, intended to arouse sympathy for the teacher and hostility for the "homophobic" parents who dared to pull their kids out of his class. The local newspaper editorialized against the "anti-gay prejudice," "homophobia," and "sexual intolerance" of those parents. Then the state labor commissioner's office issued its order: No more students would be removed from the class.

As one Bakersfield resident observed, the government ruling requires a homosexual teacher's "lifestyle choice to supersede and to discriminate against the ability of parents to choose how they want their children educated. Parents, welcome to our government-run education. You are not here to assist in the education of your children. With education being run by the state, parents forfeit their rights to choose."

What is the solution, then, to an ungodly education? Simple: A godly education! A Christian education! I know that for parents to provide their children with a Christian education requires sacrifice. A private education is not inexpensive. But, as we have seen, public education has its own human price tag—and it's a much costlier price tag than a few thousand dollars a year. The price tag for public education is often a child's eternal soul.

In Christian schools, children learn the truth about a God who loves them and values them, a God who gives meaning and purpose to their lives, and who gives moral guidance to their actions. In Christian schools, children receive a sound moral foundation, a clear view of reality, including the reality of values, virtues, and morals. They learn about sin and righteousness.

Moreover, studies have shown that students in private Christian schools are generally better prepared in academics than their public school counterparts. Certainly there are some academically inferior Christian schools, and you should carefully investigate a school before enrolling your child. But in general, Christian schools offer a superior learning environment in addition to a better moral and spiritual influence. And isn't your child worth the investment?

Step 4: Discipline your children

We live in an age characterized by lawlessness. We do not hold criminals accountable for their actions. We do not hold able-bodied welfare recipients accountable for being industrious and providing for themselves and their families. We do not hold our political leaders accountable for acts of immorality, corruption, and criminality while in office. We do not hold children accountable for being decent, respectful, honest, trustworthy, and upright.

The permissiveness of the past two decades has produced an age of lawlessness today. The Bible rebukes our permissiveness and calls us to godly discipline. Remember, we are called to be *disciples* of Jesus Christ, and we are called to *disciple* our children—and to be a disciple one must be *disciplined!* To be disciplined means to have boundaries, to know that there are things we *should* do, and things we *must not* do. Our children need discipline and (though few would admit it!) they really want and seek it. Show me an undisciplined child and I will show you a bundle of insecurities, because that child lives in a disordered, chaotic, and meaningless world; children need and crave structure and dependability in their lives. Show me an undisciplined child, and I will show you a child who feels unloved, because no one has ever taken the time to care for him by setting loving boundaries for his life.

Some time ago, a young man was caught in the act of burglarizing our church. After the police apprehended him and took him away, one of the officers said to me, "I should tell you what will happen to this boy. He'll be reprimanded by the judge, slapped on the wrist, and turned loose. You see, the juvenile hall is bulging with kids, and there is just no place to put him."

How have we managed to produce such a wonderful crop of delinquents? The police department of Houston, Texas, formulated a set of rules called "How to Raise a Juvenile Delinquent." Here are the rules:

1. Begin at infancy to give the child everything he wants. In this way he will grow up to believe the world owes him a living.

2. When he picks up bad words, laugh at him. This will make him think he's cute. It will encourage him to pick up "cuter" phrases that will blow off the top of your head.

3. Never give him any spiritual training. Wait until he is twenty-one, then let him "decide for himself."

4. Avoid use of the word *wrong*, which might cause him to develop a guilt complex. By avoiding the concept of right and wrong, you will condition him to believe later, when he is arrested for stealing a car, that society is against him, and he is being unfairly persecuted.

5. Pick up everything he leaves lying around—books, shoes, and clothing. Do everything for him so he will be experienced in throwing all responsibility onto others.

6. Let him read any printed matter he can get his hands on, no matter how vile and obscene. Be careful that the silverware and drinking glasses are sterilized, but let his mind feast on garbage.

7. Quarrel frequently in the presence of your children. In this way they will not be too shocked when the home is broken up later.

8. Give your child all the spending money he wants. Never make him responsible to earn his own way. Why should he have things as tough as *you* had them?

9. Satisfy his every craving for food, drink, and comfort. See that every sensual desire is gratified. Self-denial may lead to harmful frustration.

10. Always take his side against neighbors, teachers, and policemen, no matter what he has done. They are all prejudiced against your child.

11. When he gets into real trouble, apologize for yourself by saying, "I never could do anything with him."

12. Prepare for a life of grief. You're apt to have it.

My prayer for you and your children is that you will break every one of these rules! Tragically, all too many parents—including Christian parents—have followed too many of these rules. They, their children, and our society are reaping the ugly, often tragic results.

A failure to discipline always pays terrible dividends down the road. The disobedient, willful, rebellious child grows up to be the rebellious wife who cannot submit to her husband, or a tyrannical husband who, having never learned to obey, does not know how to lead or to love. You cannot lead until you have learned to follow, as every military commander well knows. These children who are disrespectful and rebellious at home and in school become the sociopaths, terrorists, and anarchists of the future. The child who learns to rebel against earthly authority grows up despising and rejecting the authority of God the Father in Heaven—and that child's ultimate damnation is secured.

At the same time, it is important to recognize that no parent is perfect. We all make mistakes, and God in His grace often overrules our mistakes. Because every child has an autonomous free will, many children who grow up under very bad parents turn out surprisingly well, and many children from very godly parents turn out to be shocking disappointments, at least for a season.

Rev. Lowell Lundstrom, whose daughter Lisa turned to prostitution at age seventeen, freely admits making mistakes that resulted in Lisa not feeling as loved and special as she really was. And Lisa admits that the choice to pursue a career of sin was hers alone. The Lundstroms raised four children, and one became a prodigal who eventually returned home.

Perhaps you have a prodigal child in your own life right now. If so, then Lowell Lundstrom—speaking with the voice of years of experience!—knows how you feel, what you are going through, and how you should respond to this painful crisis in your family. "I encourage you," he said, "to try these suggestions:

1. Be aware of what's happening in each of your children's lives.

2. Ask others to covenant with you in intercessory prayer.

3. Don't crucify yourself repeatedly for your mistakes.

4. Put your faith to work by helping reach other prodigal youth in your area.

5. Be patient. God has a plan and a purpose for your child's life, and He knows how long it takes to work things out.

6. Build emotional and relational bridges to your prodigal without condemning. Express your love and prayers for your child.

7. Plan a party! The father of the prodigal son told his servants, "Bring the fatted calf . . . let us eat and be merry" (Luke 15:23).

8. Hold fast to the promises of God.

"My prayer for you is that your precious prodigal will return to you as Lisa returned to us. Never—never—give up!"

Step 5: Really *love your child*

In Morgantown, West Virginia, a mother misplaced her child. It happened in the fall of 1998. How, you ask, does a mother "misplace" a child?

To begin with, she had two children and she had each of them placed in a different daycare center. Her morning routine was to drop off three-year-old John at the first day care, then take two-year-old Bruno to the second day care. One morning she switched her routine, dropped Bruno off first, then dropped John off, then turned around to check on Bruno, who is normally still in the car after dropping John off. Bruno was gone—and she completely forgot that she had already dropped him off! (If your head is spinning from just reading this, imagine how Bruno and John must have felt!)

Of course, this woman's first reaction was to panic. Assuming that Bruno had either wandered off or been snatched from the car while she was taking John into the daycare center, the mother called police and reported Bruno missing. The police organized a posse of one hundred volunteers who, accompanied by a helicopter with infrared heat sensors, spent three hours searching the rain-soaked woods for the "missing" child. Bruno, meanwhile, was obliviously playing with toys in his usual place at the daycare center!

A sheriff's deputy questioned the mother, had her retrace her steps—and figured out that Bruno wasn't missing after all! "It's a mistake anybody could make," the mother said when she learned her mistake. A lot of parents might find that statement arguable!

But in a way, she may have a point. I would suggest to you that there are a lot of ways to misplace a child, to lose track of a child, to turn around and suddenly realize that your child is not in the place you thought he was—that he has become emotionally and spiritually misplaced. It happens when we as parents become too busy, too self-absorbed, too neglectful to really take the time to love our children as they ought to be loved. Unfortunately, this is a mistake that anybody could make.

Does your child feel loved and secure? Does your child have a strong sense of belonging in your family? Or does your child feel a little lost and misplaced?

Children need to know that their parents love them. And it takes a lot more than saying "I love you" to get that message across. Many children, like Lowell Lundstrom's daughter Lisa, grow up loved and cherished—yet for some reason, the children don't feel that love, they don't receive it and internalize it. Remember Lowell's words? "I tried to reassure Lisa that she had value, that I loved her very much," he said, "but somehow it never seemed to register."

Despite their attempts to reassure her, Lisa felt as if her parents were pressuring her. "I felt that I couldn't meet the standard my parents wanted for me," she said. "I kept telling myself, 'I'm not talented, I'm not of any worth, my parents don't love me, God doesn't love me, and I'm ugly.'"

Sometimes children have a difficult time receiving expressions of parental love—but we as parents have to keep finding ways to let our kids know they are special, they are loved, and God has a purpose for their lives. We do this with our words, telling them again and again of our love for them and God's love for them. We tell them with our attention, by giving them eye contact, a nod, and meaningful, authentic interaction when they talk to us and share their interests with us; our focused, undivided attention tells our kids, "You matter to me, I'm interested in you, and you are a person of value and worth." We demonstrate our love for them by spending time with them, by doing fun things with them, by enjoying their company. We prove that our love is accepting and unconditional by forgiving them when they repent, by lifting them when they fall, by affirming them when they fail, by supporting them even when they disappoint us. Yes, we hold them accountable—but not in a harsh way, not in a way that says, "I love you as long as you please me." And when we discipline them, we do so not out of anger but out of a loving desire to see them become more and more refashioned into the image of Jesus Christ.

Do your children know you love them by the way you discipline them? Many children are only punished in anger, not disciplined in love. When a parent punishes in anger, the children suppose that the reason they are being punished is simply that the parents are annoyed, irritable, and short-tempered. Instead of thinking, *I did wrong, I disappointed my parents, and I hurt them by putting them in the position of having to discipline me,* they think, *How unfair! They're just lashing out, getting even! I bet they don't even love me! I just get in their way!*

Even when you discipline in love, children will often fuss and fume and express resentment—at least for a while, until godly remorse sets in. But over the long haul, if you discipline out of love instead of anger, your children will learn to understand the difference, and they will ultimately respect you for it—and they will know that they are loved.

Touch is another important aspect of conveying love to a child. A pat on the hand, a hug, some fatherly roughhousing, a motherly kiss on the cheek—all of these physical contacts tell a child, "I cherish you, I want to be near you, I enjoy your presence, you are important to me, I have a deep affection for you." A child is never too old to be hugged—even an adult child needs a hug now and then. How many times have you hugged your child this week? That is so important!

Psychologists tell us that appropriate, affectionate touching between a parent and child is crucial in producing a healthy parent-child bonding. A child who is not hugged and touched by his parents never develops fully in his emotions. He doesn't learn to empathize with others as he should. He doesn't learn to understand others' joys—or their pain. Many of the serial killers and violent sadists who populate our prisons were once children who were deprived of parental touching and bonding. They feel no sympathy or empathy for their victims; they kill with no conscience. So tell your children you love them—and underscore those words with a loving hug.

Another way to make sure your children know they are loved is for you and your spouse to demonstrate authentic love for each other. There is a sign in the office of one of the associate pastors at our church that says it all: "The best gift parents can give their child is to love one another." Not only are parents to love their children, but they are also to love one another, so that the child can see that he or she is growing up in an atmosphere of love. The home is the soil in which a child is planted, nurtured, watered, and grown to maturity. If that soil is enriched with love, the child grows spiritually tall and emotionally strong. If that soil is poisoned by continual bickering, resentment, and animosity, the child will grow up spiritually stunted and emotionally insecure.

So love your children—and love one another.

Step 6: Commit your children to Christ

We commit our children to Jesus Christ through the sacrament of baptism (or in some Christian denominations, the symbol of dedicating a child to the Lord), through praying for our children, and through training them in the way they should go. Neither baptism nor our prayers nor our training can provide salvation for that child. Once a child reaches the age of accountability before God, only that child can make the decision to receive Jesus Christ as Lord and Savior. Every child has a will of his or her own and may exercise that will by receiving Christ—or rebelling against God.

We do not have the power to choose the eternal destiny of any human being, not even our children. But we can influence them, train them, discipline them, love them, witness to them, teach them, and commit them to Christ.

It is important that our children know we have made a decision to set them apart for God. One way we do this is by praying very openly in their presence that they will always walk with God and fulfill His purpose for their lives. Do you pray with your child? Does your child hear you praying for him? Prayer is a crucial aspect of committing your child to Christ.

Step 7: Teach your children

The Great Commission could well be paraphrased for your home in this way: "Go therefore and make disciples of your children, baptizing them in the name of the Father and of the Son and of the Holy Spirit, teaching them to observe all things that I have commanded you . . ." The Lord has commissioned us to make disciples and to teach His commands—and His commission to us begins at home.

So it's important that we teach our children the Holy Scriptures. Read the Bible to them. Tell them the beautiful stories of God's Word when they are very young. Help them memorize Scripture passages when they are young, so they can hide God's Word in their hearts and carry it with them for life. Of course, in order to teach the Bible to your children, you must know and memorize the Bible yourself! "Your word I have hidden in my heart, that I might not sin against You" (Ps. 119:11). Are you doing that with your children? Are you helping them to hide the Word of God in their hearts as God commands you to do?

We also teach our children by setting a godly example for them. I can tell you this without fear of contradiction: If you are not a godly man or woman, your children know it. You may have hidden your ungodliness from your boss, your coworkers, your friends, your pastor, and other Christians in your church—but your kids know whether you are a hypocrite. They can see through you as if you were a pane of glass. So don't try to make something of your children that you are not. Set a godly example.

Here's an important way to set that godly example: Take your children to Sunday school. Don't *send* them. *Take* them. When I was a boy, my parents sent me to Sunday school while they stayed home. When I was about fourteen and old enough to put up a loud enough squawk, I quit going. They couldn't very well make me go at that point because they weren't going either. I said, "Why should I value church for my own life when you don't value it in your life?" They couldn't argue because they were not setting a godly example for me. So set an example for your children—take them with you to church and Sunday school.

We should also teach our children to give cheerfully and faithfully to the Lord. Teach them to tithe so that they will become conscientious stewards of Christ's riches as they grow up. It is much easier to give and tithe as an adult if you made it a habit as a child.

A man once came to Dr. Peter Marshall when he was chaplain of the U.S. Senate and said, "Dr. Marshall, I have a problem. I used to tithe regularly some years ago, but now, you see, God has blessed me to the point where I am earning $500,000 a year. Now I obviously can't afford to give away $50,000 a year—so you see my problem."

Dr. Marshall nodded gravely. "I certainly do," he said. "Let's pray about it." So the two men bowed their heads, and Dr. Marshall began to pray. "Heavenly Father, I pray that You would reduce this man's salary back to a point where he can once again afford to tithe—"

The man's jaw dropped. "Oh, no, no, no!" he said, interrupting the prayer. "Please don't pray that prayer! I'll tithe!" That is a lesson we must teach our children by both word and example.

Also, teach your children the joy of fulfilling the Great Commission. Teach them how to witness for Christ in their neighborhood and on their school grounds. Teach them to be bold and unintimidated in their testimony for Christ. Teach them how to share their faith in a comfortable, confident way. The beautiful paradox of faith is that the more you give it away, the more you have—and as your children learn to give away their faith, they will grow in their own faith and understanding and personal relationship with Jesus Christ.

Teach your children the beautiful, simple plan of salvation by grace through faith in Jesus Christ. Make sure they understand that salvation cannot be earned by works; it is a gift of God, not of works, so that no one can boast of his own righteousness. But make sure they understand that God's grace should never be trampled underfoot or taken lightly; and that they prove to themselves and others that their faith is genuine by doing good works as an act of grateful service to our gracious Lord.

Always underscore the goodness and grace of God. Never use God as a threat in order to get your children to behave: "You'd better be good or God won't love you!" Such a statement is unbiblical, untrue, and it libels God, poisoning a child's mind against our loving, gracious heavenly Father. Children should never be told that they are accepted by God on the basis of their good works. God accepts us because of who He is, because of who Christ is—not because of who we are or how we live. We are loved not *because* of what we are but *in spite* of what we are! We are loved because of what Jesus Christ has done for us on the cross.

Teach your children to walk humbly before God, because God resists the proud but He gives grace to the humble (James 4:6; 1 Pet. 5:5). Teach your children to trust Him because He is a reliable, dependable Father who can always be trusted. Teach them to be secure in His love and His provision for their lives.

Teach your children that God has a holy and noble purpose for their lives—that the reason for life is not simply to acquire a good career and make a lot of money, but to be used by God to fulfill the Cultural Mandate and the Great Commission. Teach them to cooperate with God in becoming refashioned into His image.

As a Christian parent, you want your children to grow up to love you and to honor your memory and your faith. You want your children to discover and fulfill God's purpose for their lives. With that as the goal of your Christian parenting, make it your daily goal to bring them up in the nurture and admonition of the Lord, so that they may become the salt of the earth and the light of the world.

Step 8: Invest your time in your child

A judge once received an award for his great oratorical skills and elocution. But while the judge was giving his acceptance speech, his son was sulking in a corner near the back of the hall. A friend of the judge leaned over to the young man and said, "You don't seem very happy. Aren't you glad your father is receiving this award for his eloquence?"

The young man made a face of disgust. "Oh, he's eloquent in front of a crowd of admirers, all right," he said. "But the only 'eloquence' he ever had for me was, 'Get lost, kid—I'm busy.'"

The young man never forgot the fact that his father had time for everyone in the world but him. Children never forget that. They know when a parent is too busy to love them, to listen to them, to share experiences and thoughts and feelings with them. It breaks my heart, and I'm sure it breaks the heart of God, to think of all the children who never hear, "I love you. I'm proud of you. I enjoy spending time with you."

I once read a profoundly moving and challenging magazine story by writer Michael Foster. Though I no longer recall the name of the magazine, the story itself has stuck in my memory for years. As Foster tells it, a businessman named John Carmody stood in front of a second-story window in his home, watching the raindrops splashing on the pane and thinking. At that moment, he wasn't thinking of the great plans he had for himself, for his family, for his career. No, at this particular moment, all that filled his mind was one small incident that had occurred days earlier—a seemingly unimportant event at the time . . .

John Carmody arrived home from work, his briefcase stuffed with reports for the annual meeting of the stockholders the next day. It had been a great year. The future looked bright. All the graphs, statistical projections, and marketing plans in that briefcase filled him with excitement and enthusiasm. He sat down in his den, opened the briefcase, and began reading and preparing for the next day's presentation.

Then he was interrupted by a light tapping on his hand. "Daddy!" He looked down. There was little Margie, age five, eyes wide, a bright smile on her cherubic face. "Look, Daddy!" She held out a new children's picture book.

"That's nice, Margie," said Carmody. "Now run along. Daddy's busy." His eyes went back to the marketing plan.

Seconds passed. "Daddy," said the little voice again. "Look at the pretty picture, Daddy." She held the open book before him, covering up the marketing plan. "Isn't it pretty, Daddy? Would you read me the story, Daddy? Please?"

"Not now, darling. Daddy's very busy. Ask your mother, okay?"

"Mommy's busy in the kitchen. She said she's busier than you are. Just read me one little story—please?"

"Later, sweetie. But right now I have to study these reports, so be a good girl and run along, okay?"

Margie held the open book in her hands, pondering. Seconds passed. "Daddy," she said at last, "when you get through with your work, would you just read one little story to yourself—but read it loud enough that I can hear it, too? Would you do that, Daddy, please?"

Carmody sighed. "Okay, Margie. I'll do that—but in a little bit, okay? After I finish this work. Run along and play now."

"Okay, Daddy." And with the book in her hands, Margie skipped away to play in the yard outside.

That little event from two weeks earlier, so brief and seemingly insignificant at the time, was all John Carmody could think about now. How strange that such a small event could suddenly loom so large.

He looked down from the rain-spattered window at the book in his hands—Margie's little book that had been brand-new just a few days earlier. Now it was scuffed and dirty, and had an ugly crease across the cover. The book had been damaged when a car had careened around the corner in front of John Carmody's house—just minutes after Carmody had said those last words to his little girl: "Run along and play now." The drunken man who had been driving the car that day was now sitting in a jail cell, charged with the negligent death of John Carmody's little daughter.

"It's time, honey," said a voice from the bottom of the stairs. John Carmody didn't move. "John?" said the voice again. Roused from his thoughts, he went to the top of the stairs and looked down at the strained face of his wife. "It's time to say good-bye to Margie," she said.

"Just a moment," he replied. He walked away from the stairs and found a place to sit down. He spread the book on his knees and leafed through it, looking at the pretty pictures, while a voice called to him from his memories: *Daddy, when you get through with your work, would you just read one little story to yourself—but read it loud enough that I can hear it, too?*

And he began to read. "Once upon a time, there was a little girl who was oh, so fair . . ." He read the whole story to himself, softly yet aloud—loud enough, perhaps, that Margie could hear it too.

Friend in Christ, spend time with your children.

9

GOD'S PURPOSE FOR YOUR CHURCH

And on this rock I will build My church, and the gates of Hades shall not prevail against it.

(MATT. 16:18B)

Some time ago, Rev. Donald Wildmon of the American Family Association penned a convicting essay on the role of the Church in society today. In that essay entitled "300,000 Pulpits Are Silent," he wrote:

Today, 4,000 innocent precious lives of unborn babies were snuffed out. Their arms and legs were torn from their bodies, their skulls crushed. One and one half million times each year our "civilized" society will take an innocent life. *And 300,000 pulpits are silent.*

Six hundred thousand children between the ages of three and eighteen are involved in child pornography. Twenty thousand of them will disappear each year, never to be seen again. *And 300,000 pulpits are silent.*

The networks make a mockery of Christians, the Christian faith, and Christian values with nearly every show they air. Greed, materialism, violence, sexual immorality are standard fare. Program after program, movie after movie contains anti-Christian episodes and plots. News articles condescendingly refer to the "fundamentalist, right wing

Christians." Those who speak out for the sacredness of life are brand-ed as extremists. *And 300,000 pulpits are silent.*

Teenage suicide is the highest it has ever been. The number of teenage alcoholics and drug addicts is the highest ever. Christian morality can-not be taught in schools but atheistic immorality can. Divorce is tak-ing approximately one of every two marriages. The number of chil-dren living in broken homes is fast becoming a majority. *And 300,000 pulpits are silent.*

Rape has increased 700 percent in the last fifty years, and that takes into consideration the population growth. The FBI says one in four twelve-year-old girls will be sexually assaulted in her lifetime. Pornography has become an eight billion dollar business, with some of the largest companies in America involved . . . *And 300,000 pulpits are silent.*

Rock music fills the airways and our children's minds with music which legitimizes rape, murder, sado-masochism, adultery, satanic worship, and more. *And 300,000 pulpits are silent.*

A majority of states now have lotteries. We have eliminated that crime by making it legal and putting it under the control of the state. *And 300,000 pulpits are silent.*

What important matters are being dealt with in our churches? The church bulletin says there will be a meeting to plan the churchwide supper. We are raising money to put a new floor cover in the kitchen. (The old one doesn't match the new stove and refrigerator.) The ser-mon subject last Sunday was "How to Have a Positive Attitude." We are organizing a softball team.[1]

These are convicting words, aren't they?

But the Church hasn't always been silent—by any means! Down through the centuries, the Christian Church has been on the front lines

in the battle against evil in society. Christian Churches worked tireless-
ly to abolish slavery in Great Britain and America. Two-thirds of the
members of the Abolition Society in New England were Christian clergymen. The Church has led the fight against the exploitation of child
labor and the mistreatment of women. The Church also spearheaded
such issues as prison reform, the founding of hospitals, and improved
care for the mentally ill. That is what it has meant, in past centuries, for
the Church to be the salt of the earth and the light of the world.

Today, unfortunately, this no longer seems to be the case. Many
churches in our time seem to take a "don't rock the boat" approach to
the world and its ills. In few pulpits today will you hear even a single
word about such burning issues as abortion, government corruption,
rampant immorality in our media and our society, atheistic indoctrina-
tion in our public schools, and so on. Instead, our churches today seem
to have little or no relevance to the world around them. Our pulpits do
not thunder against evil and cultural decay—they exude sweet Muzak-
like refrains of pietistic platitudes. Some pulpits merely repackage the
motivational pep talks of the secular world with ribbons and bows of
spirituality. The Church, as a force for moral and cultural change, has
been neutered.

Friend in Christ, all around us, human souls and human society are
going to Hell—and 300,000 pulpits are silent! It is time for the Church
to wake up and smell the brimstone!

The battle on the churchyard lawn

Have you heard of Rev. Jonas Clark? What's that? You haven't?!
Well, you should know him! In fact, you probably owe your freedom to
Parson Clark. If not for him, I seriously doubt that you and I would be
here today—at least, we wouldn't be free Americans.

Jonas Clark was a country parson in the little town of Lexington,
Massachusetts, in the late eighteenth century. As was so often the case in
those days, he was one of the few educated people in town. Most of the
people of Lexington attended his church, and he was a man of consid-
erable influence. From the pulpit of his little country church, Parson
Clark expounded on the great issues that faced the American colonists

in the years before the Revolutionary War—issues of personal and religious freedom, issues of the resistance of tyranny. Long before the first shot was fired in that great war for freedom, his congregation was ready to fight and die in a cause they believed was just and God-ordained—the cause of liberty.

One night, as rumors of imminent war swirled through the British colonies in America, Parson Clark sat at his dinner table with a pair of guests whose names you've certainly heard before: John Hancock and Samuel Adams. A message had been received from a neighboring village: A detachment of British marines was marching to Lexington to attack the supply and weapons storehouse. War was on the way. So these two great patriots, Hancock and Adams, asked Clark the question: Would the men of Lexington fight? Clark didn't hesitate in answering. "I have trained them for this very hour," he said. "They will fight."

So the decision was made and the die was cast. That was the night of April 18, 1775—the same night Paul Revere made his famous ride from Boston to Concord to warn of the approach of British troops. At two in the morning, the bell of Parson Clark's church was rung; within moments 150 men arrived to answer the call. A few men were selected to stand guard on the church grounds, and the rest retired to their homes to await the next alarm. Early the next morning, April 19, the British marines came marching up the road toward town. The church bell clanged, and again a group of freedom-loving, God-fearing Americans arrived, flintlock rifles in hand, ready for battle.

The two forces squared off, Americans versus British—and moments later, "the shot heard 'round the world" was fired on the very grounds of Jonas Clark's Presbyterian church. These Christian revolutionaries were not fighting for freedom from taxation or the freedom to determine their own political destinies. After sitting under the preaching of Jonas Clark, they became convinced in their hearts that resistance to tyranny was obedience to God. As followers of Christ, they were defending the altars of faith. When the British commander ordered them to throw down their guns and disperse, the Americans answered with the crack of musketry.

When the battle was over, the British were put to flight—but several stalwart members of Jonas Clark's congregation lay dead upon the grass of the churchyard lawn. Looking down upon their bodies with anguish and sorrow but without regret, Parson Clark said, "From this day will be dated the liberty of the world."

The American Revolution began in a church. It began with a preacher who was not afraid to speak out on the great issues of freedom and liberty and oppression and tyranny. He thus became one of an army of Christian pastors who helped spark the American Revolution. The pastors came to be known as "the Black Regiment" (because of their black robes), and they did not merely preach while other men went into battle. Pastor Philips Payson single-handedly captured two British supply wagons in the Battles of Lexington and Concord. Pastor John Craighead raised a parish militia, which he led in the service of General Washington in New Jersey. Lutheran pastor Peter Muhlenberg led a three-hundred-man regiment into battle against the British. Presbyterian minister and missionary James Hall of North Carolina commanded a company comprised of members of his church. Presbyterian theologian Dr. Ashbel Green served with distinction in the Revolutionary army.

Presbyterian pastor James Caldwell of Elizabethtown, New Jersey, was a militia chaplain who believed in always being ready for action— and he preached many a sermon with his loaded pistols on the pulpit in front of him! Presbyterian clergyman John Witherspoon served not only as president of Princeton University but also as a delegate to the Continental Congress and a signer of the Declaration of Independence. Samuel Davies, the "apostle of Virginia" and the pastor of Patrick Henry, once went to London and rebuked King George III face-to-face, saying, "When the lion roareth, the beasts of the forest tremble; when the Lord speaketh, let the kings of the earth keep silence."

And there were so many other courageous pastors and battlefield chaplains who believed in proclaiming the whole counsel of God boldly and fearlessly; who obeyed Christ as the rightful King and Lawgiver for all nations, including the newborn United States of America; who proclaimed God's Word not only as a rule of faith for individual lives but also as the cornerstone of a just government and godly society; and who pledged their lives, their fortunes, and their sacred honor to the cause of

God and human liberty. As American historian James Adams observed, "The political leaders may have declared independence, but the ministers turned the revolt into a holy war."

Do we have any pastors today who speak out with the boldness and courage of those pastors during Revolutionary days? Do we have any churches today addressing the great, urgent issues of our time? What is God's purpose for His Church as we move into the third millennium of the Christian era?

Friend in Christ, the times we live in demand boldness and courage on the part of God's people. God is looking for men and women who will speak out bluntly and fearlessly on the issues of our day. Martin Luther once said, "Though we be engaged in the battle, if we do not fight where the battle is the hottest, we are traitors to the cause."

Whenever I ask why pastors and churches do not speak out on this issue or that issue, the answer may be worded differently, but the bottom line is always the same. "We are afraid." Pastors and churches fear being labeled "extremist" or "fundamentalist." They fear losing members or donations. They fear losing their IRS tax-exempt status. So they avoid the real and urgent issues of the day, choosing instead to preach a "safe" Gospel that ruffles no feathers, that risks no backlash.

Don't be afraid to speak the truth! Don't be afraid of the judgment of men! Fear only the judgment of God who entrusted you with the light of His truth! Be more afraid to hide His truth under a basket of cowardice!

The battle is raging. This is no time for pastors and their congregations to hide, trembling and quivering, beneath the pews! It is time to march out boldly through the church doors and into the world. It is time to storm the gates of Hell, which—if we take our Lord at His word—cannot prevail against us. It is time for men and women of courageous faith to truly become the salt of the earth and the light of the world.

"Where there is no vision . . ."

A man passed a large construction project where workers were laying brick. He said to one of them, "What are you doing?"

The construction worker growled, "I'm laying bricks, stupid! What does it look like I am doing?"

The man went to the next worker. "What are you doing?" he inquired.

"I'm building a wall," said the second construction worker.

The man went to a third worker. "What are you doing?" he asked a third time.

The third worker beamed up at the man. "I," he said with joy and enthusiasm, "am building a magnificent cathedral that will be dedicated to the glory of God!"

All three of these construction workers were performing precisely the same task—laying bricks. But only one of them had a *vision* for the true greatness of what he was accomplishing.

"Where there is no vision, the people perish," says Proverbs 29:18 (KJV). Vision is absolutely essential for the life of a congregation and for the life of a nation. Without vision we have no collective sense of purpose, meaning, and direction. We have no life. With a grand, exalted vision, everything we do—even laying bricks—suddenly takes on eternal meaning and magnificent purpose.

What does a vision do for a pastor and a church? A vision takes all the various individual members of the church and binds them into a unified force, moving them in a single-minded direction. A vision grasps the heart of a church with fingers of steel and refuses to let go until the goal is reached and the vision becomes reality. A vision focuses the minds of the members just as a magnifying glass focuses the rays of the sun. A vision ignites the passion of a church with a white-hot sense of urgency.

Without vision, what are people accomplishing in the Church? They are just getting up in the morning and going through the motions. "Me? I'm just teaching Sunday school—you know, telling Bible stories to little kids." "Me? Oh, I just lead the choir on Sunday mornings." "I'm just an usher." "I just ladle soup in the church's homeless program." "I'm just a deacon." "I'm just a board member."

With vision, everything a church does has eternal significance. "I'm a parking attendant in the church parking lot—I help make the church an inviting place where people can come, hear the Gospel, and have their lives transformed! I'm directing traffic for the kingdom of God!" "I'm a Sunday school teacher! I'm helping children build a relationship with the Lord of the universe, so that they can be eternally refashioned into His image!" "I lead the worship in music, helping people to direct their hearts to the everlasting Lord!" "I work in an outreach ministry that is bringing scores of people into the kingdom of God, while transforming our society one life at a time!"

You see what a difference a vision makes? "Where there is no vision, the people perish." They may not die physically, but they become part of the walking dead, Christian zombies who have no sense of purpose or meaning for their activities in church.

Years ago, before the Coral Ridge Presbyterian Church was in its present spacious facilities, we met in a small building on Commercial Boulevard in Fort Lauderdale. We didn't have a large narthex or church lobby, so people would line up outside in the hot sun to file into the church service. Sometimes the line would extend for a block. Someone driving by in a car was once overheard saying, "They must be giving away something free in there!" And he was right! In the name of Jesus Christ, we were giving away the free gift of eternal life!

I was called to begin a mission church in Fort Lauderdale in 1959. I arrived with a vision and very little else. We began meeting in the cafetorium at McNab Elementary School—a place with no air-conditioning, poor acoustics, and uncomfortable seating. I sat down with the little handful of people who had come to be a part of that budding ministry, and I told them, "I know this doesn't look like much—but we can change the world from this place." I'm sure they thought that the hot Florida sun had gone to my head—but I had a vision for changing the world, and that vision has persisted through all of these years.

As I saw it, there were essentially two ways I could go about changing the world: (1) I could get a bigger megaphone so I could preach to more people; or (2) I could equip the entire church to be salt of the earth and light of the world so that *together* we could change the world for Christ. We chose the latter course. We got people involved who understood the various print and broadcast media, and the church started a daily radio ministry, a weekly television broadcast, and a publishing ministry of printed sermons, tracts, and books. We built a radio station, WAFG, which blankets our area of Florida with evangelistic programming.

We began training people in our congregation in ways to comfortably, confidently, boldly share the Gospel of Jesus Christ with others. These church members in turn trained others to do the same. We created books and training literature that eventually became a program called Evangelism Explosion. EE quickly spilled over from our church into neighboring churches. Then it spread to other cities, other states, and across the ocean to England, until today it now reaches into two hundred nations around the world.

Another part of our vision of reaching and changing the world for Christ involved establishing a school where we could train young people to be the salt of the earth and the light of the world. So for more than two decades, Westminster Academy has trained thousands of young people to know Christ, to be refashioned into His image, and to go out from here and make their mark upon the world. More recently, we have expanded upon that vision by establishing Knox Theological Seminary as a place to train people as ministers who will, in turn, train others who will, in turn, train others—fulfilling God's mandate to be "be fruitful and multiply" in a profound and spiritual sense.

It was never our intention to build Coral Ridge Presbyterian Church into a cozy little Christian enclave, safe and secure within four walls. Our vision has always been dynamic, outwardly directed, global in scope, eternal in extent. Our goal has always been to transform the society in which we live, to rescue and refashion human souls, and to glorify God. What has been accomplished so far is, I believe, nothing more than a start, a down payment on all God plans and intends to do through our church. He has given us a vision, and that vision is drawing our entire congregation toward a great and exciting future.

Vision gives significance and meaning to everything we do, and to our very existence. God has given us His vision for His Church in the form of two great mandates: the Cultural Mandate and the Great Commission—the first commandment He gave our first parents in Eden and the last commandment Christ left to us before He departed this world. In these two mandates, God has given us our assignment, our goal, our ultimate task. Because of the global and all-encompassing nature of these mandates, we cannot escape the fact that His purpose for the Church is global and all-encompassing. We are not to draw some imaginary boundary line a couple of miles to the north or south. Instead, we are to lift our eyes and see the whitened fields throughout all of the earth. We are to take the message of the Gospel of Jesus Christ to them. Our parish is nothing less than the entire world.

Even more challenging than the scope of God's vision for the Church is the profound *depth* of this vision! We are not simply to advertise a message. We are not simply to announce that Jesus has come. We are to *fill the earth*, to *subdue it,* and to *have dominion over it!* God has called us not merely to win souls but to *claim Planet Earth* in His name! We are to be involved in changing the very institutions of our society; to call for an end to the slaughter of innocents through abortion; to demand an end to the exploitation of women and children by prostitution and pornography; to restore the sanctity of the family as the foundation of a healthy society; to restore integrity and trust to our institutions of government; to expose evil and expand good in every sphere of influence and activity throughout our culture.

Let me tell you the story of some friends of mine who are staking their claim for Christ on our world: Donald and Suzy Warren. But to help you understand where Donald and Suzy are today, you should first understand where they came from—and how far their journey has taken them.

Donald was raised in a family ruled by hate. His father was a leader in a movement that preached racism and anti-Semitism. As a boy, Donald spent many hours in rallies and meetings, hearing vicious harangues about "Aryan supremacy" and death to other races. When he was old enough to break away, Donald reacted to his malignant upbringing by running in a different direction. As a seventeen-year-old secular humanist, he went to Latin America, where he witnessed the extreme contrast between rich and poor—and he embraced Marxism-Leninism and the radical Students for a Democratic Society (SDS). Thinking he was helping to build a better world, a "workers' paradise," he was unaware that he had merely traded one failed worldview for another.

As a committed radical, Donald Warren began dating the high school sweetheart who would one day be his wife. "I had accepted Christ in junior high at a Bible camp," Suzy recalled, "but I continued to live with one foot in the world and one in the Church. I looked upon Jesus as my Savior, but not the Lord of my life. I was not surrendered to Him. From the time we met when I was sixteen, I saw Donald as my soul mate, and he continued to have an influence on my life. I felt pulled in two directions. I kept two books on the nightstand by my bed—my Bible and Mao's Little Red Book, which Don had given me."

"I knew that Suzy was a Christian," Donald remembered with a wry grin, "but I chose to overlook that 'character flaw.'" After his college years, Donald, the radical SDS activist, spent time in East Germany becoming ever more steeped in the Marxist worldview and radical activism. Sometime after his return from Germany, Donald and Suzy were married. "Don was the man I always wanted to be with," said Suzy. "Despite his radical leanings and his atheist beliefs, he always had a kind heart. I knew that it was clearly, biblically wrong for a Christian to marry an unbeliever, but I thought that I could witness to Don and win him over, and everything would turn out all right. I soon found out that God had a very practical reason for saying in 2 Corinthians 6:14, 'Do not be unequally yoked together with unbelievers.' My decision, made in rebellion against God's Word, cost me years of unbelievable emotional and spiritual suffering."

The enormity of the mistake Suzy had made became real to her immediately after they were married. "I had been witnessing to Don," said Suzy, "telling him about God and the Christian life, and that I wanted to make a Christian home. And the next morning, he rolled over in bed and said four words to me: 'I don't buy it.' And I instantly knew what he meant: Don was rejecting everything I was telling him about God, about Jesus Christ, about the Christian life. He was going to live the way he pleased—and that included his intention to live a non-monogamous life while he was married to me. Of course, I could hardly blame him for rejecting the Gospel, since I had been living an immoral life myself, in rebellion against the very things I was preaching to him—that's what comes of living with one foot in the world and one foot in the Church. At the moment he said, 'I don't buy it,' I thought, *What have I done?*"

Gradually, Donald reached a point of disillusionment with Marxism. "For years, I had been working to help bring about the world-wide revolution that Karl Marx predicted," he explained, "but it gradually dawned on me that the proletariats were not going to rise up and seize the means of production in my lifetime. So I decided to point my life in an entirely different direction: I was going to get a lot of money, do whatever I pleased, gratify my senses, and seek personal happiness. I had a secular humanist worldview, so there was no God in my life. I had concluded that God didn't create man—man created God, and eventually religion would wither away as the advance of science did away with the concept of God. Since there was no God to judge my life, I decided to get everything I could out of life before it was over."

And Donald proceeded to do just that. He started an extremely successful roofing business in Florida and an equally lucrative agronomic business in Jamaica, producing aloe vera and tropical flowers. By the world's standards, he had everything he could want—plenty of money and all the materialistic "toys" anyone could desire.

"In the process of achieving those goals," Donald recalled, "I made an amazing discovery. I found out that the saddest moment in life can be the moment you reach your goals. You've been working and sacrificing, thinking, *When I get to this point, I'm finally going to be happy.* And then you get there—you've got all the money, the toys, the sex, everything that's supposed to make you fulfilled. Then you realize you're still empty inside. You think, *Is that all there is?* I kept trying to fill that empty place with money and pleasure, and nothing worked. I was on a fast train headed for Hell, and I didn't know it."

Early in their marriage, Donald and Suzy had a daughter, Breven, but a series of miscarriages in the years that followed made it appear that they would never have another child. During this time, in the late 1980s, Suzy became acquainted with my wife, Anne. A music major with a vocal performance background, Suzy had started coming to our church so she could sing in the concert choir.

"God sat me down beside Anne Kennedy," Suzy said. "Even though my heart was hardened and rebellious, there was something about the church that drew me, made me want to be a part. Anne took an interest in us—she made an Evangelism Explosion call on us, she wrote me many notes of encouragement saying she was praying for me, and she often called just to see how I was doing. I appreciated Anne's caring so much that I put the Kennedys' house on our route for regular flower deliveries—which shows how God often uses the unrighteous to bless the righteous!"

Suzy was intensely involved in Donald's business ventures, and by early 1993 the pressures of work were becoming so stressful, she feared she was having a nervous breakdown. "I was working too much," she recalled, "and not taking care of my family. I had a teenage daughter who was growing up into an atheist just like her father. I had made a complete mess of my life. Donald was so hardened in his own atheism that I considered him a lost cause—beyond all hope of salvation. I had only one hope—that Don would somehow die before I did, so that I could get back in church and get straight with God. I didn't have the strength to go against him—his personality was too overpowering. So in the midst of all this pain, fear, and failure, I cried out to God. I said, 'God, I want to be Yours, so if there's anything You can do with this messed-up life of mine, please take it and straighten it out.'"

That was in February 1993. In May, just three months later, God moved in a miraculous way to answer that prayer. First Suzy went to her doctor and received the news that she was pregnant again. But the very next day after receiving this news, Suzy's wish that her husband would die almost came true!

"The roofing business was my bread and butter at this time," Donald Warren explained. "A hurricane had just blown through Florida, and I was in constant contact with an insurance adjuster, Brian Persson, who is a Christian. Brian was always talking to me about Jesus, and I humored him because I got a lot of business through him. Once I had him over to our house, and he and I were on this high deck in the back. I was sitting on the rail, over a steep drop. 'Be careful, there,' he said. 'You might fall.' I just laughed and said, 'I never fall.' And Brian very soberly quoted Proverbs 16:18 to me: 'Pride goes before destruction, and a haughty spirit before a fall.' I just laughed—those words didn't mean a thing to me."

But the day after learning his wife was pregnant again, those words from the Old Testament came back to haunt him in a powerful way. "I was up on a two-story building surveying a steeply pitched roof for an insurance company," he recalled. "There was no wind that day—yet something reached out and swept me off that roof. To this day, I can only figure that it must have been the hand of God Himself. Whatever it was, it drove me into the ground like a stake, feetfirst, crushing my leg and ankle. And as I was on the ground, the first words that came into my mind, like a voice inside my head, were the words, 'Pride goes before destruction, and a haughty spirit before a fall.'

"Well, I still had plenty of pride left, even after falling off a roof. I looked around to see if anyone saw me fall. No one was around. So I crawled along the ground, pulled myself into my truck, and drove myself to the hospital. An experience like that should have been enough to drive me into the arms of God—but I was too hard-hearted for that! God still had some shaking to do before I was ready to come to Him."

Just a week after his fall, while he was still in the hospital, Donald Warren's world was shaken when his partner walked away from the business, taking the computers and the clients while sticking Don with all the debts and liabilities. It was a devastating financial blow. In a matter of days, Don had gone from being on top of the world to down in the dumps. During those days, his own "famous last words" echoed in his mind: "I never fall." And God's answer to those words also echoed within him: "Pride goes before destruction, and a haughty spirit before a fall."

In July, Suzy went to visit her ailing father in Washington State. Meanwhile, Donald was laid up at home with a cast on his leg and nothing to do but watch television—including Christian television. "I had always ridiculed Christian TV," said Don, "and I never would have let Suzy catch me watching Christian programming! But since she was out of the house for a month, I decided to take a look at some of these TV preachers—and I got hooked. One of the shows I watched the most was the *Coral Ridge Hour* with Dr. Kennedy. The message of God's love was hammering at the door of my heart—but I still wasn't ready to open the door."

In early August, shortly before she was to return home to Florida, Suzy called Don with more bad news: She had started to bleed again—which had always been one of the first ominous signs of an impending miscarriage. Donald had wanted this baby as much as Suzy did, and the news was an even more serious blow to him than his injuries and his financial disaster. "I thought, *Oh, no! We're going to lose another baby.* By this time, it wasn't just a pregnancy; it was a baby. So I fell on my face and made a deal with God. I don't recommend this way of praying to anyone else, but being an atheist at the time, here's what I did. I said, 'God—if there is a God—only You can save my baby. If You'll do that, I'll surrender myself to You.'"

After praying that prayer, something happened within Donald Warren. "It was as if the scales fell off my eyes," he said, "and I could suddenly see the truth with absolute clarity. Instantly, I knew that God was real and that Jesus Christ really was the way, the truth, and the life. Most of all, I clearly saw that it was my sin—my sin!—that had nailed Jesus to the cross. All I could do was drop to my face, pound on the floor, and say, 'I'm so sorry; I'm so sorry!' My life and my worldview turned upside down. All my old secular humanist views were transformed in a heartbeat—my views on morality, abortion, euthanasia, everything. My heart just underwent an instantaneous and radical change with the joy of knowing that I had received the totally undeserved gift of eternal life."

By this time, both Suzy and Donald had prayed to get right with God. True to His side of the bargain, God healed Suzy, and a few months later, a second healthy daughter was born—their miracle baby. They named her Braman. But what about their first daughter, fifteen-year-old Breven?

"I raised her to be just like me," said Donald. "My pet name for her ever since she was little was Baby-My-Baby. I loved her with every ounce of my being—yet I had made her prideful, arrogant, the captain of her own soul. I had put her on that same fast train to Hell I'd been on.

When Suzy and I told our daughter what had happened in our lives, she was adamant that she didn't want Jesus in her life. She felt Jesus had stolen her daddy. Now instead of being wealthy materialists, her parents were religious fanatics with no business and no money."

Soon afterward, Anne and I invited Suzy and Donald over for dinner one evening, and they implored us for counsel on how to reach their daughter. "You can't force Christianity down your daughter's throat," I said. "All you can do is love her where she is, equip yourselves to share the Gospel, and trust Christ." During the year after their decision to completely give themselves to Christ, Suzy and Donald became intensely involved in our church, serving faithfully every week on an Evangelism Explosion team, helping to win others to Christ. Yet throughout that time, they prayed and ached for their own daughter, who continued to reject Christ.

One night in August 1994—exactly a year after Donald came to Christ—he came home from an EE visitation. His daughter, now sixteen, asked, "Daddy, what do you do when you go on those EE things?" Suddenly, Donald's heart leaped into his throat and began pounding like a jackhammer. Breven had just given him the opportunity to share the plan of salvation with her! So he said, "Well, we go into people's homes and this is what we tell them . . ." And he shared with her the diagnostic questions, the Scripture verses relating to salvation, his own testimony, and the sinner's prayer.

"I'd like to do that, Daddy," Breven responded. "I've decided I want Jesus as my Lord and Savior too."

His eyes glistening, Donald breathed a silent prayer of thanks to God for this moment. "All right," he said, "let's pray together."

Just then, Suzy came in the door—and her heart stopped. There were Donald and Breven about to pray together! "Suzy," said Donald, "Breven is about to pray to receive Jesus as her Lord and Savior."

So the three of them prayed together, then hugged each other. Breven had come home to the Lord.

Soon afterward, Breven became involved with Youth EE, and she is now in a premed program at college, acquiring medical skills to use in service to God and ministry to others. Meanwhile God has given

Donald a burden for the spiritual needs of Haiti. In fact, our church has commissioned Donald Warren as a part-time missionary to Haiti, where he takes a number of men from our church and sets up EE programs in the Haitian churches. Through these efforts, God is bringing evangelism and revival to that spiritually darkened land.

God has also used Donald as a catalyst to transform our church's ministry to the needy during the Thanksgiving and Christmas holidays. Previously, our church would simply collect food and give it to groups like the Salvation Army and Goodwill to distribute to needy families—and there's nothing wrong with those organizations and efforts. But Donald Warren realized that by doing so, we had placed an institutional layer between our church and the needy.

He said, "Why don't we have our own EE teams distribute the holiday meals, so that we can get together face-to-face with the people who have material and spiritual needs? We can talk to them, show them we care, and if they are open, we can set up an appointment to share Christ with them." And that is what we have done. Often people pray to receive Christ on the spot. At other times, people invite their family and friends over so that the EE team can witness to them.

As a result of Don's keen Spirit-led insight, our holiday compassion has been transformed into a powerful evangelistic outreach. Many of those we reach are Haitian immigrants who are beyond the reach of social services. As Donald puts it, "God has brought a mission field to our doorstep in leaky boats." Many of these Haitians are coming out of the darkness of voodoo and the occult and into the light of God's love.

I believe that Donald and Suzy Warren are examples of what God wants to do through His Church. He is in the business of reclaiming people and calling them into the Church, bringing their unique gifts and perspectives with them so that the Church can be salt and light in the world in new, exciting, and creative ways.

What does Donald Warren say is the lesson of his story? "There is no place God won't go," he replied. "There is no person God can't reach. Do anything and everything you can to win the lost. Never give up on a 'hopeless case.'"

"Don knows what he's talking about," added Suzy. "He was once a 'hopeless case' himself!"

The kingdom of self

It is not often that I have been truly discouraged and surprised in my years of ministry. I have not been discouraged over the vicious articles that have been written in secular publications, attacking my ministry. I have not been surprised by anything that has been said by the atheists who have debated me in various public and media forums. None of the onslaughts of the world have ever seriously troubled me.

The only thing I have ever truly found discouraging in my years of ministry was the discovery that so many Christians in America do not share the vision and goals we have been discussing here. I suppose I was naive to think that everyone who came to know the Lord Jesus Christ would naturally want to share the Good News with the world. I can't understand why anyone would want to keep such a wonderful message to himself, yet I have found it to be true: Many Christians and many churches simply couldn't care less about the fact that the world is going to Hell. They don't care about lost souls in India or China or Africa or America. They don't care how many millions of babies die in abortion mills across the country. They don't care about the pornography plague and the sexual exploitation of children. They don't care about any of the urgent issues facing our society. All they want is a message to give them a warm, fuzzy feeling once a week, and maybe something to help them function a little better in their lives.

I admit my naïveté. I should have known that selfishness does not automatically end when a person joins the Church. And that is almost certainly the greatest problem within the Christian Church: The work of Christ in the world is stymied by human selfishness.

Selfishness is the very essence of sin. If the outer husks of sin were stripped off, we would finally get down to the kernel, and that kernel would be called *selfishness*. The hard core of self is where most people live their lives. All they do, they do for the kingdom of self.

This is why it is so crucial that we focus on the issue of being refashioned into the image of God, who is exemplified for us in the life of

Christ. If we would be like Christ, there would be no selfishness in us, because in Him there was no selfishness whatsoever. The example of Christ is commended to us in Philippians 2:5–8:

> Let this mind be in you which was also in Christ Jesus, who, being in the form of God, did not consider it robbery to be equal with God, but made Himself of no reputation, taking the form of a bondservant, and coming in the likeness of men. And being found in appearance as a man, He humbled Himself and became obedient to the point of death, even the death of the cross.

That is the mind and spirit that should dominate the Church, and the great tragedy of the Church is that it does not. The kingdom of self has invaded the Church—and in many churches and in many individual hearts, the kingdom of self has won the battle; it occupies the ground; it has taken entire churches prisoner. When that happens, God's vision for the Church is lost. That church ceases to be the salt of the earth and the light of the world. God's mandates, the Cultural Mandate and the Great Commission, go unfulfilled—and our enemy gains ground in the battle.

The very essence of Christlikeness is crucifixion. We are called to be crucified with Christ, to lay down our lives for His sake, to take up our cross and follow Him. As long as we are living self-centered lives, focused on acquiring wealth, security, recognition, advancement, power, and influence for ourselves, we are traitors to God's cause. We are the very antithesis of what Christians ought to be.

I am reminded of a self-centered lady named Edith. Someone said that Edith was like a small country bounded on the north, south, east, and west by Edith. She was her whole world. Everything revolved around her, and she was not interested in anything else.

What really dominates and motivates our lives? Have we surrendered to Christ, or are we ruled by self? It is not enough to be Christian in name; we must be Christlike in character. If self is on the throne of our lives, Christ is dethroned. Self is the essence of human rebellion against the Almighty. It is that which God hates. It is that part of us which has been fashioned into the image and likeness *not* of God, but of Lucifer, who said, "I will ascend into heaven, I will exalt my throne above the stars of God; I will also sit on the mount of the congregation on the farthest sides of the north; I will ascend above the heights of the clouds, I will be like the Most High" (Isa. 14:13–14).

The French have a name for a disease that they say is prevalent in the world: *la maladie de moi*, the malady of the self. It is the "me sickness." God wants us to know that it is only in dying to self that we truly live. There is no other way. "For whoever desires to save his life will lose it," says the Lord, "but whoever loses his life for My sake will find it" (Matt. 16:25).

When General William Booth, the founder of the Salvation Army, lay on his deathbed, he wanted to send a message of encouragement and direction to all of the officers and workers in the worldwide movement. His message consisted of but one word: *others*. That, my friend, is the great lesson of the Christian life.

"The best lack all conviction . . ."

One of the most important books of the late twentieth century is *Slouching Towards Gomorrah: Modern Liberalism and American Decline* by Judge Robert Bork. Bork, you may recall, was a professor at Yale University Law School who was nominated to the Supreme Court by President George Bush. His appointment was rejected after he was slandered and attacked in every conceivable way by the hostile, radical left wing. When you look at the obvious, well-known lack of morals and character on the part of some of the U.S. senators who sat in hypocritical judgment of this fine man, you have to question the sense and sanity of our nation.

If you haven't read *Slouching Towards Gomorrah*, you should. It is an indispensable guide to where our nation has been politically, socially, morally, and spiritually during the last few decades—and where it is going. If you have not read it, you will not be able to interpret the bewildering events on our social and political scene in the past few years. Read it, and not only will you understand our recent past, but also you will not be caught surprised and unprepared by coming events. The title needs little elucidation; it is clear enough that we live in a society that is *Slouching Towards Gomorrah,* toward the ill-fated city that was visited by God's judgment as a result of the unspeakable sins and evils that were tolerated and approved within its walls. There is no doubt that, barring some drastic change of social and spiritual direction, America is drifting, lumbering, slouching toward the same hideous fate that was pronounced upon Sodom and Gomorrah by a just and righteous God.

In the opening pages of the book, Judge Bork shows that the times we live in today are the obvious cause-and-effect results of forces that were set in motion in the riotous, chaotic 1960s. Where are the spoiled '60s counterculture activists who sided with America's enemies, attacked and condemned our nation in campus riots and protests on foreign soil, burned our flag while raising the flags of communist nations, took over college administration buildings, and bombed bank buildings? Those activists never went away. They never changed their beliefs. Rather, they *assumed power.* They became university professors and administrators so that they could gain power over the minds of the next generation. They joined corporations and the media, where they gained influence over the power structures and information channels of our society. And, of course, they run the government. Judge Bork writes that the decade of the '60s

> was a politicized decade, one whose activists saw all of culture and life as political. The consequence is that our culture is now politicized. It worked the other way as well: our politics is increasingly (we need such a word) culturized. We have a new and extremely divisive politics of personal identity. We have invented a range of new or newly savage political-cultural battle grounds. Democrats and Republicans have begun to line up on opposing sides of the war in the culture.[2]

It may be hard for you to recall what life was like before the 1960s, but I remember it well. Politics was very much at the edge of most people's thinking, in contrast with today, where politics is continually in our faces, where America today is almost as sharply divided between left and right as America of 1860 was divided between north and south.

Before the 1960s, people could focus on living their lives, raising their families, enjoying life, and planning for retirement. Today people have to focus, often with fear and outrage, on what the political parties are doing to each other and to our nation. The opening salvos of this culture war, which is rapidly becoming the new Civil War, were fired in the decade of the 1960s.

In the course of this decades-long culture war, the forces of sin, selfishness, hedonism, corruption, and cultural decay have steadily advanced, while the forces of godliness, morality, and cultural preservation have gradually retreated. As a result, what was unthinkable and unspeakable in the 1950s became shocking in the 1960s, then annoyingly deviant in the 1970s, then tolerated in the 1980s, and finally accepted as normal in the 1990s. This is a process that Senator Daniel Patrick Moynihan has called "defining deviancy down."

Today, without thinking critically about these issues, the mainstream culture has accepted as "normal" what once was literally unspeakable within the lifetime of most Americans. In the process, what was once considered "normal" and "mainstream"—attending church, believing in God, adherence to absolute moral standards, a sense of judgment that certain things are clearly wrong and unacceptable—is now considered deviant. To have moral standards is to be "bigoted," "judgmental," and "intolerant." In today's secular culture, there is no greater sin than being "intolerant" of other people's sin, destructiveness, and immorality.

Let me offer a case in point that will curdle your blood:

Are you aware that there is now a carefully orchestrated, politically aggressive effort under way to legalize and normalize child molestation? And are you aware that this effort is steadily progressing toward its goals? Moreover, are you aware that influential segments of the psychological community are giving their stamp of approval to the legitimization of adult sex with minor children? Though sexual exploitation of children by adults is now a serious felony, segments of the mental health community now want to redefine these revolting and destructive sex acts as "normal" and "healthy" for your children! They want to once more "define deviancy down," remove words like *child molestation, sexual abuse,* and *pedophilia* from our vocabulary, substituting "values neutral" terms such as *adult-child sex!*

These recommendations were reported in "A Meta-Analytic Examination of Assumed Properties of Child Sexual Abuse Using College Samples," published in 1998 by the American Psychological Association. One of the three authors of this report also contributed to a special 1990 issue on sex between men and boys in *The Journal of Homosexuality,* questioning the "taboo" against "man-boy sexual relationships" as "irrelevant or else biased." So it seems clear that at least one of the authors went into this study with an agenda.

Before you say it can't happen, before you say that child molestation can never be normalized in our society, consider this: In the 1970s, both the American Psychiatric Association and the American Psychological Association voted to normalize homosexuality. Once considered a form of mental illness, homosexual tendencies are now considered by the politically agendized mental health community as psychologically "normal," merely an alternative to heterosexuality. This, of course, was not a scientific decision but a political one. Having defined one form of deviancy down (homosexuality) in the 1970s, it becomes easier to redefine the next form (pedophilia) as harmless in the 1990s.

Not surprisingly, soon after the APA report was published, the North American Man-Boy Love Association (NAMBLA)—an organization of politically active pedophiles—called the report "good news" that justified its position that homosexual pedophilia ought to be legalized, normalized, and viewed as "healthy" and "harmless." Said the NAMBLA web page, "On average, nearly 70 percent of males in the studies reported that as children or adolescents their sexual experiences with adults had been positive or neutral . . . The current war on boy-lovers has no basis in science."

It is important to note that the APA report is not scientific research. It is a political con job disguised as science. The important-sounding term *Meta-Analytic* actually means that no original scientific research was conducted by the study. Rather, the authors looked up other research studies, including doctoral dissertations that had never been subject to peer review. From these studies, they took statistics they liked, threw out statistics that didn't fit their biases, and came to a preordained set of conclusions to fit their agenda—an agenda that one of the authors had already promoted in a previous article.

The authors of the APA report would have us believe that eight-, nine-, or ten-year-old children can give informed consent to sex! The message of both homosexual and heterosexual pedophiles is embodied in the APA report: They would have us believe that children like to have sex with adults—and that adult-child sex is good for them! This is not science. This is propaganda for the organized pervert underground.

Understand, too, that the APA report is not alone. There are new pro-pedophilia "reports" emerging all the time, such as this statement by world-renowned sexologist Dr. John Money (Professor Emeritus, Johns Hopkins University): "If I were to see the case of a boy aged ten or eleven who's intensely erotically attracted toward a man in his twenties or thirties, if the relationship is totally mutual, and the bonding is genuinely totally mutual . . . then I would not call it pathological in any way."[3]

The door has been opened, and a demonic flood has been unleashed upon our children—and the mental health community is pronouncing its blessing upon this Satan-inspired obscenity! "But whoever causes one of these little ones who believe in Me to sin," said the Lord Jesus, "it would be better for him if a millstone were hung around his neck, and he were drowned in the depth of the sea" (Matt. 18:6).

Woe to those who would justify what Jesus Himself has damned in no uncertain terms. And woe to the Church of Jesus Christ if we do not plant ourselves firmly in the gap, acting as salt and light, fulfilling God's purpose for the Church, obeying the Cultural Mandate, and rescuing our children from these predators and child-raping monsters.

We have been down this slippery slope before. We have seen what happens. Psychologists and psychiatrists grant their seal of approval to deviancy; liberal theologians pronounce their sanctimonious blessings; legislators declare it legal. Once it is legal, people assume that what is legal is right. They now have license to freely, openly, unashamedly commit what was once unspeakable and unthinkable.

We have seen it happen in the matter of abortion. Though abortion techniques have existed since ancient times, abortion has been a sin in the Church and a crime in society for two thousand years of Church history. In the early Church, abortion was considered such a heinous sin that if anyone had an abortion or performed an abortion, that person was excommunicated from the Church with no possibility of reinstatement. Then the government came along and pronounced the killing of innocents "legal." So now it's all right! It is even permissible to pull a baby three-fourths of the way out of a mother's womb, stick a pair of scissors in the back of neck, and kill that child—a clear case of infanticide.

What's more, when you compare the rise of the incidence of child abuse and see how it coincides with the legalization of abortion by *Roe v. Wade* in 1973, it becomes clear that the killing of children *in utero* made once unthinkable acts of violence against children suddenly thinkable and doable on an epidemic scale! By redefining abortion "choice" as "normal" and "acceptable," society unwittingly redefined and validated all acts of violence and exploitation against children.

We have seen it happen in the matter of homosexuality. I have examined a number of nineteenth-century Bible commentaries on passages dealing with homosexuality. I discovered something fascinating: No reference to homosexuality can even be found in those commentaries! The closest you can come to a mention of homosexuality in those commentaries are Scripture passages dealing with "that unspeakable sin." It was a sin so vile as to not even be mentioned by name.

Today, however, homosexuality openly parades itself in our streets and on our television screens. Activist homosexuals star in many of our television series and write pro-gay propaganda into network shows. Gay and lesbian organizations have succeeded in getting their literature promoting "tolerance" and "acceptance" toward homosexuality into the hands of children in our public schools, even in the elementary grades. As Judge Bork observed, our culture has indeed been politicized and our politics has been culturized—

And the result has been widespread, rapidly accelerating cultural decay and decline.

I come back to the title of Judge Bork's book, because it is so appropriate to our theme. *Slouching Towards Gomorrah* is an adaptation from a line in a poem by William Butler Yeats, "The Second Coming," which Bork quotes at the beginning of the book. In those lines, Yeats contrasts the second coming of Christ with His first advent, concluding that while Jesus originally came to earth as a gentle lamb, He will return as a "rough beast," a lion in judgment, loosing a "blood-dimmed tide" of divine retribution upon the world. Yeats, writing roughly a century ago, already saw that society was sliding into a mire of evil, bloodshed, immorality, and inhumanity, which would surely demand God's terrible judgment, such as John described in the book of Revelation. Yeats wrote,

> Surely some revelation is at hand;
> Surely the Second Coming is at hand . . .
> And what rough beast, its hour come round at last,
> Slouching towards Bethlehem to be born?

Truly we are seeing Yeats's prophetic words approaching fulfillment in our time, along with the prophetic words of Jesus and the book of Revelation. Civilization is caught in a moral avalanche that is roaring into the abyss, toward the greatest battle in the history of the planet. In the midst of this descent into chaos, Yeats makes this powerful indictment of those of us on the side of God and of good:

> The best lack all conviction, while the worst
> Are full of passionate intensity.

I have been all across this country. I have debated and confronted the leaders of the proabortion movement, the leaders of the homosexual movement, the leaders of the feminist movement, the humanists, the atheists, the evolutionists, and all of the left-wing cadre. I can tell you one thing they all have in common: They are full of passion. They are committed to their cause with an intensity that should shame most Bible-believing Christians. Isn't it true what Yeats writes? Don't the best, the Christians, the people of morality and righteousness, seem to lack conviction and intensity? Don't we, who are supposed to be the salt of the earth and the light of the world, easily give way and back down before the passionate, merciless intensity of the worst, the forces of cultural decay and corruption?

The forces of evil are determined to inflict their brave new world upon us all. Yet God calls us to bring His kingdom into being on this earth. Which side will prevail—brave new world or God's kingdom? And which side are you on?

Are you filled with a passionate intensity for the great cause of Jesus Christ—the only cause worthy of our passion and undying commitment? Can you get as excited and intense about sharing the Gospel of Christ and extending the dominion of Christ as you do about the NBA play-offs, the Super Bowl, or a vacation at Disneyland? If not, then these words of Yeats should be carved into your headstone as a spiritual epitaph: "The best lack all conviction."

It is the people of the greatest passion and intensity who always win. And what of those twilight-shrouded souls who lack all conviction? "So then, because you are lukewarm," answers Jesus, "and neither cold nor hot, I will vomit you out of My mouth" (Rev. 3:16). May that never be said of you and me!

Christ calls us to discipline ourselves as soldiers in His cause, passionately committed to victory in the great spiritual and cultural warfare that is now raging all around us. It is a good struggle, a just and holy war. It is a struggle for godliness, a war against Satan.

God's purpose for His Church, for you and me, is to wage that battle with passionate intensity—

And *win*.

1 0

GOD'S PURPOSE
FOR AMERICA

They won't invite Pastor Joe Wright to the Kansas state legislature again! Wright, pastor of Wichita's Central Christian Church, was invited to give the invocation for the legislative body on January 23, 1996. He accepted the invitation, he went, he stood before the legislature, he prayed—and he stirred up a hornet's nest! No sooner had he said "Amen" than three legislators jumped to their feet, grabbed the nearest microphones, and began to protest! The prayer, said one lawmaker, was "sanctimonious . . . overbearing!" And another termed it "blasphemous and ignorant."

Oh, really? Just what did the reverend say to the Lord that got these Kansas legislators all riled up? Here is the full text of Pastor Joe Wright's prayer. Read it—then you tell me if you agree with the angry legislators or with Pastor Wright:

Heavenly Father, we come before You today to ask Your forgiveness and seek Your direction and guidance. We know Your Word says, "Woe to those who call evil good," but that's exactly what we have done. We have lost our spiritual equilibrium and inverted our values.

We confess that:

We have ridiculed the absolute truth of Your Word and called it "pluralism."

We have worshiped other gods and called it "multiculturalism."

We have endorsed perversion and called it an "alternative lifestyle."

We have exploited the poor and called it "the lottery."

We have neglected the needy and called it "self-preservation."

We have rewarded laziness and called it "welfare."

We have killed our unborn and called it "choice."

We have shot abortionists and called it "justifiable."

We have neglected to discipline our children and called it "building self-esteem."

We have abused power and called it "political savvy."

We have coveted our neighbor's possessions and called it "ambition."

We have polluted the air with profanity and pornography and called it "freedom of expression."

We have ridiculed the time-honored values of our forefathers and called it "enlightenment."

Search us, Oh God, and know our hearts today; try us and see if there be some wicked way in us; cleanse us from every sin and set us free. Guide and bless these men and women who have been sent here by the people of Kansas, and who have been ordained by You, to govern this great state. Grant them Your wisdom to rule and may their decisions direct us to the center of Your will.

I ask in the name of Your Son, the living Savior, Jesus Christ. Amen.

Well, what do you think? Did you find the "blasphemy," "sancti-mony," and "ignorance" in that prayer? If you did, please tell me where it was, because I couldn't find any! What I found was an accurate and profound diagnosis of what is wrong with our nation—and a heartfelt plea for wisdom and guidance so that we can right those wrongs.

If it weren't tragic, it most certainly would be humorous. As Will Rogers once said, "There's no trick to being a humorist when you have the whole government working for you." Unfortunately, what has hap-pened to our government and our society is nothing to laugh at. It is enough to make one weep.

God's purpose for America

It would be interesting to take a survey of all the people reading this book, or even a survey of people in the street, and ask, "What is the pur-pose of America?" What would your answer be? What would most people answer? Would they even *have* an answer—or would they simply give you a blank look?

Those who first settled in America and those who founded our gov-erning institutions certainly had a profound sense of America's purpose. But over the years we have lost that driving, motivating, unifying sense of national purpose. We have lost our direction; we have lost our way. And that is why we are floundering as a nation—floundering morally, floundering spiritually, like a rudderless ship adrift at sea.

Many have tried to reframe and restate America's purpose, with mixed results. Many years ago, President Calvin Coolidge proclaimed, "The business of America is business." In other words, America's purpose is to generate profits, jobs, and stock dividends. There is nothing wrong with American business making a profit or with American workers having jobs—but I submit to you that business is not America's reason for exist-ing. This nation has been given a much higher and more exalted calling.

Ronald Reagan, when he was running for president in 1980, clear-ly had a sense of God's purpose for America in mind when he said, "I've always believed that this land was placed here between the two great oceans by some divine plan . . . Our destiny is to build a land here that will be, for all mankind, a shining city on a hill."

With those words, Mr. Reagan echoed the vision for America that was first articulated by John Winthrop, the English Puritan who sailed to America to serve as the first governor of the Massachusetts Bay Colony from 1629 to 1649. Even before he set foot on the shores of America, while he still stood upon the deck of the anchored sailing ship *Arabella*, he stated his vision for the new society that was just coming into being:

> We shall be as a city upon a hill. The eyes of all people are upon us, so that if we shall deal falsely with our God in this work we have undertaken and so cause Him to withdraw His present help from us, we shall be made a story and a byword through all the world.

Once those words expressed the hope of America, the purpose of America. Today I read those words and wonder if they have not become America's epitaph. Have we not dealt falsely with our God? And how long will He delay in pronouncing the judgment John Winthrop prophesied?

All of Winthrop's contemporaries understood God's purpose for this new land. In 1643, representatives from all of the American colonies got together in New England and ratified the New England Confederation, which declared:

> We all came into these parts of America for one and the same end and aim, namely, to advance the kingdom of our Lord Jesus Christ.

That is what America is all about! That is God's original purpose for America! Is that still our purpose as a nation? Is it the purpose of *your* life? Are you actively fulfilling God's purpose for you and for this great nation by advancing the kingdom of our Lord Jesus Christ? Are you living as salt and light? Are you fulfilling the Cultural Mandate and the Great Commission? Have you led anyone to Christ in the last twelve months? If you honestly have to answer no to these questions, perhaps you are beginning to understand what is truly wrong with America.

We can cast all the blame we like on the atheists, the agnostics, the ACLU, the NEA, Planned Parenthood, and all the other godless institutions in our society—but the truth is that we must lay a great share of

the blame for America's ills right at our own doorstep. As we have disobeyed the Great Commission to share the Gospel of Christ with the
world, we have allowed these weeds to grow up in the midst of God's
garden—godless people, ignorant of the Gospel, ignorant of the Bible.
The majority of young people in this country neither know where Jesus
Christ was born, nor where He died. A majority of them could not
name half of the Ten Commandments.

If all of the Christians in America simply led one person to Christ
this year, America would instantly become an overwhelmingly Christian
nation. Most of America's desperate problems would disappear. I have
been pleading this case for dozens of years, yet I find that even among
Christians, this message meets surprising resistance. Frankly, I am
amazed. God's purpose for our lives—this twofold directive, the Cultural
Mandate and the Great Commission, which has been the theme of every
chapter in this book—is also the theme of every page of the Bible. It was
Christ's first command, "Follow Me, and I will make you fishers of men"
(Matt. 4:19), and it was His last command, "Go into all the world and
preach the Gospel to every creature" (Mark 16:15).

Are you living in silent rebellion to that command, day after day,
year after year? Friend in Christ, the many terrible problems of this
country are the direct result of that rebellion! Judgment must begin at
the house of God.

A Christian nation

Let me ask you a question. Who said the following words: "It is the
duty, as well as the privilege and interest of our Christian nation, to
select and prefer Christians for their rulers"? Now, those are certainly the
biased, intolerant words of a right-wing extremist, are they not? They
were probably uttered by some hidebound, hard-shell, fundamentalist
TV preacher, right?

Wrong!

Those are the words of John Jay, first Chief Justice of the United
States Supreme Court, appointed to that august position by George
Washington himself and—along with James Madison and Alexander
Hamilton—one of the esteemed authors of the Federalist Papers. And

John Jay was hardly alone in professing America to be a Christian nation—not just religious, not just moral or godly or spiritual, but specifically Christian.

You remember Patrick Henry, the great golden-tongued orator of the American Revolution. (At least I hope you remember him! I was amazed, not long ago, to hear an adult say to me, "Who is Patrick Henry?"!) Patrick Henry's impassioned speech at the House of Burgesses in Virginia—"Give me liberty or give me death!"—was, of course, the spark that ignited the American Revolution. Some years after the Revolution, he observed, "It cannot be emphasized too strongly or too often that this great nation was founded, not by religionists, but by Christians; not on religions, but on the Gospel of Jesus Christ! For this very reason, peoples of other faiths have been afforded asylum, prosperity, and freedom of worship here."

Our first president, George Washington, stated his settled conviction: "It is impossible to rightly govern the world without God and the Bible." John Quincy Adams, the sixth president of the United States, said, "The highest glory of the American Revolution was this: It connected in one indissoluble bond, the principles of civil government with those of Christianity." And Andrew Jackson, the man known as "Old Hickory" and the seventh president of the United States, put it this way: "The Bible is the foundation upon which our republic rests." Even Franklin Delano Roosevelt once described the United States as "the lasting concord between men and nations, founded on the principles of Christianity."

In 1892, in the case of the *Church of the Holy Trinity v. United States*, the Supreme Court rendered a unanimous 9-0 decision after spending ten years examining every document regarding the founding of this nation. The high court's inescapable conclusion: The institutions of our nation are "based upon and embody the teachings of the Redeemer of Mankind . . . This is a Christian nation." Because of the blatant censorship that has been taking place for more than a generation in our public schools and universities, we have a vast multitude of people who know nothing about the real founding of this country and of its Christian foundations.

Now you might reasonably ask at this point, "Dr. Kennedy, are you advocating a theocracy in America?" My answer: emphatically no. A theocracy is a government controlled by a single sect, claiming to speak for God. The word *theocracy* comes from the Greek *theokratia*, meaning "a government by God or a god." Ancient Israel, under Moses the law-giver, was a theocracy; modern Iran, ruled in the name of Allah by Islamic ayatollahs, is a darker example of a theocracy. I would never suggest that America should be ruled by clergymen or ayatollahs—but I do suggest to you that the godless secular state that America has become is a far cry from the godly America that was envisioned by our founding fathers.

It is the Christian spiritual and moral foundation of our nation that guarantees all Americans of all faiths the right to worship in freedom and safety. Once that Christian foundation has been completely eroded, religious liberty will be gone as well. Fortunately, this truth is being recognized and proclaimed by an increasing number of prophetic voices in our land—including some voices from outside the Christian community. In a column carried nationwide by the Knight Ridder/Tribune News Service (March 1, 1999), Rabbi Daniel, Lapin, host of *Rabbi's Roundtable* on Radio KVI in Seattle, and founding rabbi of the Pacific Jewish Center in Venice, California, offered this perspective:

> As an Orthodox rabbi, I can state, with neither equivocation nor trepidation, that America is a nation founded by believing Christians and based upon broad Judeo-Christian principles . . . As a Jew, I am extremely grateful to be living in a country that, though founded without one Jewish signature on its Declaration of Independenc, has legally granted me full religious expression . . . America is based on the Christian faith of its founders. As a Jew living in America, I need it to remain that way.

The U.S. Constitution, and particularly the First Amendment, provide for a government that is built upon Christian principles, that expressly encourages the free exercise of religious faith, and that was intended to produce a society consisting of moral, godly people—not a secularized cultural cesspool in which God has been declared *persona non grata!* In a theocracy, one religious sect rules to the exclusion of all others. In the constitutional republic that America was designed to be, there is no ruling sect, no state church, no theocratic edicts—but there is full involvement of all sects, all churches, all believers in the operations and decisions of the government.

Though America was not founded as a theocracy, it was clearly founded as a Christian nation. It is a Christian nation no more—and whose fault is that? It is the fault of Christians! But America can become a Christian nation once more—if only Christians will be obedient and faithful to the purpose God has given them: carrying out the Cultural Mandate and the Great Commission.

"You can't legislate morality"

Adolf Hitler was not right about very much, but he was right about one thing. In his book *Mein Kampf*, he wrote,

> The size of [a] lie is a definite factor in causing it to be believed, for the vast masses of a nation are in the depths of their hearts more easily deceived than they are consciously and intentionally bad. The primitive simplicity of their minds renders them a more easy prey to a big lie than a small one, for they themselves often tell little lies but would be ashamed to tell big ones.

Hitler rightly understood that you can tell the big lie so often and so loudly that people will come to believe it. Like the phrase "separation of church and state," the big-lie mantra that "you can't legislate morality" has been recited and re-echoed so often, it has saturated the American consciousness, short-circuiting all intelligent thought. It only takes a few moments of reflection to see how obviously false this mantra is. Consider this question: If you can't legislate morality, what *can* you legislate?

The fact is, you can't legislate anything *but* morality! We have laws against murder because it is immoral to murder; we have laws against stealing because it is immoral to steal; we have laws against rape because it is immoral to rape. Our nation's legislative enactments were founded upon the Judeo-Christian morality of the founding fathers. Even Thomas Jefferson—certainly the least evangelical of the founders of this country—said in his charter for the University of Virginia that the proofs for God as the sovereign Lord and Creator of this world, and His moral requirements and laws, must be taught to all students. The legislation of this country was based upon nothing more or less than Christian morality as revealed in the Word of God. That is the standard for all right and wrong.

In recent decades, we have seen that Christian morality has largely been supplanted in American society and public policy—gradually replaced by an amoral secular humanist philosophy. Once the secularists have successfully achieved all their objectives for our society, you will find yourself living in an America that is totally alien from anything you have ever known. When their entire agenda has been transformed into legislation, you will see not only the abortion-on-demand that we see today, but the legalization of infanticide, same-sex marriage, legalized pedophilia, rampant and unrestricted pornography, state-sanctioned assisted suicide and more. You will also see the complete removal of every vestige of Christian faith and morality from the public square. These are the natural consequences that ensue when the moral and spiritual foundation of a nation is dismantled and replaced by a foundation that is supposedly "neutral" toward God, but which is, in fact, atheistic and amoral. These are the results when a nation comes to believe the lie that "you can't legislate morality."

The framers of the Constitution understood the truth of Proverbs 29:2: "When the righteous are in authority, the people rejoice; but when a wicked man rules, the people groan." And they structured the government of the United States accordingly. Our system of government is actually based on a passage from the Old Testament, Isaiah 33:22, which spells out a godly government composed of three branches: "For the LORD is our Judge [the judicial branch], the LORD is our Lawgiver [the legislative branch], the LORD is our King [executive branch]; He will save us." The founding fathers did not envision America as a secular nation, keeping God out of the business of governing the country. They would be shocked and horrified to see how far today's America has drifted from the original ideal they created.

You can go to the Supreme Court building in Washington, D.C., and you can read the Ten Commandments that are inscribed upon its walls— yet that same Supreme Court has decreed that those same commandments may not be posted on the walls of our public schools! James Madison, who helped write the Constitution that the Supreme Court interprets, has said that we cannot govern without the Ten Commandments—yet the Supreme Court would shield our children from those commandments! If that is not legal and cultural insanity, then what is?

Clearly, human nature cannot be changed by legislation. It can only be changed by the Spirit of God and the Gospel of Jesus Christ. But the law is a teacher that instructs a society in the boundaries of civilized, moral, ethical behavior. And the law is a guardrail that helps preserve society from harm. The crumbling condition of our laws reflects the crumbling condition of our moral and spiritual state as Americans. If we want to see society protected from chaos and destruction from within, then we must grasp the urgency of carrying out the Cultural Mandate and the Great Commission. We must see hearts and minds and lives changed, so that we can see our laws and our society changed. That is our task. That is our God-given purpose as Christians in America.

No room for "tolerance"

Every spring, Coral Ridge Ministries sponsors the Reclaiming America for Christ Conference in Fort Lauderdale to encourage and equip Christians to become involved in the moral issues of contemporary society. During one conference, I stood in a room that was jammed with photographers, television news reporters, newspaper reporters, and magazine reporters to answer their questions about the conference. It became clear from their questions that, as a group, these reporters were frankly incredulous over the assertion that America was founded as a Christian nation. This was an alien concept to them—and they found it absolutely threatening and abhorrent!

Of course, this is hardly surprising, given the education these journalists (as well as most other American adults and schoolchildren) have received in recent years. Today there is a mood of paranoia on the part of educators and textbook publishers concerning the religious foundations of America. Almost all references to God and religious faith have been expurgated from our textbooks. For example, many children in public schools today are taught that the first Thanksgiving was when the

Pilgrims gave thanks not to God (as history records) but to the Indians! In other words, school textbooks are *lying* about American history in order to purge God from children's minds.

I have learned that, because of the censorship of Christianity in the schools and the media, it is a virtual waste of time to try to get your point across via the print and broadcast media. None of your best points will ever penetrate their censorship grid. Even if the reporters were inclined to report your best statements, some editors and producers will make sure those statements end up on the cutting room floor. They will try to use only bits and pieces of your words, often wrenched out of context in order to twist your meaning and present their own point of view. There is little effort on the part of today's media to be objective or fair to Christianity in any way.

So as I stood in that room full of reporters, I had no great expectations. But I decided that I would still do my best to turn that pressroom into a classroom and try at least in part to remedy the failures of their inadequate educational experience. I told them, "Remember, all of the Pilgrims were Christians. That is why they came to these shores. Even 150 years later, in 1776, 98 percent of the American people professed to be Protestant Christians, 1.8 percent professed to be Roman Catholic Christians, and .2 of 1 percent professed to be Jewish. That means that 99.8 percent of Americans in 1776 professed to be Christians. I know of no other nation in the world that was founded by a group of people who so uniformly professed a single religion." I quoted to them the words of Patrick Henry and John Jay and George Washington—

And, of course, none of it appeared in the press coverage.

I once saw a man quoted in a newspaper, expressing his outrage over the idea that America is a Christian nation. "The very idea of one religion in America!" he harrumphed. "Why, that's—that's un-American!" Where has this man been? Well, I'll tell you where he's been. He's been to the public schools in America in the twentieth century—and there he was brainwashed.

Truly, America was originally founded as a Christian nation. Yes, the First Amendment forbids the establishment of a state church—but this was to ensure not the elimination of God from public life but the freedom of Christians, who were the overwhelming majority in the nation, to worship God according to the leading of their faith, not the dictates of the government. To call America a Christian nation today, however, is to invite a torrent of outrage, abuse, and name-calling from those who claim to stand for "tolerance." Their tolerance, unfortunately, is reserved only for godlessness, hedonism, and sin; they have only a zero-tolerance policy for righteousness and godliness

I recall *Newsday*'s story about Vice President Dan Quayle's speech to a Reclaiming America conference at our church in 1994. It began: "Former Vice President Dan Quayle spoke of family values to about three thousand religious conservatives, while one thousand protesters outside called for tolerance and an end to bigotry." *What* tolerance? An end to *whose* bigotry? The "intolerant" and "bigoted" message Mr. Quayle came to deliver, and which the protesters came to protest, was simply that:

- Whenever possible, families ought to be intact and monogamous;
- Children are happier and more well-adjusted in intact, two-parent families;
- Husbands ought to be faithful to their wives and wives to their husbands; and
- Children ought to be born to married couples, not to single mothers.

Incredibly, that message has become controversial in America today! Incredibly, speaking out for simple morality, marriage, and fidelity is now considered "intolerant" and "bigoted." Incredibly, the only sin in America is to be "intolerant" of the sins of others!

I ask you: Who is truly practicing bigotry and intolerance in today's America? Is it Christians—or is it those who *hate* Christians for their moral stance? I have never seen Dan Quayle picket anyone, shout slogans at anyone, or curse anyone. I have never done so myself. But both Dan Quayle and I have had the most hateful, bigoted, intolerant things imaginable shouted at us.

There is an important lesson I hope you will always remember: *So-*

called "tolerance" is the last virtue of a completely immoral society. Those who violate every imaginable standard of decency, who trample the laws of God, who expose their wickedness before the entire public in their parades, who sodomize each other in public for all to see—such people have shredded every virtue except the one virtue that suits their purpose: so-called "tolerance." And when they speak of tolerance, they don't mean that tolerance should be mutual, that they should have to tolerate a Christian's right to free speech and freedom of religion. No, they mean one thing only: "You must tolerate my wickedness. You must accept my worst excesses without criticizing me or disagreeing with me. If you disagree with my lifestyle, if you say that I am sinning, then you are hateful, you are bigoted, you are a religious extremist, you are a homophobe." That is what *tolerance* means to such people.

Understand, I am not saying that Christians should attack or persecute those who live flagrantly sinful lifestyles. The most strident extremists in the atheist, homosexual, and hedonistic camps claim Christians want to round up all the unbelievers and moral degenerates, herd them into concentration camps, and exterminate them. Friend in Christ, I don't believe God wants us to even be *rude* to such people, much less harm them! We are to be gracious but unyielding in speaking God's truth. Our Gospel is a message of love, and those who are the enemies of the Gospel today could be won over by the Gospel tomorrow. Our enemy is not flesh and blood but the spiritual forces of evil in high places.

But when a person parades his wickedness down your street, when he tries to legislate government sanctioning of his wickedness, and when he insists on rubbing your nose in his wickedness, it is not rude to say, "What you are doing is evil, it is destructive, it hurts you, it hurts the people around you, it hurts society, it violates God's law, and I will oppose you." That person will hate you for it, he will spit at you, he may even do violence to you, but you have done nothing wrong in refusing to tolerate and accept his wickedness.

We must never be intimidated by the wicked and their demands that we tolerate their sin. Almighty God is not tolerant of sin, so we must not be tolerant of sin, and America must not be tolerant of sin. "The wicked shall be turned into hell, / And all the nations that forget

God," says Psalm 9:17. This is a statement that should trouble our sleep.

God offers a choice to America: Repent or perish. There is no room for tolerance where sin is concerned.

It is time to reclaim America.

Enough is enough!

Many in our society, and in the media, and in our halls of government are appalled by the very idea of reclaiming America. "Reclaimed from whom?" they ask. The answer: from the forces of godlessness and cultural decay. "Reclaimed by whom and for whom?" The answer: by Christians, for Christ.

Christians founded this nation; Christians built this nation. America was originally a Christian nation, and to the degree that it ceases to be a Christian nation, it ceases to be America. Many people will not even understand what I am talking about in these pages, because years of censorship have blinded them to the true history and the godly purpose of America. Unfortunately, even many Christians will not understand, because they have not grasped the full import of the Christian Gospel. They are content to enjoy the blessings of the Christian life and of the American way of life without understanding the price of those blessings.

I remember the words of Dr. Francis Schaeffer, one of the greatest Christian thinkers of our time. He preached one of his last sermons at the Coral Ridge Presbyterian Church in Fort Lauderdale shortly before he died. He said that the problem in America is that even Christians seem to be living only for personal peace and prosperity; meanwhile, the whole culture around them is sliding into Hell, and they do nothing to prevent it. If God's people, who are called by His name, do not humble themselves, repent, and become salt and light in this decaying culture, we will soon see an end to both peace and prosperity in America. If we deal falsely with God, disobeying the Cultural Mandate and the Great Commission, we can expect Him to withdraw His present help from us, and this nation which was founded by godly men and women as a shining city on a hill will end up as John Winthrop prophesied—a tragic story and a byword of warning throughout the world.

So the time has come and is long overdue: *We must reclaim America for Jesus Christ today.* I say it without embarrassment and without apology: Christ is the only person in this world who is worthy of our undying allegiance. We must say, without hesitation or embarrassment, "Yes, we will reclaim America for Christ!"

You may say, "It can't be done. The forces of cultural decay and god-lessness are too pervasive, too powerful, too entrenched, too numerous, and too well-financed. We can't win. All we can do is go to our basements and hide out until the Lord returns."

You may be too young to remember this, but there was a time when many good people thought that World War II was equally unwinnable. The forces of Nazism and fascism had taken over most of Europe and were moving into Russia and Africa. England seemed ready to topple. Meanwhile, the forces of Japanese imperialism had gobbled up most of the Pacific and had moved into Korea, China, and the Philippines. The forces of evil seemed unstoppable.

Then, in the providence of God, a series of key battles were joined. In the Pacific, the backbone of the Japanese carrier fleet was destroyed at the Battle of Midway. In Europe, Allied forces launched a daring surprise attack on the shores of Normandy on D day, followed by the Battle of the Bulge and the crossing of the Rhine. Suddenly, in both theaters of the war, the tide was turned, and the forces of freedom rejoiced.

I am convinced that just such a dramatic victory is in reach in the life-and-death culture war that is now raging in our society. We have seen tremendous signs of an awakening of evangelical Christians to their responsibilities in the culture in which they live. I believe the time of national renewal is coming and soon will be upon us if we do not turn back.

Christians should feel encouraged, not defeated. We can all make a difference in the direction of this country. For decades, the godless principles of secular humanism have reigned, bringing decay, corruption, and chaos upon our society—but Christians in America are at last waking up to say, "Enough is enough! We are going to reclaim America and call our nation back to the purpose God intended for her."

What can we do?

We have already gotten a frightening glimpse of what can happen when the forces of godlessness surround the Church. It happened on Sunday, September 19, 1993, at the Hamilton Square Baptist Church in San Francisco. On that night, a crowd of homosexual activists gathered at the church to protest an appearance at the evening service by Rev. Lou Sheldon of the Traditional Values Coalition, a champion of biblical morality and an opponent of such gay rights issues as same-sex marriage.

Though the church did not advertise Reverend Sheldon's appearance, other than a notice in the church bulletin, the *Bay Area Reporter* (a newspaper for San Francisco's homosexual community) learned of the event and publicized it. Soon afterward, the church's pastor, Dr. David Innes, received phone calls and visits from homosexual activists, demanding that Reverend Sheldon not be allowed to speak—with strong undertones of a threat. Concerned for the safety of his church, Dr. Innes asked the police for protection. "We can't help you," said the police. "You have to understand—this is San Francisco." All the police would promise is that they would "monitor the situation."

Sunday night arrived and a mob of protestors showed up at around 5:00 P.M. They occupied the church grounds, shouted obscenities, and threw rocks at worshipers who wanted to enter the church. They damaged walls and fixtures, plastered obscene posters on walls and windows, and tore down a Christian flag inside the building, replacing it with the rainbow-colored "Queer Nation" flag of the homosexual rights activists. When they saw children standing in the lobby, the homosexual activists began shouting, "We want your children! We want your children!"

It was a scene eerily reminiscent of that terrible story of rampant homosexuality in Genesis 19, where we read that:

> The men of Sodom, both old and young, all the people from every quarter, surrounded the house. And they called to Lot and said to him, "Where are the men who came to you tonight? Bring them out to us that we may know them carnally." (vv. 4–5)

What began as a protest turned into a full-scale riot. The homosexual activists pounded on the doors of the church sanctuary, and the children inside the building screamed and cried in terror. Though police officers were called to the church, they stood by helplessly and arrested no one. Dr. Innes later observed, "It is impossible for a police officer to arrest a homosexual activist in San Francisco. Any policeman who arrests a radical homosexual will be immediately brought to the Office of Citizen Complaints—he'll lose his job."[1]

If you have never heard this story, I'm not surprised. Local TV stations and the *San Francisco Chronicle* pointedly refused to cover it. The story of a homosexual mob rioting and battering down the doors of a Christian church—a shocking, outrageous, secular intolerance against the Christian faith—was covered up by the dominant media in San Francisco and nationwide.

What happened to the Hamilton Square Baptist Church in San Francisco is really symbolic of what is even now happening to the Christian Church in America. The godless and the wicked are surrounding us, and they are bent on silencing us, intimidating us, and if need be, destroying us. A day may well be coming when we will be entirely surrounded, when the forces of evil will begin battering our doors while our children huddle around us in terror.

Friend in Christ, I plead with you, I implore you, don't wait until that day arrives. Act *now*. Live in obedience to the Cultural Mandate and the Great Commission *now*. Share the Gospel *now*. Get involved in the various spheres of activity in our culture, so that you can be salt and light in your neighborhood, in your workplace, in the local schools and PTAs, at the gym or on the golf course, in the city or county commissions, in elected office. Write letters to the editor, register to vote, and become active for the Lord's cause in every sphere of life.

As former Vice President Dan Quayle has said, "What the media wants and what the media demands of Christians is very simply this: your silence." We Christians have been all too willing to accept the role of "silent majority."

But I, for one, will be silent no longer. I will not be ashamed of Him upon whom my hopes of Heaven depend. I will speak the name of Christ and not be ashamed. I will speak for the principles of Christ. I will tell Hollywood I have had enough of its "sliming of America"; they have destroyed and perverted every single film and program they have laid their hands on. They have corrupted the morals of a nation, and it is past time for Christians to reclaim this nation for Jesus Christ. It is past time for us to break our silence and not be ashamed to speak out when the most vile, ungodly, immoral, and shameful things are done openly and boldly under the sun. Our silence in the face of evil is a ghastly disgrace; may that silence end, beginning today, right now.

I ask you, as you are reading these words: Would you be willing to take this moment and determine that it is going to be a turning point in your life? Would you be willing to make a promise before God that, from this day forward, you are going to (1) do more than you have ever done before to share the Good News of Jesus Christ with others around you and (2) do more than ever before to affect the society in which we live with the principles of Jesus Christ?

If so, I ask you to seal that commitment by signing your name to this pledge:

I hereby pledge that, from this date forward:

- I commit before God to be the salt of the earth and the light of the world wherever I am.

- I will take every opportunity to fulfill the Great Commission and the Cultural Mandate—that I will seek daily to be refashioned in the image of God, that I will "be fruitful and multiply" by sharing the Good News of Jesus Christ.

- I will boldly, unashamedly subdue my corner of the earth, and exercise dominion over my sphere of influence, in God's name.

Signed _____ Date _____

11

LED BY
THE CARPENTER

Let this mind be in you which was also in Christ Jesus.
(PHIL. 2:5)

On April 20, 1999, two teenagers clad in black trench coats walked onto the quiet suburban campus of Columbine High School in Littleton, Colorado. They were armed with sawed-off shotguns, a semi-automatic carbine, a pistol, and scores of homemade explosive devices. These two boys, part of a youth subculture called Gothic (or "Goth"), fascinated with darkness and evil and death, had decided to take the occasion of Adolf Hitler's birthday to massacre their unsuspecting class-mates. Striding the halls, laughing as they killed, they shot their fellow students at point-blank range while the victims pleaded for their lives. When their reign of death and terror was over, they had slaughtered twelve students and a teacher—and then they shot themselves in the head. They also left twenty-eight wounded, many in critical condition.

One of those killed was seventeen-year-old Cassie Bernall. At one time, Cassie had been an angry, troubled teenager, dabbling in witch-craft and brooding about suicide. But her parents had taken her to a youth group where she found Jesus Christ and turned her life around. The new, born-again Cassie was described by everyone who knew her as positive, cheerful, and radiant. On her backpack, in which she carried her Bible and a notebook of her own poems, she hung a pin that read,

"What would Jesus do?" On that day in April 1999, this reborn Christian teenager was confronted by a young Satan-inspired gunman, who asked her, "Do you believe in God?"

"Yes," she answered, standing up boldly and facing the gun, giving a martyr's testimony, "I believe in God—and you should too."

"Why?" asked the nihilistic, empty-souled killer, pointing the gun straight at her face. Then he pulled the trigger, and Cassie was instantly in the presence of the God she loved.

After the siege of death and terror ended, the entire nation struggled to answer the questions, "Why? Why did this happen? Why did they do it? Why didn't somebody read the clues, see this tragedy coming, and stop it?" In the hours and days that followed, politicians and pundits jockeyed for advantage on TV news shows, exploiting the moment to lobby for more gun laws, metal detectors in schools, tighter controls on the Internet, and other legislative solutions. But the American people seemed to intuitively grasp the fact that this tragedy was not primarily a problem of lax laws, lax school security, or easy access to bomb-making information on-line. Everyone understood that the school massacre in Littleton reflected something much deeper and darker in the soul of a nation. This was, after all, no isolated incident. The Littleton incident was only one of an ongoing spate of such tragedies:

- Pearl, Mississippi, October 1, 1997: A sixteen-year-old boy kills his mother, then goes to school and shoots nine students, killing two.

- West Paducah, Kentucky, December 1, 1997: A fourteen-year-old boy kills three students and wounds five others who were praying together at an after-school Bible study.

- Jonesboro, Arkansas, March 24, 1998: Two boys, ages eleven and thirteen, open fire on a schoolyard, killing four girls and a teacher, wounding ten others.

- Edinboro, Pennsylvania, April 24, 1998: A fourteen-year-old shoots a science teacher to death at an eighth-grade dance.

- Fayetteville, Tennessee, May 19, 1998: An eighteen-year-old honor student shoots a classmate in the school parking lot because the classmate was dating his ex-girlfriend.

- Springfield, Oregon, May 21, 1998: A fifteen-year-old boy kills his parents, then goes to school and fires on students, killing two and injuring more than twenty.

- Conyers, Georgia, May 20, 1999: A fifteen-year-old boy armed with a rifle and a handgun opens fire on fellow students, wounding six, then surrenders to the assistant principal.

How do we, as an American society, breed such cold-blooded monsters who have no respect for life and human personhood, not even their own? Some would be quick to blame bloody, demonic Hollywood movies, violent computer games, and the dark, sadistic filth that pollutes the Internet—and I would not disagree that those influences are factors. In fact, it is known that the boys were immersed in the Internet and in computer games like "Doom" and "Quake," in which the player stalks his opponents through dark corridors, shooting them and blowing them up with high-powered weapons.

Some would blame the hideous cult world of "shock rock" musicians like Marilyn Manson, who rips up Bibles onstage, sells "Kill Your Parents" T-shirts, and rots the minds of our youth with such songs as "Irresponsible Hate Anthem" and "Antichrist Superstar," and such lyrics as "Shoot, shoot, shoot . . . no salvation, no forgiveness!"

A few days after the killings in Littleton, former Secretary of Education William Bennett asked a probing and important question on NBC's *Meet the Press* (April 25, 1999): "If these kids were walking around that school in black trench coats, saying, 'Heil Hitler!' why didn't somebody pay attention? I guarantee you, if little Cassie Bernall—the girl who was asked, 'Do you believe in God?' and she said 'Yes,' then was blown away—if she and her friends had been walking through school carrying a Bible and saying, 'Hail the Prince of Peace and King of Kings!' they would have been hauled off to the principal's office." Absolutely true.

In the stream of psychobabble that poured forth from the TV channels following the Littleton massacre, one all-important word was never uttered: *sin!* You see, the concept of sin only has meaning within the context of God—and as a society, we have severed ourselves from God. So we have hundreds of theories as to what went wrong in Littleton, but it is all a lot of psychological drivel, because modern psychology cannot come to terms with the problem of *sin.*

We have removed God from our public life. We have removed the Bible, prayer, the Ten Commandments, and creation from our public schools. What, then, do we have left? We have a generation of young people who have no God, who see themselves as simply the accidental, spontaneous product of an amoeba in the primordial slime, slithering out upon the dry land and acquiring the ability to walk upright. Human beings have no greater value than any other animal, and therefore, no destiny, no future, no soul, no God to judge and guide their lives and give them purpose and meaning in life.

One network broadcast on the Columbine High School tragedy showed a gathering of students and parents praying and weeping. And a reporter said, "Prayer has returned to the public schools of America." Dear God, is *this* what it will take? Have we so lost our national soul that it takes *this* to shock us into a realization of the evil that results from removing God from our national life? Must we lose our children in order to regain our sanity?

Band-Aids on a cancer

On the same day the killings occurred in Littleton, the *Cincinnati Post* published a story about a baby that survived a partial-birth abortion procedure at the Women's Medical Center in Dayton. The baby girl, who was named Baby Hope by nurses at the hospital, lived for three hours after being delivered alive. During those three hours, an emergency room nurse named Connie Boyles held the child, rocked her, and sang to her. Nurse Boyles later said that other nurses in her unit had to undergo hours of counseling to cope with the pain of the experience. "Staff who cared for [Baby Hope] on the night of her birth have experienced a myriad of emotions," she recalled. "This emotional trauma inflicted on our department is deeper and will last longer than the physical frailties that we deal with on a daily basis."

You may ask, "What does a school shooting have to do with a failed partial-birth abortion in a city a thousand miles away?" Just this: We are rightly disturbed that so many of our children have fallen prey to a culture of darkness and death—that kids are actually capable of killing their class-mates, laughing about it, then killing themselves. Yet, why should we be so shocked? How has the adult world given them anything better to aspire to than the random taking of innocent life? Why should teenagers respect life any more than their parents do—a generation of parents who have done nothing to stop more than a million abortions a year? As a society, we have already said that the killing of innocents is okay—so when teens kill, aren't they just adopting and acting out the madness of a murderous culture?

These teenagers understand what abortion is and that our society even sanctions a procedure—partial-birth abortion—that allows a baby to be almost completely delivered, leaving only the top three inches of the baby's head in the birth canal, preserving a hideous fiction that the baby hasn't "really" been born. As long as three inches of the baby remains in the birth canal, it's okay to open the base of her skull and suc-tion out her brains. It is obvious that there is nothing magical about those last three inches of the baby's head that can possibly affect the life or health of the mother—for all intents and purposes, that child has already been born alive! Teenagers are not stupid, and they know that adult society has sanctioned the killing of innocent babies for the sake of convenience. They know that society allowed Dr. Kevorkian to run around the country for nearly ten years, killing the old and infirm with impunity, before he was finally sent to prison.

The culture of darkness and death that produces campus killers is merely a subculture of the larger culture of death that we in adult American society have created! I submit to you that if you look closely, you will see that America—this land of beautiful churches, gleaming shopping malls, nonstop entertainment, and boundless prosperity—is also a chamber of horrors. It is a place of nonstop abortions and killings, despair and loneliness, loveless families and teen suicides, and on and on, horror upon horror, death upon death!

I come back to the "Why?" questions that everyone was asking in the wake of the Littleton massacre. Why did it happen? Who is to blame? The two shooters themselves, of course, take the bulk of the blame with them into eternity, a stain of innocent blood that God alone must judge. But as we look around our society, we see there are other layers of blame, including parents, media, schools, and more.

And I submit to you that *we*, too, are to blame!

I submit to you that *Christians*, who in recent decades have largely lived in disobedience to the Cultural Mandate and the Great Commission, must shoulder a great burden of responsibility for the madness and death of our society. We have not been salt. We have not been light. We have not been fruitful in sharing the life-changing Good News of Jesus Christ. We have not subdued the earth in the name of God. Our disobedience is a major cause of so much suffering in the world!

I can hear your mind recoiling from that thought. "No," you say, "I am not to blame!"

But I ask you: If those two boys who committed the massacre in Littleton had been Christians, could they have possibly done what they did? If, instead of spending their time in darkened movie theaters or playing dark computer games or listening to dark music about death, they had spent their time in an after-school Bible study, praying with other Christian kids, and receiving the light of God's Word—could they have shot their classmates to death? The answer blares at our dulled consciences from Heaven itself.

We know that if every Christian in America today would just reach out and lead *one* other person to Christ this year—just one!—then this would be an overwhelmingly Christian nation. We also know that, as society now stands, there will be more school shootings in the future— probably even before this book is off the press, and possibly in your own neighborhood. What if we could reach those troubled kids before they pulled the next trigger? What if we could get to them now, today, with the message of hope and light and love that comes through Jesus Christ? How much death and misery could we prevent—just by being obedient to the Lord's command that we preach the Gospel to every creature?

If we want to see the tide of death and evil turned back in our nation, we must each do our part. We must each be obedient to the mandate of God. Increased campus security, metal detectors, gun control laws—these are just Band-Aids on a cancer. The only true cure for the cancer of human despair, rage, and death is Jesus Christ.

We can change the world

The president of one of our great theological seminaries, at a meeting with the chairman of an accreditation committee, was asked to state the purpose of that institution. Without a moment's hesitation, the seminary president replied, "The purpose of this institution is to change the world."

Surprised by that response, the committee member said, "No, you don't understand. I know that influencing the world is the general purpose of all education. But I am asking you, specifically, what is the purpose of this school?"

"The purpose of our school," the seminary president reiterated, "is to change the world."

Now, this answer still failed to satisfy the man from the accreditation committee—but repeated questioning failed to shake the gentleman from his position. The seminary president insisted that his institution served but one purpose: to change the world.

And now, having reached the final chapter of this book, I trust that you understand that God's purpose for your life and for mine is the same purpose stated by that seminary president: We are here to change the world. That is our purpose, nothing less. When I leave this world, I want to know that the world has been changed for my having been here—not because of any great powers or abilities of mine, but because, by God's grace, I was obedient in allowing the power of the Holy Spirit and the Gospel of Jesus Christ to work in me and through me.

There is a famous text that is often quoted and attributed to "Author Unknown." In fact, the text comes from a sermon preached many years ago by Dr. James Allan Francis, and it has come to be known as "One Solitary Life." Even if these words are familiar to you, I urge you to read them again and let the moving and powerful import of these words penetrate your heart:

> A child was born in an obscure village. He grew up in another obscure village, where He worked in a carpenter shop until He was thirty. Then for three years He was an itinerant preacher.

He never wrote a book. He never held an office. He never owned a home. He never had a family. He never went to college. He never set foot inside a big city. He never traveled two hundred miles from the place where He was born. He never did one of the things that usually accompany greatness. He had no credentials but Himself. He had nothing to do with this world except the naked power of His divine manhood.

While still a young man, the tide of public opinion turned against Him. His friends ran away. One of them denied Him. He was turned over to His enemies. He went through the mockery of a trial. He was nailed to a cross between two thieves. His executioners gambled for the only piece of property He had on earth while He was dying—and that was His robe. When He was dead, He was taken down and laid in a borrowed grave through the pity of a friend.

Nineteen wide centuries have come and gone, and today He is the centerpiece of the human race and the leader of the column of progress. I am far within the mark when I say that all the armies that ever marched, and all the navies that ever were built, and all the parliaments that ever sat, all the kings that ever reigned, put together have not affected the life of man upon this earth as powerfully as has that One Solitary Life.

It's truly amazing—the impact of that one solitary life on the course of human history! And He is the model for your life and mine. The Carpenter changed the world—and He expects nothing less of you and me. "He who believes in Me," said Jesus, "the works that I do he will do also; and greater works than these he will do, because I go to My Father" (John 14:12).

God has a purpose for your life, just as He had a purpose for the life and death and resurrection of His Son, Jesus. That twofold purpose, as we have examined it throughout this book, is:

1. The Cultural Mandate of Genesis 1:26–28, with its three submandates:

   • Be refashioned into His image.

- Be fruitful and multiply (evangelize).
- Subdue the earth and exercise dominion in His name.

2. The Great Commission to take the Gospel to every creature, and to disciple all nations.

We see that Jesus lived His life according to that same purpose God has given us. Of course, He did not need to be "refashioned" into God's image, because He was the very image of God in human form. "For in Him dwells all the fullness of the Godhead bodily; and you are complete in Him, who is the head of all principality and power" (Col. 2:9–10). But throughout His earthly ministry, we see that He was obedient to God's mandates in every other point: He evangelized, boldly and continually. He challenged the hypocrisy, injustice, and cultural decay of His day. Wherever He went, He exercised dominion in the name of God the Father.

We can change the world. We can spread the Gospel and multiply Christians across the face of the earth. But to do that, our hearts must be softened toward the people around us, the people God wants us to reach.

During the reign of Oliver Cromwell, lord protector of England, there was a shortage of silver coinage. Cromwell sent some soldiers to a cathedral in search of silver. They reported, "The only silver we can find is in the statues of the saints standing in the cathedral."

"Good!" exclaimed Cromwell. "We'll melt the saints and put them into circulation!"

That is what God seeks to do to you and me. He wants to melt us— all of us who are the saints of God. He wants to warm our souls, melt our hearts, and fire up our imaginations—then He wants to put us into circulation! He seeks to inflame us and send us out into our neighborhoods, our communities, and our world to share the Gospel of Jesus Christ with everyone around us.

Heroes wanted!

Suppose you were looking for employment and you read this ad: "Heroes wanted. No cowards need apply." Would you apply? Do you feel qualified? Are you a hero?

You may have never considered such questions—but you should! The kingdom of God needs heroes. Over and over, we read of valiant, mighty heroes in the Scripture. The New Testament exhorts us to endure hardness as good soldiers of Jesus Christ. It admonishes, "Fear not," "Be not afraid," "Be of good courage," and more. These are the marks of a hero. The army of Jesus Christ is to be composed of heroes. Are you qualified for the job?

In the book of Revelation, Jesus Christ declares, "To him who overcomes I will grant to sit with Me on My throne, as I also overcame and sat down with My Father on His throne" (3:21). In Romans, Paul says, "We are more than conquerors through Him who loved us" (8:37). Uncle Sam may be looking for a few good men, but God is looking for a great host of men and women who will be heroes of the cross. He is looking for successors to those early Christians who suffered and died to fulfill God's mandates for His Church—men and women who were martyred as they sought to preach the Gospel and exercise dominion in God's name.

Do the people of the world marvel at the courage of Christians today? Or do they perceive Christians as emotional cripples who use religion as a crutch because they cannot face reality on its own terms? Are we Christians thought of as heroes or cowards? I submit to you that the most common image of Christians is one of weakness and timidity—not courage.

Where, then, do heroes come from? And how can we join the ranks of heroes? I am convinced that there are two essential ingredients to heroism:

First, you must be confronted with danger. Second, you must respond to that danger by committing yourself to a cause that is greater than yourself. Merely defying danger or taking foolish risks is not enough to make you a hero. A person who flirts with danger by parachuting off tall buildings for thrills is not a hero. Most likely, he's simply a fool. But a person who parachutes behind enemy lines for the sake of his country is a hero indeed! Danger plus a great cause are the ingredients of heroism.

Where are heroes manufactured? In many places, of course—but most frequently in wars. War and heroism naturally go together. That is one reason there are so many heroes in the Old Testament—because it is filled with wars! There is the invasion of Canaan; the battles against the Canaanites and the Hittites; the invasion of the Assyrians and the Babylonians; and on and on. The Old Testament accounts read like a chronicle of continuous conflict and war! Why is that? I believe that God is showing us in physical terms that we Christians are constantly engaged in warfare. Life is warfare. We don't like to see life in those terms, but it is true.

How do most people see life? I would liken the popular view of life to a wet rag. People think of life as something that you twist and squeeze as hard as you can to wring as much pleasure from it as possible. Most people want to extract as much enjoyment out of life as they can while putting as little into life as they can get away with.

But God says that life is warfare and that we are to be good soldiers of Jesus Christ. We are to put on the whole armor of God and fight the good fight (Eph. 6:10–20). The irony of these two contrasting views of life is that the Christian, the soldier of Christ, can experience peace in his heart in the midst of war; meanwhile, the unbeliever, who shrinks from battle, has conflict and strife in his heart in the midst of worldly peace and prosperity. It is the man of God, the woman of God, the child of God who experiences God's peace in the midst of wars and conflicts who is truly empowered to be a hero for God's kingdom.

Do you trust the promises of God? Are you obeying His mandates for your life? Are you fulfilling God's purpose for your life? Our Lord has given us a promise that we will live forever in a place the Father has prepared for those who trust in His Son. Only a life built on the promise of Christ can ever overcome the fear that so easily paralyzes us.

Friend in Christ, true heroism begins when we overcome the fear of death. We overcome it by believing a promise. Have you overcome that fear? Do you believe that promise? I do! I believe that for me to be absent from this body is to be present with the Lord. I believe that to go to be with Christ is far better, as Paul said. I believe that Christ has prepared something for me that is infinitely greater than my mind or heart can conceive. Why, then, should I be afraid? You will never really begin to live until you overcome the fear of death. You will never be the courageous, valiant, heroic person Christ would have you be unless you overcome that fear. You will never truly find and fulfill God's purpose for your life until that fear has been vanquished in your life.

"We have nothing to fear but fear itself," said President Roosevelt before World War II. Those words ring even more true for Christians as we move into the third millennium. The only thing that can truly paralyze us is fear—and Jesus came to remove that fear from us. In order to carry out the Cultural Mandate and the Great Commission, we must become men and women of courage and of heroism. Today we do not face the stake or the lions, as our Christian brothers and sisters did in ancient Rome; we do not face years in Siberian slave camps, as our Russian brothers and sisters have; we do not face slavery, torture, and death, as many Christians in parts of Africa, China, Pakistan, and other nations face at this very moment.

What risks do we face? Only the lifted eyebrow of the skeptic, the condescending word, the critical response. Tragically, a mere look of disgust or a sharp word is all it takes to send Christians scurrying for cover! We must not allow such trivial opposition to silence our profession for Christ. We are called to witness for Him, boldly and at every opportunity. The culture war and the spiritual war rage around us—but are we wading into the thick of the battle, or are we AWOL, hiding and trembling like craven cowards?

The greatest hero who ever lived, of course, was the Carpenter, Jesus Christ. He single-handedly confronted not only the hosts of mankind, but also the forces of death and Hell and Satan and the demons of the pit. Most important of all, He overcame them. Those who would follow in the footsteps of the Carpenter must be courageous, as He has commanded.

There is no sign on the door to the kingdom of God that says "Cowards need not apply." Instead, Jesus Christ has hung a sign on that door with a wonderful message: "Here cowards are transformed into heroes." Remember Simon Peter in the hours before the Crucifixion? He cringed and swore a lying oath when a mere maiden suggested that he was a follower of Jesus of Nazareth! The coward! But later, after his heart was seized by faith in our all-conquering Lord, Peter stood before the entire Sanhedrin, knowing they had the power of life and death over him, and he boldly proclaimed Christ to them! Like lead being transmuted into gold, cowards are transmuted into heroes by the power of faith in the living Lord.

Now the question that confronts you is this: What will it be—fear or faith? Are you a hero—or a zero? The Lord is calling you to be a hero for His kingdom. The qualifications are simple: no age limit. No experience necessary. Just a willingness to trust God—and obey. He'll supply the on-the-job training. "Heroes wanted!" says Jesus Christ. Won't you apply, for His sake?

We follow in the footsteps of the Carpenter. His life silences all our excuses for failing to carry out God's mandates for our lives:

"But I'm only one person! What can one person do?" Jesus showed us that one solitary life, lived in obedience to the will and purposes of God the Father, can change the world.

"But what will people think of me if I open my mouth and witness? What will people do to me?" What did people think of Jesus? What did they do to Him? He went to the cross and suffered excruciating agony and death for your sake.

"But I have no credentials or position of power! How could someone like me change the world?" Jesus had no credentials, no formal education, no political power. From a human standpoint, He was "only a carpenter."

"But I don't have the resources to go out and change the world." Jesus had no money, no possessions, no home. How much does anyone need to be salt and light, to witness about the love of Jesus Christ, to have an influence in his or her own little corner of the world?

We are led by the Carpenter. He showed us how to live and how to die. He showed us how to fulfill God's purpose for our lives, to be His salt and His light in a dark and dying world. There is no unemployment in the kingdom of God. Everyone has a job to do. God has called every Christian to be His witness. He has called *you*. You cannot refuse His call and still call Him "Lord."

I once heard of a Christian scrubwoman named Aunt Sophie. She wasn't an educated lady, but she had a heart for others, and she was always ready with a word or a song about the Lord. She made the most of every opportunity to share the love of Christ with others. One day, a man made fun of her, saying that he had seen her talking about Jesus to a wooden Indian in front of a cigar store. "Perhaps I did," Sophie laughed in reply. "My eyesight is not good these days. But talking about Christ to a wooden Indian is not half as bad as being a wooden Christian and never talking to anyone about Jesus!"

She's absolutely right. If we are going to change the world, we must do so not by simply living "nice" lives, but by openly professing the Lord

Jesus. Are you a wooden Christian? Or are you actively involved in changing the world for Christ?

A *plan of action*

In closing, let me tell you a story.

Let me take you back to the mid-1980s, to a church youth group in Canton, Ohio. In that youth group was a thin, awkward boy whose face was marred with acne. The teenager, whose name was Brian, had trouble fitting in at school and at church. Some of the "jocks" in his high school liked to call him names and shove him against the lockers. A couple of times Brian was beaten up for no reason at all—just adolescent cruelty.

Even at church, the Christian kids didn't want to hang around him, talk to him, or do anything with him. All the Christian kids around him were in cliques and groups of friends, but Brian was friendless. The youth pastor tried to be friendly to him, but Brian was quiet, socially awkward, and hard to get to know. It was only natural that the youth pastor would gravitate toward the other kids in the group and spend more time with them than with this outcast kid named Brian. So even at church, Brian would just fend for himself.

One day, the youth group went on an outing to a local amusement park. The pastor wanted the kids to pair off, but no one wanted to be with Brian, even for the day, so Brian roamed the park and went on the thrill rides by himself. After Brian had been coming to church for three or four months, he finally just stopped coming. No one really missed him, not even the youth pastor.

A few years passed. The youth pastor took a position with a seminary. One day, he got a phone call from a young man who used to be in his youth group. "Do you remember a kid from our youth group named Brian Warner?" the young man asked.

The former youth pastor drew a blank. "Brian Warner . . . ?"

"He only came for three or four months, then he dropped out. Skinny kid. Pimply faced. A real loner. At the amusement park, he went around by himself because he didn't have any friends."

"Oh, yeah," said the former youth pastor. "I remember now. Brian Warner. Whatever happened to him?"

"He goes by a different name these days," said the young man. "You've probably heard of him. Calls himself Marilyn Manson."[1]

That's right. That skinny kid who was the outcast of his church youth group is now the "shock rock" teen icon Marilyn Manson. He belongs to the Church of Satan, and he blasphemes and commits obscene acts onstage while performing songs like "Antichrist Superstar." Once he was within the walls of the Church, within easy reach of the Gospel. Today he is on a search-and-destroy mission, targeting our kids with such lyrics as, "I am the ism, my hate's a prism / Let's just kill everyone and let your god sort them out."

Do you really think there is nothing you can do to change the world? What if just one person had reached Brian Warner with the message of Jesus Christ and His love before this boy turned his life over to Satan and donned the persona of "Marilyn Manson"? Could it be that instead of leading thousands of young people down the road to Hell, he might have used his life for God instead?

Of course, it's not too late to pray for him even now. And it's not too late to reach the kid in your church or your neighborhood who might otherwise be the next "Marilyn Manson." It's not too late to reach your neighbor or coworker for Christ. It's not too late to make a difference in your school or your workplace or your community. It's not too late to make a difference in your government or your society or your world.

Led by the Carpenter, we *can* change our homes, our neighborhoods, our communities, our world. The Lord has placed us in this dying, corrupt world for a reason. He has given us a finite amount of time, and He has given us a mission to perform. The task is great—too great for you and me, but not too great for the God we serve!

So join me as, together, we follow the Carpenter on this great adventure of faith. We can do all things through the Carpenter-King, because *He* is our strength. Through Him, through the power of His Gospel, we *can* change this world and we *will* change this world—

One life at a time.

It's not too late—yet.

But soon it will be. So we must act *now*—"while it is day; [for] the night is coming when no one can work" (John 9:4).

NOTES

CHAPTER 2

1. Grace Lee Whitney, *The Longest Trek* (Clovis, CA: Quill Driver Books, 1998), ix.

CHAPTER 3

1. From "There Is a Fountain," words by William Cowper (1731-1800).

CHAPTER 4

1. Patrick and Gwen Purtill, "Think Virtuously, Act Locally," Philanthropy, Culture, and Society, April 1997,Capital Research Center, 727 15th St. NW, Suite 800, Washington, DC 20005; electronically retrieved from <http://www.capitalresearch.org/pcs/pcs-0497.html> (11 June 1999); Internet.1. All quotations electronically retrieved from <http://winn.com/whee/PUTwistedRoots.html.>

2. Quotations electronically retrieved from <http://www.lc.org/lib0498.htm> (11 June 1999); Internet.

3. All quotations electronically retrieved from <http://winn.com/whee/PUTwistedRoots.html> (11 June 1999); Internet.

4. Joe Laconte, "You gotta have faith in abstinence," *Washington Times,* 15 September 1996, 33.

5. Charles W. Colson, "Volunteer Power: The Revival of Civic Associations," Breakpoint radio commentary, 3 June 1996.

6. Charles W. Colson, "Doing the Right Thing—Christianity and Compassion," Breakpoint radio commentary, 29 August 1996.

CHAPTER 5

1. Electronically retrieved from <http://www.freedomforum.org/religion/1998/3/20scpastor.asp> (11 June 1999); Internet.
2. D. James Kennedy, *Evangelism Explosion* (Wheaton, IL: Tyndale House Publishers Inc.; ISBN 0842307648, 4th edition, 1997).

CHAPTER 6

1. Wayne L. Gordon with Randall Frame, *Real Hope in Chicago: The Incredible Story of How the Gospel Is Transforming a Chicago Neighborhood* (Grand Rapids, MI: Zondervan, 1995).

CHAPTER 8

1. Electronically retrieved from <http://www.theatlantic.com/atlantic/election/connection/family/danquayl.html> (11 June 1999); Internet.
2. Kim Alexis, *A Model for a Better Future* (Nashville: Thomas Nelson Publishers, 1998), 75.
3. Electronically retrieved from <http://www.theatlantic.com/atlantic/ election/connection/family/danquayl.html> (11 June 1999); Internet.
4. Ibid.

CHAPTER 9

1. Electronically retrieved from <http://dinkum.christian.net.au/dink45.htm#BM300_000_SILENT_PULPITS.>

2. Robert H. Bork, *Slouching Towards Gomorrah* (New York: Regan Books/HarperCollins, 1996), xiii.

3 Interview: John Money, *Paidika: The Journal of Paedophilia,* Spring 1991, vol. 2, no. 3, 5.

CHAPTER 10

1. William Norman Grigg, "The Lavender Revolution," *New*

American Magazine, Vol. 10, No. 02, 24 January 1994, electronically retrieved from
<http://jbs.org/tna/1994/vo10no02.htm>(11 June 1999);
Internet.

CHAPTER 11
1. "Think About This," electronically retrieved from
<http://www.exposingsatanism.org/music> (11 June 1999);
Internet.